THE GREAT JOB SHAKE-OUT

HOW TO FIND A NEW CAREER AFTER THE CRASH

MARVIN CETRON AND OWEN DAVIES

An Omni Book

Simon and Schuster

New York   London   Toronto   Sydney   Tokyo

Simon and Schuster
Simon & Schuster Building
Rockefeller Center
1230 Avenue of the Americas
New York, New York 10020

Copyright © 1988 by Marvin Cetron and Owen Davies
All rights reserved
including the right of reproduction
in whole or in part in any form.

SIMON AND SCHUSTER and colophon are registered trademarks
of Simon & Schuster Inc.
Designed by Karolina Harris
Manufactured in the United States of America

10   9   8   7   6   5   4   3   2   1

Library of Congress Cataloging in Publication Data

Cetron, Marvin J.
    The great job shake-out : how to find a new career after
the crash / Marvin Cetron, Owen Davies.
        p.   cm.
    "An Omni book."
    Includes index.
    1. Employment forecasting—United States.   2. Economic
forecasting—United States.   3. United States—Economic
conditions—1981–   I. Davis, Owen.   II. Title.
HD5724.C43   1988
650.1'4'0973—dc19   88-21136
                                                                          CIP

ISBN 0-671-66441-7

ACKNOWLEDGMENTS

THOUGH ONLY two names appear on the cover, this book has been a group effort throughout its preparation. Of the many people who aided in this project, a few stand out for their conspicuous contributions. Our deepest gratitude goes to:

Laurie Lister, our skilled and tireless editor at Simon and Schuster, who recognized the need for this volume long before the stock crash of October 1987, guided our efforts throughout the writing, and helped us on many occasions to sharpen our thinking.

Robert Weil, literary agent *extraordinaire,* who created the idea for this book and introduced the authors for their collaboration.

Kathy Keeton, president of Omni Publications International, whose enthusiasm for this book helped inspire us to undertake the project and to see it through.

The staff of Forecasting International, and especially Charles McFadden and Rebecca Lucken, who worked diligently to gather much of the data that appear throughout this book, and Cathy Acton and Sue McGurk, who endured the tedium of keyboarding it into our computer system.

Special thanks are due to Dr. Murray Weidenbaum, formerly chairman of President Reagan's Council of Economic Advisers and now director of the Center for the Study of American Business at Washington University, in St. Louis. Though busy preparing his own book *Rendezvous with Reality* (Basic Books, 1988), Dr. Weidenbaum generously shared with us his ideas on the thorny problem of balancing the Federal budget; they form a major part of our Appendix A.

This book is dedicated to our wives:
for Glor—with love, Marv "14," and for Janice Davies,
without whose untiring patience and support
this book could not have been written.

CONTENTS

FOREWORD

"Latest forecasts from government and private economists show federal red ink rising from $165 billion this year to about $185 billion in fiscal 1988 and nearing $200 billion in fiscal 1989. Reason: Slower economic growth, higher interest rates and weaker revenue gains than had been predicted."

—*U.S. News & World Report,* July 27, 1987

"Any rebirth of inflation will trigger a recession. This will occur late in 1988 or early in 1989."

—Stanley Kauffman, managing director of Salomon Brothers, in *Wall Street Week,* August 7, 1987

"Among those suffering most will be those who regard all current warnings with the greatest contempt. . . . The wise course is to assume the worst."

—John Kenneth Galbraith, from "The 1929 Parallel," *Atlantic Monthly,* January 1987

POLITICS AND ECONOMIC POLICY are balancing acts in which our leaders try to build a bright national future from the many conflicting forces within society. This book is about one of their failures and its consequences, which may shape our lives for many years to come. It is also about a future in which the job market we know will be radically transformed. Even if we escape a grave economic downturn, the list of so-called "sunset industries" will grow longer. Many familiar jobs will vanish and be replaced by new and very different opportunities. Of these, some will require higher levels of training; the remainder will provide only a much lower standard of living than middle-class workers have come to expect. In the 1990s, our lives will change and all things will be different.

Many factors have long held the American economy in a tolerable balance, so that since World War II, we have enjoyed long periods of healthy growth punctuated by relatively minor recessions. But in the last ten years we have allowed our national debt to grow out of control, and this has so weakened our long-standing economic stability that the balance is now slipping. Unless Washington's power brokers can tip the swaying structure back toward solvency, collapse may be nearly at hand.

A number of capable economists now believe that we can hope, at best, for only one more year of prosperity. Then inflation will reappear, business will retrench, foreign trade will begin to dry up, and we will enter the worst recession of the last six decades. Some believe this slide will quickly overwhelm traditional protective measures, and the world—led by the United States—will plummet into a universal depression like that which followed the stock-market crash of 1929 and the Smoot-Hawley Tariff Act the following year.

Our economy is not yet beyond saving. Yet its wounds can be healed only by prompt, effective action by our government, with the cooperation of our trading partners. The consequences of failure would be so grave and enduring that it is difficult to believe the problems will not be solved in time. Yet the policy measures required are enormously unpopular with large blocs of voters, and our leaders in Washington have a poor record when it comes to risking their jobs in order to do what is necessary for the common good. Their performance in the budget-cutting negotiations of November 1987 was not encouraging.

So it is time to shore up our personal economies to weather whatever storm may come. Above all, we must look to our jobs. Unless we hold the right jobs, in the right geographic areas, we may not have them much longer.

Even without a depression, the job market has been in chaos. Many factors are to blame:

• New technology is eliminating two-thirds of manufacturing jobs, throwing our industrial regions into poverty and unions out of power. This trend is now beginning to strike the service sector and other formerly secure job markets.
• Low oil prices have plunged much of the once-booming Southwest into its own regional recession.
• Government policies and shortsighted business management have

combined to destroy our markets overseas while opening our domestic market to intense foreign competition.

• Deregulation has fostered a two-tiered economy in which big businesses grow and the smallest businesses survive, while mid-sized businesses die. Witness the death of many airlines while both industry giants and tiny regional carriers prosper.

• Mid-sized farms, once a refuge in time of trouble, are disappearing in record numbers. So are the farm-equipment dealers and other businesses that depend on them.

• The growing service sector has created jobs, but most are ill-paid positions for unskilled workers. Foreign competition is now beginning to damage those service industries which do offer middle- and high-income jobs.

As a result, for the first time, most families now include two full-time wage earners, yet they find it difficult to make ends meet. An estimated 70 percent cannot make their debt payments without scrimping on necessities.

Few businesses and fewer individuals are prepared to meet further adversity.

For too many of us, the bad years are already here. Hundreds of thousands of former steel puddlers, production-line workers, and farmers have learned in the last decade what it is to lose an established career and find yourself qualified only for menial jobs. Many more of us may soon join them, including the white-collar executives who thought unemployment could strike only the blue-collar workers they once managed. If you are one of them, or understand that you soon could be, this book is meant for you.

Unless you are very young, the chances are that you have gone job hunting before, and more than once. Each time, it was probably among the least pleasant experiences of your professional life.

This time will be different. And in some ways better. If you are fired this time, you can be sure it's not your fault. Nothing you did cost you your job; nothing you could have done would have saved it. Like others on the unemployment line, you will have lost out to global forces truly beyond your control. There will be no reason to doubt your own worth.

But in some ways it will also be worse. This time you will be looking not just for a new job but for a new career that may be like nothing you have known before. You will have to look deeply into yourself for neglected talents. You may have to go back to school to learn new skills—this while unemployed or trudging daily to a menial job that once you would not have considered taking. The task may drag on for months or years. And if you are near the beginning of your working life, you may have to repeat this chore periodically as changes accumulate ever more rapidly. Many forecasters predict that in coming decades most people, either out of preference or by necessity, will seek out new careers every ten years.

All will not be gloom, however, even if the economy lives down to our worst expectations, for the forces now closing the doors on many once-rewarding careers are now opening other opportunities. For example, by the year 2000, an estimated 3 million openings will appear for computer-aided design technicians alone. The continued aging of our population will bring ever-greater demand for medical technicians and support personnel. And a recession itself would broaden the market for repairmen of all kinds. Somewhere among the new opportunities presented in this book, you will find your next career.

No book can completely prepare you for the time ahead. Nothing can cushion the loss of the only career you have ever known or make it easier to build a new one. But this life-changer's manual for the new decade can help you to endure the coming shock and find the tools to build new prosperity.

If you are already convinced that your job is in jeopardy, and perhaps our national economy as well, you can skip the first two chapters. If not, attend them well. Nothing will focus your attention on the uncertain future like the understanding that your old lifestyle may be nearing its end.

Chapter 3 looks at the changes we can expect from Washington and from society in the coming decades. Though some are specific measures for coping with a depression, most will come to pass even if we avoid disaster. Economic collapse would simply hasten their arrival and make the transition far more difficult.

We then focus on the job market and the preparations to be made if we are to prepare for its inevitable changes.

Chapter 4 is the key; it examines industries and job categories likely to decline or prosper. You will find a heavy emphasis on computer skills, even in fields that do not now require them. (Appendix B offers a more detailed look at Commerce Department employment classifications with prospects notably better or worse than average. If your job is not listed in the first section, it probably will not soon vanish, but neither will it offer the growing opportunities of the expected winners.)

There was a time when career-minded people viewed the idea of going into business for themselves with skepticism bordering on suspicion. Entrepreneurs were seen widely as strange, cranky people unable to get along in a respectable corporation—the business world's answer to the mad scientist. Today, they are more often romanticized as self-reliant, all-American heroes who take on challenges too difficult for most of us to face, and in so doing provide much of the power that drives our economy. As always, the truth contains elements of both extremes. One thing is certain about entrepreneurs: Whether American business sinks or soars in the 1990s, they will find many opportunities to develop new companies. For a look at those chances, and how to take advantage of them, turn to Chapter 5.

Chapters 6 and 7 examine the ultimate defense against hardship: Lace up your walking shoes, and go where the economic sun shines brighter. In the 1970s and early 1980s, many former industrial workers from the Rust Belt states reluctantly took that route out of adversity and found new careers in the Southwest. In the 1990s, many of us will look to other pockets of prosperity dotted around the United States. And for the truly hard-pressed, who nonetheless have something to offer, there are other countries whose economies may prove more hospitable than our own. These chapters will guide you to them.

For those who have ready capital, hard times always offer unbeatable opportunities to snap up investments that will bear profits when the economy recovers. Chapter 8 tells what to look for.

Chapters 9 through 11 offer tools with which to evaluate your own prospects and take advantage of the opportunities you find. What are your assets? What are your marketable skills? How hard will it be for you to find a new field in the turbulent job market of the coming decade? How can you position yourself to take advantage of the new economy that will grow from the ashes of the old one in the late '90s? This section will help you plan your personal survival strategy.

Though it may already be too late to prevent a temporary decline in our standard of living, there are at least two dozen steps that our leaders in Washington could take to clean up the mess they have made. If they act decisively, we could yet suffer no more than a minor downturn. Appendix A presents the measures we believe could head off the depression of the 1990s and explains why each is necessary. Read them. Use them as the standard against which to measure the performance of your elected representatives. If you can convince our national leaders that their shortest route to unemployment is to continue playing politics with your economic future, the job shake-out of the 1990s could yet become the business boom of the century.

Before looking closely at the economy and job market of the 1990s, we should answer an obvious question: Do we really believe an all-out depression looms in the world's near future? Or even a major recession? Not quite. What we do believe it that it is a significant threat and one that we must all prepare to face.

As we said earlier, economic collapse is not inevitable. At the moment, Forecasting International's computer gives us only a 10 percent chance of a major recession and a 5 percent chance of a depression like that of the 1930s. That is not a huge risk, but it's not a tiny one; it is roughly the same as your chances of tossing a coin and having it come up heads three or four times in a row. What makes it so important to every jobholder is the size of the disaster if depression does strike—loss of job, and very possibly loss of career. If you are in an obsolescent trade and a depression strikes, you might never work again.

If the threat still does not seem real, think about how eager you would be to play Russian roulette with a one-in-ten or one-in-twenty chance of blowing your brains out. Thanks largely to many years of inept, shortsighted government, that is roughly the economic position you are in today. We'd like to help you find a way out.

PART ONE

A BAD TIME TO BE FIRED

APOCALYPSE NOW?

IF YOU HAVE READ a newspaper or seen a television news report since the Wall Street crash of October 19, 1987, you already know what America's foremost economic problem is: Since the dawn of Reaganomics in 1981, the United States has been living far beyond its means. Uncle Sam is not merely broke, but in hock up to his stovepipe hat, and a frightening number of American consumers are equally in debt. Add to this a massive trade deficit, poor industrial productivity, loss of manufacturing jobs, low capital investment, the virtual disappearance of private savings . . . the list is nearly endless, and it constitutes a recipe for economic collapse.

Our leaders in Washington—the same geniuses who got us into this mess—announced late in 1987 that thanks to their wisdom, courage, and dedication, the danger had been turned aside. By a combination of politically safe budget cuts, limited tax increases, fees for services, and onetime sales of government property, Congress and the Administration cobbled together a program that shrank the fiscal 1987 deficit by little more than $23 billion that the Gramm-Rudman Act would have cut without their efforts. They even passed further reductions for the following year.

For the short run, they probably did enough—though just barely enough—as demonstrated by the relative stability of stock prices and the dollar's value on international currency markets since late 1987. A deficit reduction of less than $23 billion after the stock-market crash that October would have told investors clearly that the United States lacked the political will to bring its economic problems under control; a reduction greater than about $30 billion would have slowed the economy enough to threaten an immediate recession. Though more of the current deficit reduction should have come from spending cuts rather than from onetime sales of government assets, the overall result is adequate—barely.

Yet these accomplishments will not significantly reduce our one-in-ten chance of entering a severe recession within three to five years. An outright depression, though only half as likely, remains frighteningly possible.

Though economic policy has taken a disastrous turn for the worse since President Reagan took office, we had plotted our course toward the precipice long before that. President Lyndon Johnson, to pick one culprit from among many, promised the American people a Great Society, in which social programs would eliminate poverty and injustice; then he found himself sinking into the economic quicksand of Vietnam. Discovering that America could afford either guns or butter, he simply printed the money he needed to give the illusion of paying for both. Three presidents after him struggled to control the inflation triggered by his indecision, yet none found it politically feasible to cut government spending to affordable levels. As a result, by 1981, the nation's long-standing budget surplus was quickly eroding, the country had racked up some $200 billion in foreign debt, inflation had reached double-digit levels for the first time in American history, and the prime lending rate had topped 20 percent. Business, if not collapsing under the load, was clearly facing hard times.

Several very bad decisions in the 1970s and '80s made the long term problem dramatically worse. One was a change in the way Federal budgets are set in Congress. It used to be that government spending was controlled directly by the House of Representatives; if money was to be spent, the House had to make the decision explicitly. Further, tradition demanded that government operate on a pay-as-you-go basis. Congress could not habitually spend money that it had not raised from taxes and other revenue sources. That made it difficult to build up a large deficit.

But it also meant that any loss of revenue—for instance, from a politically popular tax cut—had to eat into equally popular Federal programs. It also meant that Congressmen willing to slash benefits had to go on record by voting for the cut. So, in the early 1970s, Congress invented the entitlement programs. In the name of protecting the poor, *nonpoverty* benefit programs suddenly became untouchable. No one would ever have to face the voters' wrath for enacting a benefit reduction, because the law made any such cuts impossible. And to protect the middle class against losing these benefits to inflation, cost-of-living adjustments (or "COLAs") were added to the programs. Not only had Congress eliminated the one relatively simple —if politically unpopular—method of correcting deficits, it had guaranteed that entitlement costs would go up.

Legislators then enacted a second blow to fiscal responsibility: the Congressional Budget and Impoundment Control Act. Until 1974, when Congress appropriated more money than the President had requested in his budget, the Chief Executive could impound the excess—simply refuse to spend it. The new law required him to spend it all. In preventing some possible abuses of Presidential power, it stripped away one more frail control on government spending.

In the world financial system as well, the controls of the 1960s and early 1970s have been replaced with less inconvenient rules. Gold was still king in those days; the value of paper money was measured against that fixed standard. If one ounce of gold was worth $35, and other currencies were similarly pegged against gold, everyone could be sure that a dollar was worth a given number of Italian lire, Japanese yen, or French francs. Fixed rates made life easy for international business, because there was no danger of signing a contract to sell, say, ten computers in Italy and discovering when the time came to deliver that a drop in the value of the lira had cut your profits in half. But that stability had a price. Countries with healthy export businesses tended to build up stocks of foreign money, while net importers ran short of their own currencies. Thus, balance-of-payments crises periodically shook the system, forcing abrupt changes in the exchange rates.

To avoid such cataclysms, the world's central banks cut themselves loose from gold in 1971. Since then, currencies have been pegged only against each other. In 1973, the finance ministers took the obvious second step and dropped fixed exchange rates entirely. From then on, dollars and lire and yen and francs have floated against each other as the currency markets please, moved only by such "natural" forces as the country's inflation rate and balance of trade. Capital has flown across national boundaries with ever-greater ease in the fifteen years since then.

So long as a nation's economy is strong, floating exchange rates make it easy to borrow foreign capital to finance a temporary budget deficit. Unfortunately, the supply-side economists swept into power with the Reagan Administration had found their economic policy on a T-shirt that read, "I can't be overdrawn. I still have some checks." The deficits that had been economic poison when President Reagan's Democratic predecessors were responsible for them suddenly were discovered to be good for America. Our economy still looked strong, so other nations were more than willing to lend to us. In the United States, the end had become inevitable.

In his first Presidential campaign, Mr. Reagan promised both to cut taxes and to reduce drastically the government spending he found so wasteful. Because Americans would then have more money to invest, the economy would grow, tax revenues would rise even as tax rates fell, the budget would be balanced at last, inflation would finally come under control, and the American economy would be sound again. Instead, declaring in effect that it was more important to feel good about America than to save it, he cut taxes and aimed defense spending toward space.

Let's give credit where it is due, however. Inflation dropped sharply when the new economic policies took effect. Though consumer prices rose at 5.4 percent in the first half of 1987, up from only 1.1 percent the year before, even that was less than one-third of the Carter-era high; in 1979, we had an inflation rate of 18 percent, and a prime interest rate of 21 percent. It is true that we benefited during most of this period from the militantly anti-inflationary stance of then–Federal Reserve Board Chairman Paul Volker, a Carter appointee, and from a sharp drop in the price of oil, which had touched off our inflation problem in the first place. In fact, the moderate rise in consumer prices last year was due largely to the recovery in oil prices. But it would be less than generous to deny the Reagan Administration any credit for reducing inflation.

Another improvement: As of 1986, some 61 percent of American adults were employed, the highest proportion in history. By the end of 1987, we had enjoyed sixty months of relative prosperity. The U.S. economy created 9 million jobs in the first six years of this decade. This was markedly below the 15 million jobs created in the comparable period of the 1970s, and many of today's new jobs are found in poorly paid service industries rather than in yesterday's well-paid manufacturing fields—but we could have done worse.

Yet the decline of inflation and rise of employment are the rare bright spots in an unprecedentedly ugly economic picture. The combination of high defense spending with uncontrollable entitlement programs, massive government borrowing, a strong dollar throughout the mid-1980s, and a truly remarkable personal spending spree have nearly destroyed what was once the strongest economy in the world.

There is blame here for all; not just the Republicans, who have brought us these final steps of our course; but the Democrats, who did so much to prepare the way in previous administrations and have steadfastly defended costly government programs we can no longer afford to let grow out of control. But perhaps the real guilt lies with the American public itself. Not only have we failed to turn our leaders out of office for self-seeking incompetence, we have demanded that Washington give us all the benefits of prosperity without accepting the work that true prosperity would have required. In short, we have asked for economic collapse, and we have almost gotten it. Here are the gruesome details:

• Federal spending rose from roughly one-fifth of our Gross National Product in 1979 to nearly one-fourth in 1986.

• Our Federal budget deficit rose from a relatively controlled 1.7 percent of the GNP, on average, during the 1970s to 4.9 percent of the GNP in 1986. Last year it totaled $148 billion. At best, the nation's leaders hope to reduce their annual deficit to roughly $100 billion by 1990.

• Our national debt tripled from the $645 billion amassed from 1776 through the end of fiscal 1979 to $1.745 trillion at the end of fiscal 1986. That debt is still rising at the rate of $350,000 per minute.

• Federal entitlement programs, paying benefits largely to the middle class, totaled $200 billion in 1979. They have doubled in the Reagan years. The Social Security, Medicare, and Federal pension programs are already committed to paying out nearly $10 trillion to current beneficiaries—$100,000 for every worker in the country. In only four years, a worker retiring in 1981 received in Social Security payments every nickel he and his employer paid into the system during an entire career.

• In 1981, the United States was a creditor nation, and the rest of the world owed us a total of $141 billion. By the end of last year, we had frittered away that credit balance and owed the world roughly $400 billion, nearly one-third of our Gross National Product. Brazil, Argentina, Mexico, and the rest of the Third World debtor nations combined do not owe half as much as the United States. Because interest payments on our debt grow ever faster, the deficit could reach $700 billion in 1989. Most economists believe that our debt to other countries will exceed $1 trillion before it starts to shrink, sometime in the early or mid-1990s. There is reason to fear that it could go much higher and last much longer.

• America's foreign-trade balance disintegrated from a surplus of $17 billion in 1980 to a deficit of $170 billion in 1986. The deficit mounted still further last year, even though our trading partners bought 12 percent more American products in 1987 than in the year before. The cause: a rise of 8.2 percent in imports to the United States, with a total value twice that of our exports. Even more ominously, the 1986 figures included the first deficit ever seen in the high-technology products long dominated by U.S. manufacturers. By August 1987, the trade imbalance had reached a dizzying $15.7 billion per month.

• Personal savings have fallen from about 7 percent of disposable income as recently as 1984 to barely more than 2 percent in the summer of 1987. (Compare that with a savings rate of 23 percent in Japan!) As a result, we can no longer maintain even the minimum level of investment needed to support our public infrastructure and meet the needs of business. Savings rates are rising a bit, but are not expected to average more than about 3.2 percent this year. It is not enough to help significantly.

• Unwilling to do without the goods that savings might have bought, we have let credit-card bills and other consumer debt skyrocket to nearly $600 billion. The interest alone on installment debt now amounts to about 3 percent of the average American's income. These figures do not include the value of home-equity loans, which have become increasingly popular because interest on them can still be deducted in the calculation of Federal income tax.

• Private domestic investment, already at a sickly 6.9 percent of our Gross National Product in the 1970s, has declined to 4.7 percent of the GNP in the first seven years of this decade. The cause was our Federal budget deficit, which consumed the equivalent of 90 percent of our savings in 1986. Among the industrialized nations, only Britain has a lower investment rate.

• • •

None of these are signs of a healthy economy; none can be repaired by the timid stopgaps we have seen from Washington to date. The standard of living in America has been gradually slipping for several years now; we all know that the Baby Boom generation will not live as well as their parents did, and the generation to follow will face even grimmer times. Fifteen years from now, if we play our cards right, those fears will have evaporated in the warmth of a growing economy. But not even heroic measures can nurse the U.S. economy back to health without prolonged pain. The wrong measures, or simple inaction, will turn us from a convalescent nation into a chronic invalid.

For a better look at what the combination of Reaganomics and free-spending entitlement programs has done to the American economy, picture what would have happened if you tried to run your family economy the same way:

Start in 1981. You have always worked hard, tried to put something into the savings account every month, built up a few small investments. It hasn't always been easy, and you've occasionally had to borrow to make ends meet; in fact, you owe a few thousand dollars right now. Your mortgage and car payments are under control, your credit cards near their limits, but not yet over them.

But living on a budget has gotten pretty tiresome. It's time to trade in the car. The stereo needs a new turntable. And it's getting on toward December; it's time for Christmas shopping, and a few weeks in St. Thomas look a lot better than winter in Duluth. But this year's raise won't pay for more than a third of that. Where will you get the rest?

Half of it is easy. Drain what's left of the savings account; it was just sitting there, anyway. And forget about the investments; the hope of profits tomorrow doesn't do a thing for your life today. For the rest? Your credit is still good. Just go down to the bank and borrow what you need. In fact, borrow from every bank in town. Inflation will mean that you get to borrow fat, healthy dollars today and pay back in cheaper dollars tomorrow.

But, you say, the house needs painting, and the bathroom faucet leaks? They will hold for a few more years. Today is what counts. Enjoy.

• • •

That is economic policy as we have known it for the last eight years, and on the national scale it has led to the same result it would in your personal life: to crushing debt.

In the real world, the price for the great spending spree of the '80s is breathtaking. As a country, we have had our raise: We produce more than in the past, about $950 more per worker per year now than in 1979. It amounts to about $100 billion (in 1986 dollars) for the country as a whole. In the past, we would have spent about $855 of that, or $900 million, on increased government purchases and personal consumption; the rest would have been saved and invested. Under Reaganomics, we have spent fully $3,100 per worker per year —$300 billion for the country at large. That extra $2,150 per worker, $200 billion for the nation, has been borrowed from abroad. Last year alone, offshore money bought a grand total of $143 billion in American assets, most of them in one form or another of IOU. In effect, all the houses built in the United States last year, and 40 percent of all business investments, were paid for by borrowing from Japan, Germany, Saudi Arabia, and other countries that still manage to live within their means. One-fourth of our entire national debt in the '80s has been financed through a single company, Nomura Securities, of Tokyo.

It is not impossible to pay off such a debt, but it's not nearly so easy as it was in the days when the government owed its deficit to American citizens. Back then, all we had to do was cut government spending a bit, raise taxes a little, and the taxpayers would end up paying for the services they'd already received. But foreign debt can be repaid only from the profits on foreign trade. Now we must export more of our own goods and services than we import from other countries. In fact, we must do that merely to pay the interest on what we already owe.

Unlike Third World debtors, we actually have goods and services to export. The problem is, we do not export nearly enough of them. Far from making enough profit on our foreign trade to pay our debts, we run a deficit that since 1975 has risen to $170 billion per year.

It comes back to our budget deficit. To borrow money to rehabilitate World War II battleships, operate overseas military bases, meet Social Security and welfare payments, and pay the million other debts the Federal government incurs, we have to pay high interest rates.

High rates push up the cost of borrowing for American companies, making it difficult for them to finance business expansion and pushing up the cost of their products. Pushing our interest rates down aids American business. Pushing them down too far, however, would cut off the government's supply of borrowed dollars and leave no way to pay immediate bills. The only solution would be to drive interest rates up again to draw back foreign investors. The blow to American industry would surely plunge the economy into a severe recession.

High rates also help to keep the value of the dollar high in relation to other currencies, and that makes foreign products cheaper than ours. (It is true that Japan and many other countries also maintain artificial barriers against American imports, but most analysts estimate that this accounts for only 10 percent of our international trade deficit, and perhaps less.) Thus Japanese and French consumers buy relatively few American products, but American consumers buy Japanese cars and French wines at the rate of $270,000 per minute.

In the last two years, the dollar has fallen on world exchange markets, and exports have risen dramatically. But the change is not nearly great enough to solve our budget problems.

How much chance do we have of raising our exports enough to pay the debt in a reasonable time—say, within fifteen years or so, shortly after the turn of the century? Look at the numbers:

Let's say that we manage to wean ourselves from overseas borrowing within six years. Given today's level of foreign debt, and the growing interest on it, our overdue bills will still peak at $1 trillion in 1994. And to accomplish even that, we must improve our trade balance by $20 billion a year, every year, for the next decade—a total of $200 billion. Either we must sell the entire $200 billion in new exports, or we must make up the difference by cutting our imports.

Remember the great oil crises of the 1970s? American drivers and homeowners shrieked in pain as consumer dollars flowed out of the industrialized countries toward the Persian Gulf and made a few oil sheiks the richest men in the world. The total flow of money sucked from the United States in those two unpleasant episodes was less than one-third of the sum that we must now draw back into the country.

It amounts to $200 a year, every year, for every worker in the country. That money can come only from added productivity. Every worker in the United States must make an extra $200 worth of merchandise next year, $200 more than that the following year, and so on. That does not take into account the rising cost of interest on foreign-debt payments. Add another $40 per worker per year to cover those bills. And raising productivity means finding money to invest in new factories and modern equipment; call it $60 per worker per year. It totals $300 more per worker per year needed to bring our foreign debt under control.

There is one more factor to consider: oil. It sells, as this is being written, for $18 per barrel. That is up nearly $6 per barrel in the last year, but well below the cost of producing and marketing oil from American wells. Unless Iranian fanatics manage to depose the governments of Saudi Arabia, Kuwait, and the Trucial States, there is virtually no chance that oil prices will rise high enough in the next decade to bring American wells on-line. In fact, they are expected to fall to only $12 to $15 per barrel by 1990. Thus, barring the unexpected, U.S. production will continue its decline. So instead of importing 25 to 30 percent of our oil in the 1990s, we will import at least half. The best available estimate holds that oil imports, which totaled $44 billion in 1985, will climb to at least $130 billion by 1995 if oil prices remain stable; even at $12 a barrel, the total will be $100 billion. Add that to the total foreign debt we must repay.

Unfortunately, worker productivity in the United States is growing at the anemic rate of $135 per year. That leaves $165 each year to be made up, not counting the possible cost of rising oil imports. How will we get that extra money? By spending less. It does not sound like much of a sacrifice, really, but Americans have long since grown used to being able to spend more, not less, each year. We have not had to face a shrinkage in our disposable income for more than two decades. It's not going to be a pleasant change.

And that assumes that we can actually improve our balance of trade by $200 billion in the next decade. When you try to figure out just what it is we are going to export to earn that money, things look much worse.

More than one-fifth of our foreign trade consists of wheat, corn, and other agricultural products. "Breadbasket of the world," we used to call the American Midwest. Not anymore. Early in this decade, farm exports accounted for nearly one-fifth of all overseas sales; in

1981, we made a profit of $25 billion on our agricultural exports and sales of raw materials. By 1986, farm exports made up only 11 percent of our foreign trade; the total profit from agricultural products and raw materials had fallen to $3 billion.

That sharp drop is not just the product of high dollar values that have driven our prices up. Over the past ten years, most of our traditional markets have managed to improve their farm production dramatically. India, Pakistan, and China once would have faced widespread starvation without American grain; today they actually export farm products. The Common Market countries too have become food exporters. In 1976, they had to import some 25 million tons of grain, most of it from the Unitied States and Canada. Now they actually export about $16 million tons per year. And even the Soviet Union, long plagued by inefficient farms and bad weather, hopes to meet its own food needs by the turn of the century. The declining dollar will raise our agricultural exports temporarily, but farm products will not help to repay our foreign debt. Chances are that in the long run their declining market will make it worse. The same is true for lumber, steel, and other bulk commodities.

The service industries have become the "Great White Hope" of many economic forecasters. The sluggers from the East may have beaten our automakers and computer manufacturers, they say, but travel, shipping, insurance, and the other service industries will surely make up for those losses. After all, isn't America quickly becoming a "service economy"?

Yes and no. It is true that services will acount for about 44 percent of our economy this year and will grow to 88 percent by the year 2000. About 44 percent of people working in the service sector deal with information; they are data-entry personnel, computer operators, and so on. Another 44 percent fix things; they are plumbers, electricians, computer repairmen, and the like. But today, we are actually exporting jobs in the information industries, just as we have done in manufacturing for many years. For example, an insurance company with masses of financial information to digest can send the paper to the Caribbean, have the data entered into computers by people earning $.50 an hour, and get it back by satellite at a total price of $1.25 for an hour's work—one-third of the cost here in the States. If this trend continues to grow, as seems inevitable, the information services could be one of our most disappointing economic sectors.

Further, service exports are not nearly the gold mine that statistics suggest. When economists calculate the value of service exports, they include so-called "debt service"—principally dividend payments to stockholders overseas and interest payments on our foreign debt. Stripped of those unproductive components, our service exports amount to less than $50 billion per year. If service exports double, they still will not make much of a dent in the mountain of debt that we must pay off.

In the long run, it will be manufacturing that bails us out of our international debt. The key is automation. Over the next fifteen years or so, American manufacturers will be forced to adopt all the time-saving, cost-saving methods of cutting-edge industrial engineering: computer-aided design and manufacturing, so-called "flexible manufacturing cells" that can be adapted to turn out a variety of products on short notice, and of course, robots. As a result, we will gradually begin to turn out better products at lower prices. And that means a dramatic renaissance for American exports. But though the new technology is already bringing prosperity to many individual companies, as our economy is now being managed it will be at least ten years before widespread benefits are felt in the general economy.

And in the meantime? If all goes well in agriculture and the service industries—not merely well, but far better than we have any excuse to hope—we will have to sell an extra $275 billion in manufacturing exports over the next ten years. That amounts to a growth rate of 10 percent per year, even without inflation. Just breaking even will be an improvement. Compensating for inflation, exports of manufactured goods have actually shrunk in the 1980s. Manufacturing is not likely to bridge the trade gap before the pain sets in.

Let us say, for the moment, that the dollar remains cheap enough to promote trade, yet does not drop low enough to provoke a recession. There remains a hidden assumption in our discussion thus far which presents the biggest problem of all. What if our trading partners don't want the exports we hope to sell them?

There are only two ways in which other countries can absorb the products we are counting on to pay our debts. Either their economies have to grow rapidly enough to spur demand. Or the value of the dollar must fall dramatically against other currencies—much farther than it has already—so that our products can be sold at bargain-basement prices, yet still earn the huge supply of dollars we need. Neither solution is feasible.

Rapid growth is easiest to discount. The world's economies are growing at a rate of about 2.5 percent per year. Assume that we can add a full 1 percent to that for the foreseeable future. (Don't ask how. There is an old joke about an economist stranded on a desert island with nothing but a crate of canned peaches saved from his ship. After staring at the problem for a few minutes, he mumbles, "Assume a can opener. . . .") Then assume that none of that growth depends on trade with the United States. Even in that best of all possible worlds, we would be lucky to raise our export income by even 3 percent—less than a third of what we need.

Lowering the value of the dollar might theoretically help, for we know that cheaper dollars eventually make it dramatically easier to sell our goods abroad while raising the cost of imports to our own consumers. But that requires cooperation both from our trading partners and from American industry that we have not seen in the past. When the dollar began to drop from its recent peak in 1985, Japanese companies reacted by stockpiling in U.S. warehouses nearly a year's supply of automobiles, consumer electronics, and other products. Thus, they could continue to sell at their old, low prices and maintain their hold on the American market. Our own manufacturers, meanwhile, raised their prices to match the changes they expected to see among Japanese products. The automakers were among the worst offenders. By trying to make a few more dollars on each car, Ford and General Motors threw away their chance to win customers back from Toyota, Nissan, and Honda. Thus it was two years before the cheaper dollar had any significant effect on our balance of trade.

By contrast, the dollar's succeeding drop against foreign currencies in autumn 1987 was so abrupt and unexpected that Japanese manufacturers had no chance to defend against it, and American competitors had no time to squander their advantage. So the record monthly trade deficit of $15.7 billion in August immediately dropped to $14.1 billion in September. How much more improvement we can expect is uncertain, in part because the drop in the dollar's value against the Japanese yen and the German deutschmark has not been matched by similar declines against the currencies of other nations. It has fallen, for example, less than 5 percent against those of Canada and Korea, both major trading partners. Most economists believe—or at least hope—that our export markets would be virtually limitless if the dollar were to fall far enough and our products seemed cheap enough. But even if possible, that solution will not be painless, for it means an end to the low-priced imports on which many American sales and marketing jobs depend.

There is another side to the declining dollar, as well. One primary reason our trading partners are prosperous is that they can sell their products in the United States. Whenever the dollar falls and our exports grow, their exports shrink and competition from our products reduces their sales at home. According to one estimate, a 10 percent fall in the value of the dollar cuts economic growth in France by roughly half a percentage point. That is enough to hurt, and the other trading nations would be equally hard-hit. When the dollar fell to new post war lows against the yen in November 1987, stern-faced Japanese businessmen actually picketed government offices in Tokyo, protesting the loss of a major trading advantage.

If the dollar falls far enough to help significantly in repaying our foreign debt, those Japanese businessmen are likely to opt for armed revolution. Businessmen in other nations that depend on foreign trade would probably be close behind, for what we are asking of them is an enormous sacrifice. At a reasonable guess, Japan alone stands to lose about $50 billion per year in export profits—roughly one-third of its entire manufacturing trade surplus! Such a drop of the dollar could be enough to send some nations into a severe recession.

Our trading partners could soften the shock of that decline by easing interest rates to stimulate demand in their own countries, but they have shown little inclination to do so. Stimulating demand would both reduce the national savings rates that power their industrial production and risk the rise of inflation. In Germany, where inflation after World War I so lowered the value of the deutschmark that it took a wheelbarrowful of bills to buy a loaf of bread, the fear of a recurrence is so ingrained that a significant reduction in interest rates is politically almost impossible—this despite a current inflation rate of less than 1 percent. Japan will find it even more difficult to reduce its interest rates. Its industrial growth has been financed by lending to corporate borrowers at interest rates of only 2.5 to 3 percent.

National economies today are so intertwined that a deep recession

in the United States—the kind we can count on if we reduce our foreign-trade deficit by drastically cutting consumption rather than by promoting exports—would surely destroy our trading partners as well. We saw proof on October 19, 1987, and in the following days, when the record fall of the New York Stock Exchange triggered declines as great or greater in stock markets around the world. So we tend to assume that Japan, Germany, and the rest of the industrialized world, acting in their own self-interest, will adjust their economies to save ours. It is far from certain that they can.

The depression of the 1990s, if it comes, will not be quite the same as the Great Depression of the 1930s. After that grim lesson, the United States enacted a wide variety of programs designed to protect both the national economy and private individuals from future disaster. Unemployment compensation, Social Security, the Federal Deposit Insurance Corporation, and the Federal Savings and Loan Insurance Corporation were all born of the Depression, and they have functioned well ever since. Because of those programs, bank depositors this time around will not mob the teller's windows demanding money that the banks have irretrievably lost. The elderly will not find themselves bereft of both savings and income. The unemployed will not have to line up at soup kitchens—at least, not until their checks run out.

But we will have massive unemployment. And this time, there will be no world war to jump-start our economy by replacing one misery with another, the remedy for which was better understood.

In another world, there would be almost no chance of ever seeing another depression. That world would be inhabited by model citizens willing to put their nation's interests before their own, governed by cooperative leaders more concerned with the welfare of their countrymen than with their own reelection. Further, it would be a world where both citizens and leaders can recognize the mutual cost of national competition and, when absolutely necessary, sacrifice short-term profits for long-term survival.

The government policies that would prevent the crisis of October 19, 1987, from growing out of control are obvious to any economist or politician willing to accept them. (For a close look at them, turn to Appendix A.) But those measures are political dynamite, for they threaten the cherished privileges of every special-interest group in every developed country of the world, and most especially in the United States. They are opposed by what the operations-research community calls Savage's Law of Minimum Regrets: People, and most especially elected officials, make their decisions not according to how much good they will bring their company or country in the long run, but according to how much immediate harm they personally willl suffer.

The Senators and Congressmen who cut entitlement programs and raise taxes—and their counterparts in other countries—will face angry voters eager to turn them out of office. Yet without such painful measures we face a future of growing constraints at best, and bitter poverty at worst. Whether this country and its trading partners are led by men and women willing to sacrifice their political careers merely to spare their nations the inconvenience of depression is something that readers can best judge for themselves.

2

HOW YESTERDAY'S WARNING COULD TURN INTO TOMORROW'S ECONOMIC MELTDOWN

ON MARCH 28, 1979, the worst commercial nuclear accident in the United States history drained the coolant from one of the power reactors at the Three Mile Island (Pennsylvania) generating station, causing a partial core meltdown. Both equipment failures and inattentive, poorly trained human beings were to blame. Yet for all the "I told you so's" that antinuclear activists heaped on the power industry, and for all the gargantuan cost of repairing the facility—a task still far from complete—as potential accidents go, Three Mile Island was something of a bust. Even badly damaged, the reactor did not explode; the amount of radiation released was negligible. Despite a depressing array of errors by the plant's too-human workers, the last of the reactor's safety systems—the steel-and-concrete containment vessel—had done its job.

In April 1986, the Soviet Union was not so lucky. The Chernobyl reactor was of a type long considered obsolete in the United States, with relatively primitive safety systems and no containment shell at all. By all accounts, Soviet technicians were not trained even as well as those at Three Mile Island, and safety procedures had grown almost unbelievably lax. Thus, what should have been a controllable malfunction destroyed most of the installation, killing dozens of technicians and emergency workers and spewing radioactive gas that soon covered much of Europe.

On October 19, 1987, the world economy, led by that of the United States, had its Three Mile Island. The next such shock could quickly become an economic Chernobyl from which it would take years to recover. As we saw in the last chapter, many of the safety systems intended to protect against economic disaster are not working. Either they have been dismantled or, particularly in the United

States, they have fallen into the hands of politicians who seem far less interested in the welfare of their nation, and world, than in taking the greatest possible credit for the least possible accomplishment. At this point, the U.S. economy needs only the right combination of accidents and negligence to trigger an economic meltdown, and many such combinations are possible.

Take a moment to review just part of the sorry list of problems:

• Pay-as-you-go spending in the United States has been replaced by entitlement programs with automatic cost-of-living adjustments that make it impossible to hold popular government programs to affordable budgets. Thus the Federal budget has soared out of control and shows no sign of being stabilized. When our leaders in Washington claim to have cut the budget, what they really mean is that they have not raised it quite so much as they wanted.

• The once-traditional gold standard, and the exchange controls that replaced it, have been replaced in turn by a nonsystem of floating exchange rates and free passage of currency between the world's developed nations, making it easier to finance national debts with international borrowing. The Louvre Agreements signed by the seven major Free World industrialized nations late in 1987 represent an attempt to regain control over foreign exchange markets, but in large part the damage has already been done.

• The U.S. debt to other countries has grown so large that not even radical budget cuts and unprecedented trade growth can keep growing interest payments from pushing it to $1 trillion by 1994.

• Raising American exports enough to bring our foreign debt under control could so reduce the profits of our trading partners that they can no longer afford to buy our goods, driving us all into a deep recession.

• Though Americans have begun to save a little more of their money —just over 4 percent in early 1988, up from less than 3 percent in the previous summer—four years of frantic spending have left them with little to fall back on if their jobs and income vanish. Private investment has also fallen to its lowest point in memory, in part because savings are so low, and in part because they are being absorbed by Federal borrowing; in future years, this will cut into the job-creating power of private industry.

• • •

To this catalog, we can add several other problems, both immediate and potential. One is the response of our trading partners to American pressure for open markets. Faced with demands that Japan lower its trade barriers in many key areas of its economy, and especially in politically important farm markets, Japanese businessmen now feel the relationship between our countries has gone from good to very bad indeed. For this, they blame American politicians and businessmen, who are unwilling to take responsibility for the economic problems they—definitely not Japan—have created. In one recent poll, Japanese citizens forecast that if their nation were ever again dragged into a war, it would not be against the Soviet Union, but against the United States! Korean surveys mirror Japan's discontent with American pressure tactics. If the United States acts upon threats to match our trading partners barrier for barrier, these partners may well decide that not even the giant American market is lucrative enough to justify tolerating the conditions of doing business here. In that case, our hopes of paying off our foreign debt—not just in the foreseeable future, but *ever*—would vanish overnight.

The so-called "tax reform" of 1986 threatens equally severe domestic problems. Virtually all the new jobs created in the United States in the past decade have appeared in small, fast-growing companies. Much of the credit for this growth goes to just two pieces of tax legislation enacted early in the Reagan years: our relatively low capital-gains taxes and the investment tax credit. Tax breaks for the rich? Perhaps. But low capital-gains taxes encourage investors and venture capitalists to buy stocks. And that gives companies the money required to finance their growth—in short, to create new jobs which people sorely need. The investment tax credit lowered corporate tax bills when they put money into new production capacity, another strong boost to future job growth. The Tax Reform Act of 1986 did away with both these fertile measures. Repeal of the investment tax credit was made retroactive in 1986. And from 1988 on, capital gains will be taxed as ordinary income.

There is no way to tell exactly what impact loss of the investment tax credit will have on the American economy; it's never happened before. But we have all too much experience with changes in capital-gains taxes. In 1969, Congress nearly doubled the maximum tax on long-term capital gains from 25 percent to 49 percent. Venture capital, the lifeblood of risky new businesses, dried up. In 1969, under the old rate, investors had put $171 million into high-risk new ventures; by 1975, the flow had shrunk to only $10 millon, and new business start-ups had dropped sharply. In 1978, Congress came to its senses and cut the capital-gains tax back to 28 percent. Three years later, venture capitalists were funding new companies to the tune of $1.3 *billion*—an increase of 13,000 percent in only six years! Reducing the capital-gains tax to 20 percent early in the Reagan years spurred a similar job-creating leap in funding of new ventures.

Now Congress has returned us to 1969. All things being equal, confiscating one-third of an investor's patiently earned profits should be less discouraging than taking half his earnings. But today's tax change is more damaging than that of 1969. Even at 49 percent, capital-gains taxes were lower than ordinary income-tax rates then in force. That should have given investors a reason to put their money into risky new businesses. Yet they fled the venture-capital market almost to a man. The new tax law gives potential investors no incentive at all to put their capital into hazardous new start-up companies. It is a good guess that they will therefore seek out safer ways to make their capital grow. Entrepreneurs will soon find it much more difficult to obtain the money they need to enter business. Jobs which the American economy might have had, and will sorely need, will be lost as a result.

No, neither of these blunders will plunge the United States into recession tomorrow. But they deprive us of two more life preservers that have buoyed up our economy in a sea of troubles. They put us that much closer to going under.

As this is written, talk of a depression, or even a minor recession, seems alarmist and perhaps out of touch with reality. Since the Black Monday scare in October 1987, the economy has rebounded strongly. The Dow Jones index is up well over 2000, just when the gloom-and-doom brigade once said it would be reaching new lows, and Wall Street analysts are beginning again to sound as if they believe it will remain forever high. Housing starts were off a bit in January 1988—in fact, they hit their lowest levels in more than five years—but overall residential sales are still running strong. Even America's poor, downtrodden manufacturers have found new prosperity, thanks to soaring exports spurred by the decline of the dollar. Factories are running at well over 80 percent capacity, and shipping companies report that their cargo haulers are booked up three sailings in advance. Automakers expect to sell 100,000 cars in other countries, more than twice their 1987 performance. (Admittedly, that isn't very impressive when compared with the 3.1 million foreign cars that will be sold here, but at least the trend is promising.) Even Honda has taken to building its cars here and shipping them home to Japan. And USX, the former United States Steel, says that it is planning to resume large-scale steel exports for the first time in years. It seems that as long as the dollar remains low, there will be jobs and prosperity for all.

Yet it is alarmingly easy to find the symptoms of underlying sickness in this seemingly healthy post–Black Monday economy. Start with a minor item, the low value-added of our exports. Japan and Korea and Taiwan bury us in cars and consumer electronics. And it's true that our manufactured goods are recovering their markets abroad, now that the dollar is down. But do you know which of our exports to the Pacific countries ranks number one? It's wastepaper. They use it to make boxes for the products they sell to us. There is not much profit for us, nor many new jobs, in wastepaper.

Look at some more evidence:

Though Federal taxes were cut in the early Reagan years, state and local taxes have risen to compensate for the lost revenue. As a result, the percentage of the Gross National Product consumed by total government spending has climbed steadily. At the end of 1987, it reached more than 30 percent, its highest level in history. (For comparison, the United States managed to fund the entire Second World War with taxes that equaled less than 25 percent of the GNP.) The so-called "tax simplification" enacted in 1986 resulted in substantially higher effective tax rates, most of which will come into effect in 1988 and '89. In part, this was accomplished by plugging nearly all the loopholes through which people formerly shielded their earnings from the tax man. Most of the remaining revenue was gained by sharply raising corporate taxes—in effect, by taxing investors' income before they got to put their hands on it. (Of course, this can also be viewed as a hidden national sales tax, because much of the cost to the company is passed on to consumers.) In addition, the compromise budget plan agreed to by Congress and the Administration early in 1988 raised the Federal take by $9 billion in unspecified new taxes and nearly $9 billion more in other revenues. The end result will be to shift still more of the GNP into government hands in future and leave private citizens with still less money to keep the economy growing.

Personal income rose in 1987, but farm subsidies accounted for much of the gain. Once adjusted for inflation and tax increases, disposable income has not risen so slowly since 1982. Manufacturing workers actually earned less in November 1987 than they had a year earlier. As a result, consumer spending grew progressively weaker throughout 1987. Spending for clothing, gasoline, and even food dropped for the year. Not even last-minute Christmas shopping in the country's high-tech and financial centers compensated for the weakness in the rest of the country. Consumer spending makes up fully two-thirds of the Gross National Product, so any continuing decline could easily wipe out the benefit of gains in export sales. Manufacturers are already bracing for the worst. In late 1987, the Commerce Department forecast that spending by producers for new plants and equipment would jump sharply in the year's last quarter. In fact, their durable-goods spending dropped by more than 7 percent.

If it continues, this trend alone could be enough to tip us into recession. Weak sales mean slower hiring. If sales weaken further, companies begin to lay off workers. Jobless workers can't afford to buy the way they used to, so consumer spending drops still further, in a deadly circle. We have passed this way before.

But that is not all. There are signs that inflation could be making a comeback. Energy prices were up slightly in January 1988, largely because the price of natural gas was up, offsetting a drop in the cost of oil. Food and housing cost more as well. The same low dollar that has given us new export markets has raised the cost of imported consumer goods by almost 20 percent since early 1987. Foreign cars are up more than 25 percent in two years, and American automakers (ever shortsighted) have followed their lead with double-digit price hikes. And sharply rising prices in such industrial basics as steel, aluminum, chemicals, and plastics during 1987 are being translated into higher prices of consumer goods in 1988 and '89.

To date, low oil prices have kept the overall inflation rate down, and Forecasting International does not expect the cost per barrel to rise significantly. (It costs only $5 to lift a barrel of oil from the bottom of the North Sea, only $2 more to have it refined and delivered. In Saudi Arabia, lifting costs are only $1.38 per barrel; refining and delivery cost little more than $1.) But there is at least one factor that could change this prediction: Oil prices are fixed in U.S. dollars. As the dollar drops against other currencies, oil exporters receive fewer yen, francs, and lire for their crude. If the dollar again begins to head for new lows, the day will come when OPEC is forced to raise its member nations' prices in American dollars simply to shore up their profits from sales elsewhere. At that point, a sharp rise in inflation is inevitable. (Later in this chapter, we will look at another painful possibility that could accomplish the same end.) It was the dollar's decline in the early 1970s—augmented by sheer greed on the part of OPEC members—that triggered the rise in oil prices from $2 per barrel to $40 per barrel, sending the U.S. inflation rate into double digits.

At some point, rising inflation would require a hike in interest rates that would cut into housing sales and make it still more difficult for business to finance expansion, or even its existing operations. In fact, the economy can keep going even if interest rates slowly rise to 10 percent. But if the rise is quick, it becomes much more difficult to adjust. And manufacturers may choose to cut back well before they need to rather than risk further spending when they cannot predict how high inflation will go. In that case, all bets are off.

As we saw in the last chapter, America's debt burden is so large that paying it back will almost inevitably weigh down our standard of living for years to come. Combine that drain on our spending money with the signs of weakness already appearing, and there are many forces that could turn our current sluggish economic progress into a full-fledged rout.

Let's take a look at the worst of all possible worlds. It could yet turn out to be the one in which we live.

The single most important fact about the American economy in 1988 is not really economic, it's political: 1988 is an election year. Therefore, the Federal Reserve Board will hold interest rates down in an effort to keep the stock market looking healthy after its heart attack in 1987. This will have the added benefit of propping up housing sales, which would drop alarmingly at the first sign of a significant increase.

More importantly, none of the hard choices will be made. None of the politically sensitive programs will be hit with budget cuts, and most especially not the most expensive, fastest-growing burden of all —Social Security. In fact, when the President's budget proposal for the 1988 fiscal year arrived, virtually all of it having been hammered out in negotiation with Congressional leaders, it carried an admitted deficit of $139 billion. Privately, a few relatively honest Washingtonians conceded that the government would run closer to $170 billion in the red. In short, the deficit may actually be larger in fiscal 1988 than it was before all that well-publicized budget cutting.

It is generally bad policy during an election year, but we will venture one firm political prediction: Democratic Congressman Richard Gephardt's get-tough-with-Japan trade policy won him so many votes in Presidential primaries that at some point Congress and the next President will decide that it was not such a bad idea after all. In one form or another, the U.S. government will push Japan and Korea even harder to abandon the trade restrictions that politicians and businessmen like to blame for our balance-of-trade deficit.

So let's look forward to 1990.

The last two years have not been kind to the American economy. All the improvements of 1988—the export boom that promised to cure our trade deficit, a growth rate that unexpectedly touched 4 percent, the recovery on Wall Street, the brief and deceptive glow that resembled economic health—all of them depended on low interest rates and the falling dollar. But low interest rates did more than stimulate our economy; they also discouraged foreign investors from buying American Treasury bonds. So did Washington's refusal to reduce the Federal budget deficit. (Why lend good money at low rates of interest to a government that has little hope of being able to pay it back?) In an effort to lure those investors back, so that the government can continue to spend money it has not taken directly from the pockets of American voters, the Federal Reserve Board has been raising interest rates a bit at a time for more than a year. As a result, the dollar has risen on foreign-exchange markets, but exports have lagged and stock prices have begun to drift downward. Though we have managed to avoid recession, GNP growth has slowed to less than 1 percent per year, its lowest level in recent memory. Inflation is edging upward again. But worst of all are the twin deficits.

Long, hard negotiating sessions between Congress and the Administration have eliminated the last-minute budget battles that plagued the Reagan years, but an air of grudging cooperation is about all they have produced. Each year, the President and Congressional leaders congratulate themselves for enacting huge budget cuts and avoiding major new taxes. But when examined closely, most of the spending cuts turn out to be illusory—fraudulent might be a better word—and revenues have been raised largely by selling off government assets, a practice that cannot continue. Our leaders still forthrightly refuse to cut the spiraling cost of popular entitlement programs. As a result, the Federal budget has ended up further in the red after each round of so-called "cuts."

The trade deficit also remains high. Imports from the "Four Tigers"—Hong Kong, Singapore, South Korea, and Taiwan—actually rose when the dollar fell, because their currencies fell with it on the world market. As prices of Japanese and European imports soared, theirs held steady. And after a six-month decline, imports from Japan also rebounded as manufacturers there struggled successfully to lower prices. As this was happening, the great surge in American exports lost its momentum. As exports went up and the deficit came down, the dollar rose on exchange markets, and American products lost much of their competitive advantage over products from other countries. Export income is off slightly and promises to fall further. Hopes that exports will ever bring America's economy back to health have largely faded.

Employment statistics are also signaling trouble. Unemployment rose slightly during the third quarter for the first time in three years. Government economists attribute this to the slowdown in exports and consumer spending, which has led a few companies to lay off some of the workers hired during the boom of 1988. Others note that fewer new jobs are being created with each passing month. Fewer new companies are being born this year, apparently because investors have withdrawn from the venture-capital market.

All this is mirrored in the Consumer Confidence Index, which has declined slightly with each new report that interest rates and inflation are going up. Recently, consumer sales have begun to fall, and inventories have begun to build up in the stores. Throughout the country, most major retailers report that the Christmas season was their most disappointing in the last decade. Housing sales are down as well. Ominously, the much-respected Index of Leading Economic Indicators now forecasts at least a small recession within six months.

• • •

Spring 1990. The first of the crises comes early in the year, at the GATT talks, the semiannual planning session of the General Agreement on Tariffs and Trade, in which economic leaders from the major Free World trading nations bicker over policy. The meeting begins as business as usual, with each delegate trying to manipulate world trade to his government's political advantage while avoiding an all-out trade war.

As always, the talks focus on an old argument: The representative from the United States demands that Japan drop the complex network of tariffs, quotas, quality standards, and other trade barriers that American leaders blame for our inability to penetrate Japanese markets. He presses other demands as well. Japan, he says, must stimulate its economy, so that its citizens will buy more American products. It must cut its taxes and reduce its already-low interest rates so that they will have more money to spend.

Some of our demands are disguised as concern for the Japanese people. In simple decency, Japan should establish a national pollution-control program, so that its citizens can breathe clean air—and, though our negotiator does not say it, so that Japanese manufacturers will be burdened by the same costly regulations that help drive up the price of American products. And it's time that Japan "reform" its educational system to give its people a broader view of the world than mere technology and commerce. (Again, the real purpose is unstated: If Japan's educational system more closely resembles ours, maybe its graduates will resemble ours as well—virtually unable to read, write, or count above ten without removing their shoes, and hopelessly ill-equipped to deal with an increasingly technological world.) Further, the government should establish a national social-security program, not just rely on corporate retirement programs. And surely Japan can afford to pay for its own defense, even if America continues to provide the military manpower.

None of this is new. America has trotted out the same list of demands at every opportunity since the mid-1980s.

In the past, Japan has negotiated hard and then done its best to give the image of change without the substance. In 1988, for example, it made a show of stimulating its economy with a budget increase. On close inspection, it turned out that the previous year's budget had been followed by several supplementary appropriations, much like Washington's habitual continuing resolutions. When those appropriations were taken into account, 1988 spending was no larger than in 1987.

This time, there is a dramatic change. Japan's central banker flatly rejects the American demands. According to his figures, once Japan's trade statistics are adjusted for inflation, the country has actually been running its own trade deficit of 5 trillion yen per year (about $40 billion) ever since the dollar plummeted in 1987. Beyond that, he announces, Japan is through paying for America's free-spending lifestyle. Japanese insurance companies alone lost more than $17 billion when the fall of the dollar cut the value of U.S. Treasury bonds they had purchased—far more than American banks stand to lose from all the bad loans they have made to inept governments throughout the world. If the United States cannot bring itself to balance the Federal budget, Japan will make no more concessions on trade or any other subject.

The talks end with a threat from the United States: Japan has one year to eliminate its trade restrictions. After that, America will raise barriers of its own, just as Congressman Gephardt proposed two years earlier.

In the Middle East, Iraq has made two bad mistakes in the same month. One of its fighters fired a Silkworm missile at an American frigate. Unlike the ill-fated *Stark,* the ship destroyed the missile in midair. Two weeks later, a second Iraqi fighter managed to shoot down an American F-16 well outside Iraqi airspace. America's stated policy of neutrality in the Iran–Iraq war is now truly neutral. Throughout the country, Iraq is viewed no more favorably than the dying Ayatollah's Iran.

Autumn 1990. During the U.S. budget negotiations, another long-standing quarrel with our allies has flared up: the cost of our military commitments to them. In all, the Pentagon spends, directly and indirectly, some $280 billion per year to defend our allies. Included in this is some $7 billion per year spent to guarantee the passage of Kuwaiti oil through the Persian Gulf to Japan, a particularly sore point with House Democrats. Congress has long pointed out that America's dependents are no longer frail states impoverished by world war, but among the richest countries in the world, with huge surpluses in their trade with the United States. Japan spends only 1 percent of its GNP on defense, a huge advantage over us in maintaining economic health. Even West Germany, bordered by the Iron Curtain, spends less on defense than we do. It is time, Congress declares, that both countries paid far more of their own defense costs, even if American troops continue to do the actual work. Over the President's objections, this becomes part of next year's budget plan. From now on, both Japan and West Germany will be billed at least $10 billion per year each for American military services, or America will bring most of its troops home.

The move provokes loud protests from both countries. Japan points out that it is already paying $4 billion per year to help defray America's military expenses in the Far East. Congress is unmoved. West Germany agrees to raise its contributions. Japan does not.

American trade statistics look worse than they have since 1986, when the dollar's value on exchange markets was at its all-time high. Japan and, to a lesser extent, Germany, are shipping goods into the country at record rates, stockpiling merchandise to soften the blow if the United States goes through with its threat to erect harsh new tariffs and other trade sanctions. Japanese firms begin to lay off workers at their American plants and shift their operations to other countries.

Both inflation and unemployment continue to edge slowly higher, while consumer spending eases. Factories, too, are buying fewer machine tools and less of other capital goods.

In West Germany, natural gas begins to arrive through the newly finished pipeline from the Soviet Union. In one move, the country becomes nearly independent of oil from the Middle East—and very dependent on the Soviets.

Spring 1991. In late January, the Commerce Department announces last year's final economic statistics. Inflation averaged 4.9 percent in 1990, but rose steadily to end the year at 5.7 percent. The budget deficit has finally broken $200 billion. The December trade deficit reached $19.4 billion, a new high. Unemployment totaled 7.5 percent in December. The Dow Jones Industrial Average loses 268 points in two days.

After months of heated debate, Congress passes a trade bill that subjects Japan to import restrictions much like its own. Its sponsors claim the measure will cut our trade deficit by more than $25 billion in the first year alone. The President signs the bill into law immediately, but the barriers will go into effect only if Japan fails to eliminate its tariffs and quotas by the end of the upcoming conference on international trade.

West Germany signs a new trade agreement with the Soviet Union. Its exports of computers, automated machine tools, and other high technology to the Soviets are expected to total more than $100 billion within the next decade.

At the GATT talks, the spokesman for Japan denounces America's new trade policy and declares that his sovereign country will never be ruled by blackmail from Washington. The trade bill takes effect, and imports from Japan drop sharply. In response Tokyo enacts new trade restrictions that virtually prohibit American imports and forbids the purchase of American government bonds by Japanese corporations. Tokyo further decrees that profits earned by Japanese divisions of multinational corporations must remain in Japan.

Desperate to attract foreign investors to American bonds, the Federal Reserve Board hikes interest rates by a full percentage point, to 10.25 percent.

The stock market suffers its second 200-point one-day loss. For the first time in history, trading on the New York Exchange is halted for two days.

In the Middle East, the fragile Iran–Iraq truce suddenly erupts into war. For nearly three years, it has been rumored that a major European government with a taste for foreign trade has sold Iran a nuclear reactor. When West Germany sold Iraq a reactor, Israeli bombers destroyed it before completion; this time no one has interfered. Iran's reactor is now confirmed to have been operating for two years—almost long enough to produce atomic weapons and smuggle them into Baghdad. Recognizing that it faces extinction, the Iraqi government renews its combined gas and infantry attacks at Abadan, at the mouth of the Euphrates River, near the border of Kuwait. Iran's bombs are not quite ready, but its armed forces are. In a massed counterattack, Iranian troops pour into Iraq, crushing the Iraqi army and recruiting most of its survivors to the cause of Islamic fundamentalism. The combined hordes move on into Kuwait and the Trucial States. In Saudi Arabia, the ruling family prepares to flee as Shiite Moslems riot in the streets of Riyadh.

At this point, you can see what happens next. The Dow heads toward zero, oil prices aim for infinity, and international trade virtually disappears. First in America, and then throughout the Free World, the jobless threaten to outnumber those still employed.

It's the worst of all possible worlds. But it *is* a possible world. The Great Depression of the 1930s was not caused by the stock-market crash in 1929. Rather, it occurred as a result of two blunders in the year that followed. The Hoover Administration made the first when it tightened credit after Black Thursday and stopped business in its tracks—an error that Fed Chairman Alan Greenspan avoided in 1987. The United States and its trading partners compounded the damage by passing trade restrictions such as the Smoot-Hawley Act of 1930. Some legislators still seem eager to make that mistake. This time around, it would almost surely tip our economic balance toward recession.

The frightening end of our scenario is also possible. Rumors have floated through the international community since late 1987 that one of the NATO countries has supplied Iran with a nuclear reactor suitable for the production of bomb-grade uranium, supposedly to produce defoliating chemicals. (What use a desert nation has for defoliants has never been explained.) Never mind that to give Iran access to nuclear weapons is an act of criminal stupidity, if not outright madness. No one has ever accused the country in question of being less than stupid in its eagerness to placate terrorist nations—or in its grasping for money.

We do not believe that more than a few of the events sketched above will actually come to pass. Which few? It remains open to question. The problem is not that any one event will, if it occurs, drive us into a new depression, but that there are so many factors which could aim us toward economic catastrophe. And once the slide begins, there is no telling how far it will go. It is not a future we would wish to face unprepared.

3

HOW OUR LIVES WILL CHANGE
AND ALL THINGS BE DIFFERENT

ECONOMICALLY, SOCIALLY, PERSONALLY, the 1990s will change our lives more than any decade in recent memory. Many of us will experience the next twelve years as a time of dislocation, destroying lives we once thought secure and leaving only chaos behind. Others will find the 1990s a period of liberation, of retraining for a lifestyle of greater freedom and prosperity. For them, economic hardship will be a difficult part of an unavoidable transition which in the long run will be worth the inconvenience it brings. Staying out of the first group and becoming part of the second will require foresight and planning. We will leave planning for the last three chapters of this book. For now, let's peer into the future to find out just what changes we face. Many of them are easily predicted.

Do you remember the difference between a recession and a depression? When the other guy is out of work, it's a recession; when you are out of work, it's a depression. Given competent leaders, both in the United States and in other Western trading nations, the 1990s could be a time of growing prosperity. Yet many people would still suffer their own personal depressions. Many would be out of work.

In the industrialized, unionized states of the "Rust Belt," we can already see what the coming crash will mean for the rest of the nation. More than half of the manufacturing jobs that existed in this country in 1960 have been lost. By the year 2000, half of the remaining jobs will be gone. With them will go the supporting roles that depend on them; local markets, appliance stores, real estate agencies, and similar enterprises will be forced to cut back or go out of business, as many have done before them, adding to the unemployment rolls.

In the recession of the early 1980s, many of these lost jobs could be blamed on foreign competition. Yet even now, when the low dollar has given American manufacturers new export markets, only 15 percent of the workers who lost manufacturing jobs six or seven years ago have gotten them back. Another 35 percent have found other work, mostly in poorly paid service industries. Fully half remain unemployed. Even in the deficit-financed good times of the Reagan boom, unemployment in some Midwestern cities remained near 25 percent—as high as in the Great Depression. There may be worse to come.

The reason is automation. American manufacturers simply cannot compete on the world market with traditional methods; too often, they have even lost their customers here at home. The newest, most automated equipment lets them turn out higher-quality products, faster, at much lower prices, and that is their only chance to survive in the face of competition from foreign companies with highly automated plants and employees willing to accept lower salaries than American workers are used to. Companies that have automated their plants have grown rich in the new low-dollar economy. Companies that have not automated continue to struggle; many have died. Either way, they need—or can afford—far fewer human workers than in the trade booms of past decades.

Recession can only make this inevitable transition to "steel-collar" workers—robots and flexible manufacturing cells—harder on the human beings they replace. In a sound economy, even unhealthy companies can struggle to survive, and thereby carry a few more workers on into their retirement years. In a waterlogged economy, marginal companies die, throwing all their employees into the job market. And in a severe recession, not even low-wage service jobs will be open to them.

Millions of white-collar workers around the United States have already joined the blue-collar pioneers on the unemployment lines, displaced from unproductive management positions as large, top-heavy companies trim themselves to leaner, more competitive forms. Many more face the same fate. Automation, foreign competition, and simple bad management are already slowing the growth of employment, both in high-tech fields that Americans once thought secure and in some of the better-paid service industries. This trend will grow worse as the 1986 tax changes and the coming rebirth of inflation stifle already meager capital spending and drive investors out of the stock market.

One trend that will add to unemployment in many job markets is the decline of the middle. In one industry after another, corporate giants prosper; little companies prosper in market niches too small for the conglomerates; but the mid-sized companies either merge into the giants or wither and die, unable to compete.

Look at American agriculture, for example. Large, commercial farms are the only segment of the industry still growing. In 1985, there were some 23,000 farms with more than $500,000 per year in gross sales; they accounted for one-fourth of all farm products raised in this country and made half of all farm profit. Mid-sized farms, with sales between $100,000 and $500,000, number 250,000, grow 40 percent of our crops, and make one-third of all farm income. And today there are still 2 million farms with annual sales of $100,000 or less; they grow 35 percent of our crops and take home 15 percent of all farm income.

By the year 2000, these figures will have changed dramatically. There will be 50,000 giant corporate farms growing two-thirds of American crops and making 75 percent of the profit. Most small, part-time farms will also survive. By the year 2000, they will grow only 15 percent of the country's agricultural products and earn only 5 percent of the profits; but three-fourths will still be in business. But fully 60 percent of the mid-sized farms will be gone. Some will have grown into corporate giants; most will have vanished. The few that remain will be slowly dying.

The same trend can be seen in the airline industry. Today, there are ten major domestic carriers; by the year 2001, only three will be left. Yet there are many dozens of tiny regional carriers and commuter airlines, each flourishing within its local niche.

It is at work also in the hospitality industry, where the top 25 chains now control half of the nation's hotel rooms. Eventually, only three or four giant chains will dominate the industry. Yet there will be room still for independent hotels and resorts with a unique personality and a strong emphasis on service.

And in the health-care industry. In 1985, there were 300,000 separate health-care providers. By the year 2000, only 20 giant systems will provide medical and hospital care and health insurance to more than half of the American population. At one point in 1987, Louisville-based Humana Hospital Corporation was buying up one hospital every day. Hospital Corporation of America was buying five to six hospitals a week. Small ambulatory-care and "surgicenters" are also growing rapidly. There were 2,000 of these small, neighborhood facilities in 1985; they treated 45 million Americans and billed almost $2 billion per year. By the year 2000, there will be 10,000 "doc-in-a-box" operations, and they will own one-fourth of the national market for health care.

We can expect similar changes in many widely differing industries: department stores, restaurants, banks, and financial institutions. In each case, the industry consolidates, either driving mid-sized players out of business or merging them into one of the competing conglomerates. Small companies with specialized, service-oriented market niches prosper as well. But mid-sized companies disappear.

Unfortunately, the loss of jobs is disproportionately high when mid-sized companies go under, because most of them need more people to get their work done than smaller or larger operations would. Again, farming is typical of industry in general. Tiny farms, often run as a hobby or to carry on family tradition, can seldom afford to hire many laborers; but with small crops, they don't need many. Huge farms are well automated and therefore need less manpower to grow their produce. Mid-sized farms cannot bring in their crops without more hands than a family can provide and cannot afford the machinery that keeps commercial agriculture humming; they rely on hired labor. That makes for smaller profits when harvest time comes and a greater threat of failure when prices fall. And when several mid-sized farms go under, they take far more farm jobs with them than one large corporate farm would.

Again, this trend can only be made worse by recession. When prices drop, mom-and-pop operations can adapt, because they need relatively small profits to survive. Giant corporations prosper because they can afford the best automated equipment to help them cut costs and they can build a single, integrated corporate staff to manage their many divisions with relatively little overhead. But mid-sized companies lack any saving advantages.

Just what this will mean for the employees varies widely with their field. The medical industry is growing so quickly that health-care professionals will have no trouble finding new jobs. Hotel and motel employees who once worked for mid-sized companies may actually find themselves earning more after being hired by large conglomerates. But few manufacturing workers will find any demand for their skills; they will have to retrain for new industries. Many former executives will be in the same position.

Even industries that thrived throughout the 1980s will be hard hit by an economic downturn. One of the darkest areas will be in housing and construction, where a contraction seems to have begun already. In October 1987, a relatively minor rise in mortgage rates drove new-housing starts down by a startling 8.2 percent. Home sales also dropped in November and December 1987 and January and February of 1988. We can expect far worse if, as is all too likely, Washington leaders eventually find themselves forced to push up interest rates in an attempt to draw foreign investors back to the U.S. financial market. Individual carpenters, plumbers, and electricians will still find work in repairing homes and making inexpensive additions, but many mid-sized building concerns will collapse along with their market, sending added thousands looking for work.

It is not inevitable, but it would take only a few mistakes to trigger a dramatic rise in joblessness. If the most pessimistic estimates prove accurate, there could be 25 million unemployed in the United States by 1995.

It is not difficult to figure out what unemployment would mean to most people's lives. Those of us who are young enough or lucky enough never to have been jobless can look to virtually everyone they know for examples. But a few details may make it clearer just how vulnerable we have become.

Personal income ought to be one measure of our ability to withstand adversity. Assuming we have handled our money wisely, the more we have earned, the more we should have saved, and the better we should be able to hold out while searching for a new job. By that standard, things have not been going well for us these last few years. The 1960s and '70s look brighter in our memories not simply because we were twenty years younger or because we have forgotten the old struggles to make ends meet, but because our economic lives really were better.

Cheerleaders for the American corporate system often point to the Gross National Product as proof of how well the economy has served us all. GNP per person has grown constantly for decades—by 2.6 percent per year, on average, throughout the 1960s and 1.6 percent per year since then. It sounds like a healthy economy, if not as buoyant as it once was. And there is a good deal of ~~~~~~ since the 1950s, prices have soared, if you calculate you look at the number of hours most people them, most goods are cheaper. A kitchen range what it did in the '50s. An average man's suit is half it was thirty years ago. So is a six-pack of beer.

Unfortunately, the 1950s were a long time ago, and our expectations have changed since then. For the generation that grew up in the 1960s and '70s, life is looking markedly less comfortable than it did when they were children. Adjusting for inflation, the average household lost 8 percent of its income between 1972 and 1985. Hourly wages have fallen by nearly 9 percent. They're dropping still. And some things actually do cost more than they did thirty years ago. People worked 30 percent longer in 1986 to pay for a visit to the doctor than they would have in 1956. Car insurance is up by 50 percent. A movie ticket has risen 7 percent.

Worse yet, it is taking more people to earn that income. Back in 1970, only 40 percent of Americans held jobs. Today, it's 46 percent. That does not sound like much of a difference, but it means that 33 million new workers have entered the job market in the last fifteen years. Two-thirds are women, many of whom once would have stayed home. It is true that many women today would have taken jobs even if they had a choice, but that is a choice they do not really have. Without their income, many families could not maintain what we have come to think of as a normal standard of living. In 1987, the Congressional Joint Economic Committee took a look at what would have happened to family income if women had not taken on some of the breadwinner's burden. In 1973, they found, the average thirty-year-old man earned $25,253 (figuring it in 1986 dollars). By 1984, his income had fallen to $18,763; more than one-fourth of his purchasing power had evaporated in just a decade. Because more women had gone off to work, family income fell by only 3 percent; without their income, it would have dropped three times as far. And again, the decline is continuing today.

In short, it takes two people now to earn a middle-class income. If one of us loses a job, having that second salary in the family won't keep us out of poverty. The new poor person is the single head of household.

In fact, on average our situation is even more fragile than that.

Unwilling to let our lifestyles decline with our real incomes, many of us have been borrowing heavily. Consumer installment debt equaled more than 16 percent of personal income in 1987; that October, American consumers owed a record-high $609 billion, up more than 5 percent from a year earlier. In the twelve preceding months, consumer debt had skyrocketed more than 13 percent; overall, it is up by more than 75 percent since 1982. So-called "home-equity loans" —doesn't that sound less frightening than "second mortgage"?— raise the total debt even higher.

Again, in the industrialized North-Central States we have already seen the predictable results of this massive debt load. When the economy turns down and jobs begin to disappear, a wave of bankruptcies and foreclosures will leave many families in poverty. The only defense is to pay off those debts before the crisis arrives, but an estimated 70 percent of American families already have trouble making the minimum payments on their credit cards and installment loans.

Declining real income and high debt don't leave much chance to save for bad times, and (as noted in Chapter 1) Americans have done predictably little saving these last few years. As recently as 1984, we were saving about 7 percent of our income. At that rate, with today's earnings, an average family would add about $1,960 to their savings account this year. It's not much compared with the $6,440 that an average Japanese family would save from the same pay, but at least it's something. Instead, Americans are saving at a rate of little more than 3 percent, or $840 for an average family. Lose even one salary, and that will disappear almost overnight. And that is only an average. For every family that saves more, another saves less. Too many find it impossible to put any money aside at all. In a recession, unemployment insurance and welfare will be their only hope of survival, and most workers will find that their unemployment checks run out long before they can find a new job.

If you are like most homeowners, your house is the largest, most profitable investment you've ever made. For most of us, it represents a kind of savings-account-of-last-resort. Reluctant as we might be to tap into it, if our lives fall apart we can always sell the house and survive on the proceeds while learning some new way to earn a living. That may not be true for much longer.

If the American economy is as badly mismanaged in the 1990s as it has been during the 1980s, real estate values will plunge as people lose the ability to pay high prices for houses and condominiums. In early 1988, the average price of an American home neared $150,000 for the first time in history; the last time it failed to climb from one year to the next was between 1978 and 1981, when national-average new-home prices actually fell by some $20,000 (calculated in 1987 dollars). But even before a recession strikes, home sales are falling off; too many people have already found themselves priced out of the housing market.

Again we can see what will happen to property values in the 1990s by looking to the "Rust Bowl" and the oil states in the early 1980s. In the North-Central States, three-story Victorian houses can be had at prices as low as $40,000. And throughout much of Texas and Oklahoma, almost anyone with a job can buy a luxurious home with only a small down payment. Just walk into a bank, and talk to the loan officer in charge of repossessed houses. If he can sell a house that once cost $350,000 and get one more bad debt off the bank's ledgers, he will have done his job, no matter how low the sale price. But once you own the house, don't expect to sell it. Even without a depression, it will be many years before Oil Belt real estate recovers its former value.

Some of the social changes we can expect to see in the 1990s have also made their first tentative appearances. It used to be that men married at age twenty-two, women at about twenty. Today, the average man is four years older when he marries, the average woman about three years. Having children is delayed even longer. Women who had their first baby at age thirty-five used to be a rarity. Today, they are almost common. The reason has as much to do with economics as with new sexual mores. Smaller real incomes make it harder to set up a home and to support children today than it was twenty years ago. In a recession, it will be more difficult still. People will marry even later, and more couples will delay having children until late in the woman's childbearing years.

Once married, though, couples will stay together longer. There is something very steadying in the knowledge that it takes two incomes to survive. In the 1990s, divorce rates will fall sharply.

Recession will bring back another custom from past generations: the extended family. Rather than searching for an affordable house, new couples will move in with their in-laws. Rather than trying to maintain a home of their own, grandparents will move in with their children, freeing their daughter (-in-law) to look for work while they take care of the kids. We saw a small trend toward this new family unity in the recession of the early '80s, particularly in the industrial states of the North. If the economy falls apart, it will return on a large scale throughout the country.

Children will remain part of this extended family far longer than they do today, because they will not be going to college as soon as everyone expected. They may not go at all. The reason, of course, is cost. Short of getting a full scholarship, they won't be able to pay for tuition, books, housing, and the hundred other costs of going off to school. Scholarships may still help the best students, but they will not be as readily available as they are today. In addition, families will need all the breadwinners they can produce. So when they graduate from high school, or drop out, young men and women will go straight to work at whatever jobs they can find. For the first time in years, fast-food franchises will be able to take down their "Help Wanted" signs, and colleges will be as they were in the '30s, the province of the rich and nearly rich.

Recession will force the government to act at last to correct many long-standing problems. In the 1990s, it will move both to clean up the mess it made of the economy in the '80s and to minimize the suffering of its citizens until the repairs take effect. Many of the measures it will enact can be found in Appendix A; they are things that should have been done long ago to avoid the problems we now face.

As we saw in Chapter 1, the government's insistence on spending money it does not have is at the root of our economic troubles. Therefore, most of the changes to come will be aimed at balancing the Federal budget. Until that is accomplished, there is no hope of escape from a long and painful recession. Trying to tax our way to a balanced budget would deprive people of the money they need to live and take from business the capital required to create new jobs. So the first obvious step will be across-the-board spending cuts. Without them, any other efforts will be wasted.

The easy, politically safe cuts have already been made; all the programs with few defenders have been slashed, from employment training to the school-lunch program. So new savings will have to come from programs that have been largely exempt from budget problems:

defense and the entitlements. And most of those cuts must affect the politically popular entitlement programs—Social Security, Medicare, and the Civil Service and military retirement systems. The reason is obvious: in the 1988 budget, defense accounts for $291 billion, the entitlement programs for a whopping $506 billion—47 cents out of every tax dollar. Until that burden is reduced, there is no hope of balancing the Federal budget.

By far the easiest way to cut entitlements, and therefore the one that Washington will choose first, is to place a means test on Social Security and Medicare. These entitlements were intended to shield retirees from a life of poverty. In practice, perhaps one-fifth of the money doled out under these programs goes to people who truly need it; the remainder has turned into a kind of welfare for the wealthy. (See Appendix A for details.) Limiting entitlement payments to people with a median income or less would save roughly one-third of every tax dollar the Federal government receives. That alone would be more than enough to balance the budget.

However, Social Security and Medicare are defended by tight-knit organizations with tremendous political power. Thus, it seems unlikely that whatever means test is eventually enacted will eliminate any but the richest recipients. Therefore, some other means of saving on these programs will be needed. The only one that seems politically feasible is a small cut in the cost-of-living adjustment. As things stand, whenever inflation raises the cost of living by at least 6 percent, Social Security payments rise as well. In fact, in 1987, when the inflation rate was barely 4 percent and no COLA was required, Congress raised the payments anyway. In future, COLAs will be limited to 80 percent of the inflation rate. By the year 2000, this will save at least $50 billion.

We can expect a wide variety of cuts in other parts of the Federal budget as well. There will be long-needed cuts in pork-barrel construction projects that destroy the environment and serve only to produce temporary jobs for the constituents of powerful Congressmen. Foreign aid is likely to shrink a bit. Expect some minor cuts in farm subsidies as well. And new volunteers for the military will face retirement at age fifty, not forty, after at least twenty-five years in the service.

On the other side of the ledger will be "revenue enhancements"—taxes and fees designed to avoid still more budget cuts. So-called "sin taxes'' on liquor and tobacco products will be easiest to enact and among the most lucrative. Add in a higher tax on gasoline, and the total take should come to at least $12 billion per year. We will also bill our allies at least $20 billion per year for the troops and other military aid we supply.

If these measures leave the Federal budget in the red, Washington will follow Europe's lead and enact a value-added tax (VAT), a kind of national sales tax that bills companies for the amount of value they add to their product. For example, in the long process of building a car, the government would take its cut of the value added at each stage on the route from iron ore to auto: The smelter would be charged for turning ore into steel, rolling mills for turning bulk steel into sheet, subcontractors for their contributions, and the carmaker for all the parts it makes and assembles into the final product. We can expect stiff resistance to this massive new tax, and to the bureaucracy needed to oversee it, so the VAT will be saved as a last resort. It will be delayed until late in the 1990s, if it is enacted at all.

At least three new pieces of legislation will be designed to protect American citizens from destruction by a failing economy. A few years ago, farmers faced with losing their land asked Congress to place a moratorium on foreclosures. In the 1990s, consumers will succeed where they failed. Faced with a growing wave of foreclosures among the increasingly jobless middle class, Congress will call a three-year halt to the real estate auctions so that homeowners can get back on their feet. Credit-card debt is in for a similar moratorium. For three years, strapped consumers will be allowed to pay only the interest on their Visa and MasterCard bills, leaving the principal for a time when the economy has recovered and their income has returned to normal. Finally, government will join with private industry to create a nationwide retraining program for displaced workers. Under the plan, people who have lost their jobs as a result of economic changes will be given new skills fitted to the growing high-tech industries.

Finally, one long-overdue measure that we expect to pass is enactment of Federal educational standards designed to make America's future generations better able to compete on the world labor market. Japanese students learn under conditions that would horrify most American parents. In Tokyo, for example, each classroom holds an average of forty-five students, all working with a single teacher. Yet they learn more of the hard subjects—math, science, and foreign languages—by the end of high school than most American students pick up in four years of college. The Japanese culture and the high motivation of the students are only part of the reason. Simple exposure to learning is another. In the United States, high school students spend an average of 180 six-hour days per year in school; in many cases, there is little or no homework. In contrast, Japanese students spend 240 days per year in school, eight hours per day, and take home at least two hours of work per day. In addition, most go to special "cram schools," where they spend another four hours per day, and all of Saturday, reinforcing the lessons learned in public school. Theirs is a harder curriculum as well. In Japan, high school students master elementary statistics and calculus; in the United States, it is possible to graduate from high school without having mastered finger counting. American students may not face such stiff standards as the Japanese, even by the year 2000. But at least they will spend a bit longer trying to learn whatever is demanded of them. Expect at least seven-hour school days and a 210-day school year throughout the United States before the 1990s are over. A national core curriculum and common standards of teacher competence are two more changes that would improve our school systems, but they face such heavily political opposition that their chances of passage seem mediocre at best.

Almost surely we will see one major addition to school curricula throughout the country: genuinely effective computer-literacy programs. For all the billions of dollars' worth of personal computers and software purchased by the nation's school systems to date, very few high schools send their students into the world qualified to deal with the intimidating array of spreadsheets and databases, expert systems and automated machinery they are forced to master at work even today. How could they do better? Educators themselves have never had to deal with computers and therefore have no idea what to teach their students. Within ten years, that will change dramatically as a generation of teachers who grew up with their own computers enters the schools. This will do more to improve our competitiveness in the world economy than any other development in American education.

This chapter has offered only a broad overview of some of the things that will happen during the next recession. No more than that is possible, for the details of the crash will vary widely from the industrialized North-Central region to the information-industry centers of both coasts and from Wyoming's broad ranchlands to the retirement meccas of Florida. It is those missing details which will determine how well you can survive a recession, given your job and place of residence.

Fortunately, the information you need should be relatively easy to find. Just go to your nearest library, and read back issues of your local newspaper for the years 1981 through 1983. Concentrate on the business news. As it happened in the early 1980s, so it will occur in the 1990s. If you find that your industry and region fared significantly better than most during that decline, you can hope to survive the next in relative comfort. If you find your local paper filled with stories of urban decline, of massive unemployment and a standard of living in free fall, it may be time to consider looking for another locale in which to live.

Do not trust to your own memory or to the recollections of co-workers. In retrospect, the recession of the early 1980s may seem better or worse than it actually was. Special circumstances that influenced your life or the lives of your neighbors may no longer hold true. If your job has changed or your business has found new markets, your experiences in the next recession could differ markedly from those of the past. The only way to prepare for them is with hard information and careful analysis of your position today.

PART TWO

SURVIVING THE 1990s

4

VICTORS AND VICTIMS OF THE
COMING SHAKE-OUT

IN CHAPTER 2, we looked at the many changes in our economy that have destroyed a wide range of traditionally lucrative jobs. Now let's examine the factors that will transform the job market in the next decade and answer the crucial questions: Which jobs will vanish? Which will survive? Which will flourish? How tough will the competition be? Who will get the good jobs?

• One trend of the 1970s and '80s that will continue in the 1990s is the decline of manufacturing and growth of service industries. As long ago as 1980, according to the U.S. Labor Department, more than 65 million people worked in the service sector. By 1990, that will have grown to nearly 84 million. And by the turn of the century, nearly 90 percent of American workers—more than 120 million— will hold service jobs. An estimated 22 percent of these will work in their homes, connected to their employers only by computer networks and their paychecks. The remainder will be evenly divided between blue-collar workers and information processors. Though manufacturing industries will still contribute more than one-fifth of the Gross National Product, as they have for almost forty years, they will employ a little less than 5 percent of the American labor force— about the same portion as agriculture.

This change will not mean a mass descent into poverty for former manufacturing workers forced to move into service areas—*if* they can manage to retrain themselves. Nor do the high school graduating classes of 1995 necessarily face a lifetime of flipping hamburgers for salaries smaller than the average welfare check. It's true that the clerk who served your last Big Mac was a service worker, but so are your doctor, the physics professors at MIT, and the Wall Street whizzes who manage billion-dollar pension funds. In fact, slightly fewer employees in service industries fall into the bottom third of the income spectrum than in manufacturing, and about 10 percent more earn their way into the top third. Fully 12 of the 24 fastest-growing jobs offer average starting salaries in excess of $15,000 per year, 13 provide median salaries of $25,000 or more, and 3 average at least $50,000. All are service jobs.

• Demographics are one key influence that will be radically different in the 1990s than in the past. By the year 2000, the U.S. labor force will total between 135 million and 140 million, up from only 115 million in 1985. That sounds like a rapid change, and yet this growth rate is actually slower than at any time since the 1930s. It portends a severe shortage of workers, particularly for entry-level positions.

In the last ten years we have seen the change begin. During the 1970s, when the last of the Baby Boom generation was entering the job market, the U.S. population grew at an average rate of 1.9 percent per year, the labor force by 2.9 percent. Those numbers meant that employers could afford to pick and choose among job applicants. In 1980, there were still more than 25 million new workers between the ages of sixteen and twenty-four. By 1987, population growth had slowed to roughly 0.9 percent, and there were only 23 million new workers. In 1995, with a smaller generation yet, the figure is expected to be barely more than 21 million. In anything but an all-out depression, the supply of new workers will barely keep pace with the number of new jobs opening up for them.

The effects of this trend can already be seen in falling unemployment figures. Though the American economy added only 9 million new jobs between 1980 and 1986, compared with 15 million in the comparable period a decade before, unemployment rates have dropped to less than 6 percent. For white males, the rate was only 4.9 percent in January 1988, while in the executive and professional categories it ranged from 2.4 percent to 2.6 percent. In 31 major metropolitan areas, overall unemployment totaled less than 4 percent. For employers, clearly, the easy days are at an end.

This change will bring major advances for groups traditionally disadvantaged in the job market. Of the 25 million or so people who begin their careers by the year 2000, nearly 16 million will be women.

More than 60 percent of women then are expected to hold full-time jobs, and a healthy fraction of the remainder will work part-time. Many of these women will be shunted into the same ill-paid jobs they occupy today; they will become salesclerks, secretaries, and so on. But an ever-growing number of women are fully qualified and aiming for professional and technical careers. In some leading universities, one-fourth of the students majoring in scientific and technical disciplines are coeds.

In theory, minorities should make rapid gains as well. Nonwhites now make up about 14 percent of the work force. By the year 2000, roughly 29 percent of first-time job seekers will be members of minority groups. Unfortunately, it seems unlikely that this will translate to economic gains for today's disadvantaged. One reason is that blacks and Hispanics simply don't live where the jobs are. According to the U.S. Census Bureau, about half of Hispanics and somewhat more blacks are city dwellers. New jobs are concentrated in the suburbs. As a result, teenage unemployment in cities like Detroit may top 50 percent, while entry-level jobs go begging a few unbridgeable miles outside town. Until this problem is solved, minority unemployment will remain high.

An answer may already be in sight, however. In fact, two possible solutions are being tested, with encouraging results. Some suburban employers, unable to fill minimum-wage openings in their own communities, have begun to bus workers from nearby cities, providing jobs for many who had given up hope of finding work. And some county governments are helping low-income people move from cities with high unemployment to suburbs with a shortage of service workers. Under these plans, the county either offers a tax break for low-income housing in the suburbs or pays part of the housing costs for new workers. Fairfax County, Virginia, and Montgomery County, Maryland—among the richest communities in their states, but with pockets of urban poverty—have both found subsidized housing a practical way to put workers where the jobs are.

These programs will be widely copied in the coming decade. Many businesses will begin busing inner-city residents as the shortage of service workers tightens still further. And while busing to an entry-level job seldom offers much hope of advancement, it may be the only route away from welfare that many inner-city residents will find. Subsidized housing will grow more slowly, in part because it is costlier than busing, and in part because wealthy suburbanites are loath to open their towns to less fortunate neighbors. Yet it promises a permanent escape from the hereditary dependence on welfare that has grown up in the inner cities. How many minority workers share in the opportunities to come depends largely on how quickly these programs are adopted throughout the country.

• Education will be another obstacle for many job hunters. According to the Hudson Institute, jobs open to high school dropouts—and even high school graduates—are growing ever scarcer, while demand for workers with a junior college education and above will soar in the 1990s. In part, this is because the fastest-growing fields (see Tables 2, 3, and 4) are those which require long training: computer science, health technology, the legal profession, and so on. In part also, it results from a kind of educational inflation that has struck existing jobs. As new technology changes the way in which work is accomplished, more training is needed to function in the workplace. Manufacturers used to be able to hire almost anyone off the street to run machines in their factories; today virtually all job openings require a high school diploma, and a few crucial shop-floor positions require an engineering degree. Even a department-store salesclerk today must have at least minimal competence with computerized inventory-control systems. And at the bottom end of the employment ladder, the National Restaurant Association forecasts that by 1995 a million jobs could go begging, in part because too many first-time job seekers are too poorly educated even to become waiters, cashiers, or hamburger flippers. Yet each year, more than 500,000 high school graduates drop out before graduation. Of those who do graduate, perhaps 700,000 are effectively illiterate.

EDUCATION FOR TOMORROW'S JOBS

SCHOOLING REQUIRED	TODAY'S JOBS	NEW JOBS
8 Years or Less	6%	4%
Some High School	12	10
High School Diploma	40	35
Some College	20	22
College or Advanced Degree	22	30

Data from the Hudson Institute

THE CHANGING OCCUPATIONAL STRUCTURE, 1984–2000

OCCUPATION	JOBS IN 1984 (000)	NEW JOBS (000)	GROWTH RATE (%)
Total	105,008	25,952	25
Service Occupations	16,059	5,957	37
Managerial and Management-Related	10,893	4,280	39
Marketing and Sales	10,656	4,150	39
Administrative Support	18,483	3,620	20
Technicians	3,146	1,389	44
Health Diagnosing and Treating Occupations	2,478	1,384	53
Teachers, Librarians, and Counselors	4,437	1,381	31
Mechanics, Installers, and Repairers	4,264	966	23
Transportation and Heavy Equipment Operators	4,604	752	16
Engineers, Architects, and Surveyors	1,477	600	41
Construction Trades	3,127	595	19
Natural, Computer, and Mathematical Scientists	647	442	68
Writers, Artists, Entertainers, and Athletes	1,092	425	39
Other Professionals and Paraprofessionals	825	355	43
Lawyers and Judges	457	326	71
Social, Recreational, and Religious Workers	759	235	31
Helpers and Laborers	4,168	205	5
Social Scientists	173	70	40
Precision Production Workers	2,790	61	2
Plant and Systems Workers	275	36	13
Blue Collar Supervisors	1,442	−6	−0.4
Miners	175	−28	−16
Handworkers, Assemblers, and Fabricators	2,604	−179	−7
Machine Setters, Operators, and Tenders	5,527	−448	−8
Agriculture, Forestry, and Fisheries	4,480	−538	−12

Data from the Hudson Institute

THE FASTEST-GROWING JOBS, 1985–1995

JOB TITLE	GROWTH (PERCENT)	NUMBER NEEDED (000)	STARTING SALARY (000)	MEDIAN SALARY (000)
Paralegal Assistant	98	—	$ 9	$16
Computer Programmer	72	258	$19	$35
Computer Systems Analyst	69	260	$25	$45
Medical Assistant	62	—	$ 7	$14
Computer Service Technician	56	93	$18	$28
Electrical or Electronics Engineer	53	367	$22	$33
Actuary	51	—	$13	$30
Electrical or Electronics Engineering Technician	50	359	$12	$14
Computer Console and Equipment Operator	46	558	$10	$18
Health Service Administrator	44	220	$19	$50
Travel Agent	44	52	$10	$18
Physical Therapist	42	34	$17	$27
Physician's Assistant	40	10	$18	$22
Podiatrist	39	12	$22	$50
Financial Services Sales	39	—	—	—
Engineer	36	—	—	—
Attorney	36	487	$21	$60
Accountant or Auditor	35	1,047	$17	$25
Correctional Institution Officer	35	103	$12	$25
Mechanical Engineer	34	237	$20	$28
Registered Nurse	33	1,302	$14	$20
Public Relations	32	131	$12	$32
Computerized-Tool Programmer	32	200	$12	$20
Occupational Therapist	31	—	$15	$22
Medical Records Technician	31	20	$12	$23

Data from the Bureau of Labor Statistics and Forecasting International

THE 24 LARGEST JOB CATEGORIES

JOB TITLE	NUMBER NEEDED (000)	STARTING SALARY (000)	MEDIAN SALARY (000)
Food Service Worker (Commercial Cook)	4,436	$ 7	$20
Secretary or Stenographer	3,490	$ 9	$12
Sales Worker, Retail	3,300	$ 7	$14
Salesclerk, Retail	2,435	$ 6	$14
Truck Driver	2,275	$17	$27
Bookkeeper	1,904	$10	$17
Computer Software Writer, General	1,830	$20	$30
Housing Rehabilitation Technician	1,750	$14	$24
Waiter or Waitress	1,700	$ 7	$12
Assembler	1,670	$ 8	$20
Teacher, Elementary School	1,600	$17	—
Cashier	1,554	$12	$17
Energy Conservation Technician	1,500	$13	$26
Hazardous Waste Disposal Technician	1,500	$15	$28
Farmer or Farm Manager	1,485	—	—
Registered Nurse	1,302	$14	$20
Blue Collar Worker Supervisor	1,300	$16	$19
Teacher, Secondary School	1,243	$18	—
Farm Worker or Supervisor	1,218	$13	$22
Auto Mechanic	1,197	$ 9	$14
Carpenter	1,185	$16	$28
Accountant	1,047	$17	$25
Typist	1,023	$ 8	$12
Sales Representative, Wholesale	1,001	$18	$33

Data from the Bureau of Labor Statistics and Forecasting International

NINE LARGEST SERVICE-INDUSTRY JOB MARKETS

Retail Trade	12.5 million
Education	9.1 million
Health Care	8 million
Government	7.7 million
Finance, Insurance, and Real Estate	6.4 million
Bars and Restaurants	6.0 million
Wholesale Trade	5.9 million
Transportation and Public Utilities	5.8 million
Business Services	5 million

Data from U.S. Bureau of Labor Statistics

During the last decade, industry has begun to cope with the deficiencies of modern schooling. Nearly all of the Fortune 500 companies have set up large educational departments to train their employees; many operate remedial classes to help their workers master such basic skills as reading and arithmetic. And many firms are solving personnel problems by providing crutches for the educationally disabled. The military showed the way with shoulder-fired missiles that operate with the simplicity of a "point-and-shoot" camera: The infantryman simply lines up the cross hairs on the target, adjusts a range control until a red light in the sight turns green, and presses the trigger. Similarly, as factories grow ever more automated, their equipment is becoming easier to operate. On some modern assembly lines, the worker simply watches his machine, waiting to press an "Emergency Stop" button if something goes wrong. And in many information-oriented jobs, workers are guided by computerized "expert systems," which condense a skilled employee's knowledge and judgment into a piece of software. One of the most successful expert systems helps unskilled bank employees to evaluate loan applications just as a trained loan officer would. This trend has put off into the future the day when it becomes impossible to find a good job without technical training.

Yet smart machines also have their dark side. When companies hire poorly educated workers, they offer bargain-basement salaries, and there is little hope of promotion for employees who cannot read their own paychecks. And the automation that allows an illiterate worker to run an assembly line sharply reduces the number of employees that plant will need. In the 1990s, the only jobs in high demand will be those which require special training and the minimum wage, going-nowhere jobs for unskilled labor. Minority workers, with far higher dropout rates and lower average reading and math scores than whites, will find themselves on the wrong side of this division.

For most of this century, the driving force in the American economy, and that of the developed world, has been technology. Technology it will remain in the next decade. In this section, we'll focus on some of the fields where new technology offers the fastest-growing employment opportunities.

First, though, a minor disclaimer: Just how much any new technology will change the job markets of the 1990s depends on how quickly each new development moves from the laboratory to the marketplace, and that is never easy to predict, even when the idea is capable of spawning a whole new industry within a few years. Similarly, some technologies that now seem promising may well fail to turn a profit. And even if they are profitable, they may yet add few jobs to the American workplace.

It's getting harder to make such forecasts every day, for two reasons: The product-development cycle is moving ever faster; and some of our competitors have gotten better at crucial parts of it than we are.

Any product goes through four steps in its life cycle: idea, invention, innovation, and imitation.

The idea is the basic science behind the product; for example, one of the ideas behind today's computers is the science of solid-state physics, which gave scientists the notion that they could build microchips. Invention is the creation of the prototype, the proof-of-concept machine that first turns the idea into a working reality. Innovation is product development—putting a glossy finish on the rough prototype so that consumers will buy it. Imitation spreads the product through the marketplace, as the original developer adds new features and competitors produce their own versions. It is imitation that creates the most jobs.

In the last twenty years, that cycle has shrunk dramatically. At the beginning of this century, it often took forty years to move a product from idea to imitation. The huge chemical industry that was the high-tech of World War I and the 1920s grew out of basic science learned in the 1880s. By mid-century, the cycle was down to twenty years. The giant plastics industry that flourished in the 1960s had its origins in efforts to devise substitutes for hard-to-get natural materials during World War II. By the late 1970s, biotechnology companies were springing up to exploit the discoveries geneticists had made only five years earlier. And in some market niches, firms have to move even faster: Software companies that specialize in tax-preparation programs have just three months to update and sell their products from the time Internal Revenue finalizes its regulations for the year until they become obsolete on April 15. At this point, today's theories could become marketable products almost before this ink dries.

But there is another factor to consider as well. An old business joke carries the painful truth: "You can always tell the pioneers. They are the ones lying in the sand with arrows in their backs." Ideas, inventions, and innovations all cost money; this side of a Las Vegas craps table, there is no easier way to go broke than in developing a first-of-its-kind product. Innovators at least can make a profit, usually after years of costly work, but it is their imitators who really clean up. For them, success is as close to a sure thing as can be found in the business world.

Unfortunately, Americans tend to specialize in the first three steps. There is no one better at new ideas than the United States. Since the end of World War II, 43 American scientists have won the Nobel Prize in physics, 27 in chemistry, and no fewer than 57 in physiology and medicine. (Only 16 Germans and 3 Japanese have won Nobel science awards in the last forty-two years.) We're not bad at invention and innovation, either, as companies like Xerox, Polaroid, and Apple Computer clearly demonstrate.

But more and more, we've left the profitable, job-creating process of imitation to others. For proof, just look at your VCR. American and British engineers patented the first video recorders in 1954; those first prototypes cost $1 million each. Broadcast-quality video recorders reached the market ten years later, carrying American labels and $10,000 price tags. The innovation step that brought their cost down to home-appliance levels took most of another decade. All that engineering-development work was carried out in the United States. Yet by 1974, imitators from Japan and Korea, working under licenses from the American inventors, had spent $5 billion to perfect the technology and production processes, and they dominated the market with cheaper, equally serviceable products. Today not a single VCR is built here, not a single manufacturing job has been added to the American economy.

Here are three more cautionary examples of how hard it is to predict the fate of a new product:

About four decades ago, a little-known inventor asked the famed consulting firm of Arthur D. Little to analyze the prospects for his latest creation. The Little staff found no possible market for it. Unconvinced, he asked them to try again, but this more exhaustive study also pronounced his device worthless. A few years later, it was the first Xerox copier.

In 1977, Steve Wozniak and Steve Jobs were developing their first Apple computers. Upon hearing of them, Kenneth Olson, founder of Digital Equipment Corporation, declared that there was no reason for anyone to have a computer in his home.

In stark contrast was the fate of the Rollamite, an odd mechanism developed in the early 1960s at Albuquerque's government-sponsored Sandia Laboratories. In essence, it was a bearing that virtually eliminated both friction and slippage. Engineers hailed it as the first new basic machine, comparable to the lever or pulley, invented in several hundred years, and they designed it into hundreds of products, from thermostats to flush-toilet mechanisms. Only one ever made it to market, a shock-sensitive switch used to trigger emergency radio beacons in crashed airplanes. Everything else the Rollamite could do was already being accomplished more cheaply by other mechanisms.

You get the idea.

There is no doubt that we have overlooked a few promising technologies which will create thousands of new jobs in the next ten or fifteen years; some may not yet exist. Almost certainly some developments that now show promise will prove disappointing, at least in the short term. And all too often, the bright ideas that pay off best will go the way of the VCR, creating jobs for Japanese and Korean workers, but doing little for Americans.

But at least five areas of innovation seem sure to flourish in the 1990s. Two are already huge industries, but are destined to grow ever larger. Three are still in their earliest stages of development. And a sixth field closely related to technology is also on the launch pad, though it is being driven by social and economic forces more than by new product development. To make it in any of these fields, would-be career builders will need special training.

COMPUTERS AND DATA PROCESSING. The biggest of the big, the electronics industry employs nearly 2.5 million American workers. Computers and data processing are by far the most vital segment of this industry. Computer companies have grown at a steady rate of 20 percent per year for fully three decades now; they are still growing at a rate of roughly 15 percent per year. Because of this, the computer industry has created nearly 900,000 new jobs since 1978. Just how long this vast employment market can continue to grow is unclear, but even slower growth in so large a worker population means a vast number of new jobs in the next dozen years.

As in the past decade, one of the deciding factors will be foreign competition. Employment in the consumer segment of this industry faces relatively little threat from overseas, if only because nearly all of the vulnerable jobs—nearly all of the jobs outside marketing—have long since emigrated to the Far East. Firms that produce computers and related products have been by far the most vigorous segment of the American electronics industry, yet they too have had a good deal to worry about.

Little more than five years ago, American semiconductor manufacturers dominated the world. Today, Far Eastern electronics firms supply an ever-larger portion of our microchips. They virtually own the multibillion-dollar market for memory chips and are slowly beginning to compete in microprocessors, the "brains" that give computers their "intelligence." Only the market for special-purpose, semicustomized chips still seems relatively safe for U.S. manufacturers; as long as exchange rates for the dollar remain low, it will probably remain in American hands.

A similar trend can be seen in the market for computer peripherals. Ten years ago, American manufacturers produced virtually all of the computer printers sold in the United States. Then Epson entered the field. Today, they and a few other companies from the Far East produce nearly all the dot-matrix printers sold in the world. Canon and Ricoh—both Japanese—make the central mechanisms for most laser printers, the fastest-growing part of the printer market.

For U.S. computer manufacturers, overseas competition is also growing. Toshiba, Sony, Sharp, Hyundai, Olivetti, and a host of anonymous "generic PC" makers all sell here. Leading Edge, a prominent computer marketer from Massachusetts, lends its all-American image to products made in Korea. And it is growing increasingly difficult to tell where a supposedly American computer was really made. As noted earlier, the vast majority of chips plugged into computers built here now come from the Far East; in many cases, hardware "built" here is pieced together from boards, boxes, and power supplies imported as finished subassemblies.

Yet the picture is brighter than it might appear. Many of the transactions now recorded as computer imports actually occur within companies that are primarily American. Almost all major computer manufacturers now own component factories overseas, where cheaper labor cuts the cost of parts; even in IBM's all-American computers, 39 percent of the parts are made overseas, many of them in factories throughout the Far East. Ireland has recently emerged as a major source of computer components, largely because American companies have set up subsidiaries there. All products shipped from these subsidiaries to their American parents count as imports. It is true that each of these overseas subsidiaries represents jobs lost to American workers; yet it is the American firms that earn the final profits and boost the American economy.

Even taking these transactions into account, American firms still build more than half of the world's computers and own more than 40 percent of the export market. In the most profitable end of the microcomputer market—for small business machines and home computers with a base price in excess of $1,000—they still outsell all foreign competitors at home and abroad. In fact, American companies have sold more than half of the computers installed in all the Free World nations with the exceptions of Japan and Britain. Even in Japan, the second-largest computer company—close behind Fujitsu—is IBM. And in Britain only large-scale government support keeps the major local manufacturer, ICL, Ltd., in business; the firm has actually been losing money for many years.

America's dominance in the world computer industry is not likely to vanish with the 1980s, in part because the United States itself remains the world's largest single market for data-processing equipment; there are more than 500,000 large computer installations in this country, more than in Europe and Japan combined. In addition, the dollar's continuing decline against other currencies should dramatically improve our share of overseas markets. Both these factors will foster greater employment in this key industry.

The real driver of job growth, however, will be technology itself. It's no secret that computers have found their way into an ever-greater variety of products, from automobiles to toasters. This trend can only move faster in the years to come.

By the year 2000, office computers will take a letter, transcribe it with nearly flawless accuracy, and translate it into any of a dozen foreign languages. (The day is long past when an experimental translator began with the phrase, "The spirit is willing, but the flesh is weak," converted it to Russian and back, and emerged with "The wine is fine, but the meat is rancid." Yet as recently as 1987, an English-to-Japanese translation program did reduce "Out of sight, out of mind" to the unlikely "invisible idiot.") Kurzweil Applied Intelligence, of Cambridge, Massachusetts has been marketing a "voicewriter" with a vocabulary of 1,000 words since 1985. More advanced models are now available; IBM has a prototype capable of understanding 30,000 words. One physician who uses the 1,000-word device says that his radiology reports go out faster and with fewer errors than when he taped them and gave them to a human secretary for typing. And many technical writers these days turn their copy over to a merciless electronic "editor" that rejects any words not found in its preprogrammed dictionary. The procedure not only ensures that product manuals will be easy to understand, it lets a computer translate them automatically into seven foreign languages.

Robots have already driven two-thirds of human workers from the nation's assembly lines, and there are only 30,000 of them in the United States today, about half as many as in Japan. Twelve years from now—equipped with depth perception, a sense of touch, and the beginnings of artificial intelligence—robots will be picking tomatoes, loading trucks, and serving meals to the handicapped. Already, surgeons at the Long Beach (California) Memorial Hospital use a robot to perform delicate brain operations. A company called Denning Mobile Robotics sells a $110,000 mechanized security guard for factories and other large installations. And Transitions Research Corp. is testing both a robot vacuum cleaner and a "nurse's aide" that can deliver meals to hospital patients and may soon learn to retrieve medical files and even help patients walk down the hall. The company hopes to develop a $50,000 robotic butler/handyman capable of cleaning the house, cooking meals, shoveling snow, and even repairing household appliances. By the turn of the century, there could be upwards of 1 million robots in the United States.

Within the computer industry, these developments mean an evergrowing demand for systems analysts, design engineers, programmers, assemblers, technicians, and repairmen. In all, computer-industry employment should continue to grow by 15 percent per year. Outside the industry, these new computer-based technologies will be a mixed blessing. They could mean hard times for some workers who have been tracked into a job fast becoming obsolete; secretaries, for example, are likely to find that good shorthand skills are not as desirable as they once were. Yet they will also create jobs—more than 1 million of them every year, counting positions outside the computer industry that will grow up around new computer applications.

For many specific jobs, the future looks bright:

Computer console and equipment operators. It's a step above typing on an old manual typewriter, but the basic skill required is the same. Frankly, this is probably the lowest rung on the data-processing ladder and the only job in the field more likely than not to turn out to be a dead end. You'll learn your employer's software and procedures, but that knowledge may not travel well if you decide to change jobs. To move up in the computer world, you will need to train in your off hours to become a programmer or service technician. But the demand for console and equipment operators is stronger than in almost any other segment of the job market. After all, someone has to get all that data into the system and back out. More than 500,000 of these entry-level jobs will open up in the next decade. The pay scale is relatively low for the high-priced computer field, not over $20,000 per year even after several years of employment. But it's a place to begin.

Computer programmers. Look into the "Help Wanted" pages of almost any metropolitan newspaper today, and the chances are that the largest section you'll find will be for computer programmers. Perhaps the strongest impulse behind the programmer's ascendancy in the job market is the growth of the personal-computer industry. A decade ago, personal-computer software firms were for the most part kitchen-table operations, with sales that would barely buy the morning paper. Today, multimillion-dollar corporations abound. By 1990, personal-computer programs will account for half the total software sales in the United States. Add to this the rapid growth of the tele-communications industry and more than 250,000 programmers will be needed by the year 2000. Entry-level jobs for people with two years of college-level training are nearing $20,000. Mid-career sala-ries are about twice that, on average, but people with good experience in desirable specialties are regularly earning $70,000 or more, with a few reaching six figures. Consultants and temporary workers willing to give up job security and fringe benefits in exchange for higher immediate income make up to 50 percent more than the staff pro-grammer doing the same job at the next terminal.

Computer service technicians. With computers rapidly becoming al-most as common as people, it's obvious that someone has to keep all the complex hardware working. Nearly 100,000 new openings will appear in this job category by the year 2000. Though most of these people will be employed by computer makers themselves, a growing number of companies will find that their installed base of computers, and particularly personal computers, has grown so large that they must hire their own repair staff. Independent computer-repair ser-vices are also growing rapidly, and in the right area the entrepreneur-ially minded should find it fairly easy to set up their own business or buy into a franchised operation. Salaries for computer service tech-nicians begin at about $18,000, and still top out at less than $30,000 unless the worker can make the transition to a management role. We expect these figures to climb significantly faster than the inflation rate for the remainder of the century.

Computer systems analysts. Systems analysts are the planners of the computer-software world, charged with the task of figuring out just what it is new software should do, how it must operate, and how to fit it in with existing systems. Though it is still possible for program-mers to work their way up into the systems-analyst positions, some-one deliberately entering this profession will need more technical education than the programmers start with; most have at least a college degree in computer science, and many have advanced train-ing. But in return, pay scales are higher. An entry-level systems ana-lyst can begin at more than $25,000, and mid-career salaries of

$50,000 are not uncommon. Some 260,000 will be needed in the next twelve years.

TELECOMMUNICATIONS. The second electronics revolution of the 1990s will transform the telephone from a simple link to other people into the centerpiece of a new information economy. Technologically, this change is already well under way; worldwide sales of new, ever-more-sophisticated telecommunications equipment will top $100 billion by 1990. As a generator of new jobs, it is only just beginning.

You've already seen some parts of the telecommunications revolution. For more than a decade, stock-market information has been no farther away than the little terminal on the corner of your broker's desk; today, for a few hundred dollars down and a few hundred a month, we can receive real-time price information from every major stock and commodities market in the country. (Make that a few thousand down if you live in a remote area and need your own satellite link to receive the data.) Cellular car phones now keep the well-to-do in touch with their offices even when they are on the road; in the next few years, prices will drop far enough to make them practical for the rest of us, and by the year 2000 they will be standard equipment on most automobiles. Cable TV now serves almost 80 percent of the households in its viewing areas. And electronic mail services allow computer owners to send a letter at the speed of light; already, they have taken more than half of all long-distance business communications away from the U.S. Postal Service.

Deregulation of telephone service in 1983 has turned AT&T's monopoly on long-distance communications into one of the most hotly contested markets in all of technology; the new and improved long-distance networks resulting from this competition are quickly welding the United States into a single electronic neighborhood where virtually any information can be had at a moment's notice. Over the next two or three decades, this flow of information will expand geometrically, as the billion miles of copper wire now strung across the United States is replaced by hair-thin optical fibers. Where expensive copper now carries about a dozen calls per wire, a cheap glass fiber carries up to 6,000, and that number is expected to increase several hundred thousand within the next few years. By the end of this year, AT&T will have linked cities along the East and West Coasts, Chicago, and the Sun Belt cities from Atlanta to Tucson with more than

10,000 miles of optical fiber. Five years later, glass strands will tie the entire country together, and more fibers will span the Atlantic and Pacific. At least nine other companies are installing similar networks. Chances are that between 1995 and 2000, the Federal government will decide that the country's need for more efficient communications outweighs the evils of a monopoly; AT&T and the so-called "Baby Bells" will be allowed to reunite into a single company, linking many of these networks into a single system. The result will be cheap, reliable, long-distance communications with capacity equal to about twenty of today's telephone systems.

An alternative cable network is already in place. In 1987, half of all American households were hooked up for cable TV; by 1991, the figure will be 92 percent. And by order of the Federal Communications Commission, all the television cables installed since 1973—all but 2 percent of the cables now in use—have included two lines, one bringing TV programs in and one ready to carry information back out. There have already been a few limited experiments with two-way cable, whereby viewers can take part in polls or can respond directly to advertising by pressing buttons on a primitive terminal attached to the TV set. By the year 2000, these services will have become a major data carrier.

One fast-growing industry sure to use this new capacity packages information into the computerized on-line databases now delivered over the phone lines. More than 2,000 on-line databases today market information ranging from newspaper articles to medical research reports and from agricultural statistics to engineering standards for home construction. At least 350 companies are now compiling and maintaining databases, and another 350 provide related services; they serve at least 500,000 on-line customers, 20 times as many as their corporate ancestors did a decade ago. Total U.S. sales of on-line information were a mere $1.2 billion as recently as 1983. According to the market researchers at Link Resources Corporation, they should reach $5 billion this year. Nearly 10 million homes are now equipped for on-line data searches, so that growth rate should continue for the foreseeable future.

Business services make up by far the largest segment of this industry today. One of the biggest is TRW's credit-reporting service. Apply for a loan this morning, and your bank will have it checked with TRW by this afternoon; the slow part of the process will be finding time to make the call. Other major services include stock-market databases from Quotron, Dow Jones, and others, and the legal and news files from Mead Data Central.

Yet the fastest expansion in the information market is in the consumer databases. Growing at well over 50 percent annually, services with names like The Source, CompuServe, and Oracle now offer stock-market data, on-line stockbrokers, weather reports, video games, and on-screen conversations with other users. Computerized home banking systems from Citibank, Chemical Bank, and others have been less well accepted—in fact, Chemical Bank discontinued this service when consumer demand proved too disappointing—but are sure to grow as providers fine-tune their offerings and the equipment needed to use them grows ever less costly. In all, these services will have nearly 8 million subscribers within the next year. One conservative estimate puts the total potential market at some 45 million homes. By the year 2000, virtually all of us will have joined the revolution.

The other major new tele-industry of the 1990s will be telemarketing. We can see the beginnings of this trend in today's televised shop-at-home services, wherein consumers sit for hours on end, half mesmerized by the video catalog, telephoning orders to the numbers flashed on their screens. In its new incarnation, telemarketing will move from TV screen to computer screen. In part, the change will come because increasingly sophisticated computer graphics are making it possible to display merchandise on a CRT display with all the color and detail of a TV picture. But the real appeal is that computerized communications are interactive. With these systems, there will be no need for customers to dial their telephones to place orders; there will be no delay for sale-killing second thoughts to form. Customers will just sit at their terminals and type in their orders as the impulse moves them. Within the next decade, up to one-fifth of U.S. retail sales may be made through telemarketing.

The rapid growth of telecommunications has already made itself felt in job markets across the United States. Washington, DC, alone is home to corporate headquarters and regional offices of more than 200 telecommunications firms. Another 75 law offices and 45 consulting firms specializing in this field are based there. If all goes well —that is, if Washington itself manages to avoid economic disaster— the 1990s will see new jobs opening up for more than 100,000 advertising personnel specializing in telemarketing, another 60,000 computer programmers for telemarketing services, about 80,000 people to write, edit, and direct computerized teletext information services, and an endless stream of related opportunities.

BIOTECHNOLOGY. A revolution delayed, biotechnology will not remain so much longer. In the early 1980s, it seemed that every other biology professor was setting up his own company to banish hunger, cure disease, clean up pollution—and, not incidentally, to convert the microbes in his culture dishes into cash in his bank account. A few of these early start-ups, firms like Cetus, Genentech, and Biogen, have grown into substantial corporations. Too many others, underfunded and poorly managed, have fallen into bankruptcy, and the Wall Street analysts who once touted biotechnology companies as the IBMs of the '80s have written them off as an idea whose time has not yet come, and may never do so. In fact, biotechnology will not be the computer industry of the 1990s either. But its long sojourn in the wilderness of research will soon begin to pay off in the rich, relatively comfortable environs of the marketplace.

Even in its infancy, the biotechnology industry has scored some impressive successes:

• Ten years ago, insulin was laboriously extracted from the organs of pigs and cattle; some diabetic patients found that their bodies eventually rejected the drug and forced them to discontinue the lifesaving therapy. Today, it is grown in bacteria, and the result is in every way identical to the natural human hormone. In the United States alone, the insulin market is worth roughly $200 million per year. Growth hormone, somatostatin, and several other costly human hormones are similarly available.

• Ten years ago, the experimental anticancer drug interferon would have cost $22 *billion* a pound, if anyone could have obtained a pound of the rare protein. Today, several forms of interferon are cultured in bacteria at prices that make them available to any researcher with a plausible experiment to perform. A growing variety of similar research compounds are also in production.

• Physicians are now using tiny bits of artificial DNA known as gene probes to identify the microbes that infect their patients. Until gene probes appeared, doctors who suspected that their patients might

have tuberculosis had to wait three months for the bacterial culture that would confirm the diagnosis. Today, the test is done in minutes.
• Monoclonal antibodies, synthetic versions of the chemicals the body uses to fight off invading pathogens, are used in a wide variety of diagnostic exams, including the home pregnancy tests that have appeared on drugstore shelves in the last decade. Other monoclonals are being tested as weapons against cancer and other diseases that have resisted traditional drugs with dramatic success. Annual sales of monoclonal antibodies are expected to top $1 billion by 1990, with the $2 billion mark not far behind.

If all these examples are drawn from medicine, it's no coincidence. Biotechnology research is expensive, and health care is one market-place in which the investment is easy to recover. By 1990, bioengi-neered medical products will form a business easily worth more than $1 billion per year. But as the 1990s pass, biobusiness will finally penetrate some markets that for one reason or another have remained elusive.

Agriculture may be the most obvious. Researchers have developed bacteria that can protect crop plants from frost damage, new plant varieties that can grow in areas too hot or cold or dry or in earth too salty for natural strains, and synthetic hormones that will help cattle produce more milk or beef on the same amount of food. In the long run—say, within fifteen years—they expect to produce new plants that can grow their own fertilizer, resist insect pests and plant dis-eases, and produce more food from a given quantity of water, air, and sunlight. The unreasonable fear that gene-spliced plants and bac-teria, if released into the environment, will wreak unforeseeable dam-age to the ecology is slowly dying away, or at least losing its political clout; in future, technology assessment will be used to rule out gen-uine risks, not as a means of harassing innovators. So these new developments can be expected to reach the farmer's field well within the next decade. When that happens, world agriculture will become vastly more productive.

Heavy industries have also been looking into genetic engineering and related technologies. Mining companies in the United States, Canada, and Australia have been studying bacteria that can leach valuable metals from low-grade ore that is not worth processing by normal methods. Other bacteria promise to clean the sulfur from coal, eliminating a major source of air pollution and acid rain. Still others manufacture a reasonable facsimile of crude oil, though not yet at marketable prices. And chemists are convinced that bacteria will soon produce many of the industrial chemicals now manufactured synthetically, at lower cost and without pollution. Traditional chemical companies such as Du Pont, Dow, and Monsanto all have biotechnology research departments larger than most independent companies; Monsanto has redirected about half of its R&D budget into bioengineering.

All this adds up to soaring demand for biologists, technicians, and salespeople with a scientific bent in the 1990s. It may well be, however, that the growth of biotechnology spells job losses in other fields. Greater agricultural productivity on top of already-large gluts in world produce markets could further reduce the need for farmers, while workers in traditional chemical plants are also likely to find themselves displaced by the new technology.

SUPERCONDUCTIVITY. In early 1987, a costly scientific curiosity suddenly became the hottest technology since the computer. Dr. Paul Chu, a University of Houston physicist, and his colleagues had announced the discovery of a new superconductor—a material that conducts electricity without resistance or losses. In theory, superconductors offer dramatically greater efficiency in electrical-power transmission. Even the most efficient high-voltage long-distance power lines now in use lose about 5 percent of the electricity sent through them; for most lines, the waste runs closer to 15 percent. That useless drain costs utility customers billions of dollars per year in the United States alone.

Superconductors have been known for nearly a century, but it took Dr. Chu's breakthrough to make them practical. Previous materials became superconducting only at exceedingly low temperatures, not higher than 4 degrees above absolute zero. And that meant they worked only when cooled by liquid helium, worth about $4 per liter, even in quantity; it made them far too expensive to use outside of high-budget research projects, such as superpowerful particle accelerators. But Chu's material lost all resistance at 36 degrees Kelvin, and soon afterward people were reporting superconductors that functioned at 77 degrees Kelvin. At that temperature, they could be cooled by liquid nitrogen; it's only $.40 per liter, cheap enough to open many new uses to superconductors. Since then, new alloys have been discovered that appear to promise loss-free power transmission at well over room temperature.

Already, many possible uses for room-temperature superconductors are obvious:

They are most likely to appear first in a new generation of computer, replacing the copper and aluminum that now link microchips. As a result, computer power requirements will drop significantly, and less chip-destroying heat will be generated. There is even a chance that the computer itself will work faster, because the superconductors will carry signals between the chips more rapidly than metal wiring.

The next step would be so-called "Josephson junction" computers. Josephson junctions are a kind of superconducting transistor that operates far more rapidly than modern circuitry. Computers incorporating them would be many times faster than today's biggest number crunchers. Even when they had to be cooled in liquid hydrogen, Josephson junction computers were so attractive that IBM spent twenty years and an estimated $1 billion trying to develop one. The firm eventually gave up, reportedly because there was no way to build a computer that would not immediately stop working as its own waste heat built up faster than it could be carried away. A practical room-temperature Josephson junction would put the program back at the top of almost every computer designer's wish list.

It is worth noting that IBM now has one of the world's most active superconductor research programs; company scientists have already learned how to make superconductors that will carry enough current to operate a computer—scientists had regarded that as a difficult technological hurdle—and to form them into simple printed circuits.

In the long run, far more dramatic developments are possible. Magnetically levitated trains, or "maglevs," offer intercity transportation at speeds of up to 350 miles per hour, with much greater energy efficiency than air travel can provide. With superconducting magnets, their efficiency would be greater still, their construction costs significantly lower. Economic and political obstacles may well block construction of maglev trains in the United States, but Japan has firmly committed itself to their development. (Ironically, maglev trains were invented some thirty years ago by Henry Kolm, of the Massachusetts Institute of Technology. Once he had demonstrated his idea with small models, further experiments were never funded. Japan and Germany are now the world's leaders in maglev development.)

Just what superconductors will do for job markets in the 1990s is not yet clear. At the least, they are likely to create openings for a few thousand chemists, physicists, and technicians. But the odds seem good that they will soon begin what eventually—say, by the year 2010—will be a dramatic change in the way that we use one of our most crucial forms of energy. And that kind of transformation is always good for entrepreneurs and workers who can adapt to the new way of doing things.

ADVANCED MATERIALS. Technologically, it is easy to see what new materials can do: Just look at your car. In the last three decades, the average weight of American automobiles has fallen by more than half a ton. It's not just that today's cars are smaller than the gas-guzzling land yachts of the 1950s and early '60s. It's that the heavy steel in them has been replaced. New, lighter alloys easier to form than sheet steel have found their way into body panels—when metal is used at all. Plastics have replaced metal in trim, moldings, and other applications; in some models, the body is virtually all plastic, with the car's color not just painted on but mixed into the material so that a minor scrape hardly shows. And they are not welded or bolted together; they're glued, each car using about two dozen different adhesives, most developed within the last fifteen years. In the next decade, more and more new synthetics will replace metal in many applications, and surely will find novel uses of their own.

Ceramics are one of the most obvious winners. Cheap, lighter and harder than steel, able to survive higher temperatures, they promise uses limited only by the imaginations of the engineers who work with them. In fact, they have been making that promise for more than twenty years. Carmakers have worked for more than fifteen years to build an all-ceramic auto engine—Ford alone has nearly 100 patents in the field—and still the lightweight, superefficient power plant remains a dream. Yet ceramics have found their way into ovenproof cookware, artificial tooth implants, turbine blades and other high-precision moldings for high-temperature applications, and even a few knives and scissors. The 1990s may well be the decade in which the ancient craft of pottery reaches its true potential.

Bet also on new composites, high-strength compounds of plastic or ceramic mixed with reinforcing materials. Most materials fail in use when a crack forms on the surface or at some inner imperfection and then propagates through the entire piece. Composites can be far stronger for a given weight of material because cracks do not form; a few reinforcing strands may break, but the gap is not propagated through the supporting matrix. Wood is nature's own composite, with long, strong cellulose fibers supported by a matrix of relatively weak, but durable, lignin. Fiberglass is the classical man-made composite, with glass threads replacing the cellulose of wood and plastic resin replacing the lignin. These days, a wide variety of compounds are used for the matrix, and the reinforcing fibers may be fine carbon threads, boron filaments, hair-thin tungsten wire, or almost anything else that materials science has to offer. The resulting composites are used in everything from spacecraft to artificial hips. If a ceramic engine ever reaches the market, it will probably be made from a reinforced ceramic composite.

Materials that sound far less likely are also working their way toward daily use:

"Metallic glass" was discovered at the California Institute of Technology more than twenty years ago and has finally reached commercial production. It's not a glass in the usual sense, but as scientists use the word: a substance in which the atoms are distributed at random, rather than in the orderly arrays of crystals found in normal metal. The difference gives metallic glass some useful properties. Engineers at GE and Westinghouse, for example, suspect that transformers made with it could save about 75 percent of the energy now lost in switching; such losses cost U.S. electric customers about $1 billion per year.

Even stranger is a discovery from the Soviet Union: a way to deposit thin films of diamond on the surface of other materials. Such diamond coatings could make your spectacles virtually scratchproof and harden knives to keep them sharp for years. Their biggest use may be in semiconductors; a thin diamond film carries heat away from computer chips much faster than other materials and greatly increases their reliability. Many researchers also believe that chips made from diamond could operate far faster than the materials now in use. Alas, as usual, Japan has been far quicker to pick up on this opportunity than American industry. Several Japanese firms are already selling eyeglasses and airplane windows coated with diamond, and Sony has test-marketed a high-fidelity loudspeaker that uses a diamond-coated speaker element for much better sound quality.

How many new jobs will result from these developments and others like them? Again, it is difficult to guess. New materials seem an ideal market for the technology-minded entrepreneur looking to start a small company in a field with big potential; several have already done so. There will be golden opportunities here for job hunters with an eye for start-up firms whose rapid growth could soon carry them to the top.

Best bet for the late 1990s: affordable houses factory-built of high-performance plastics and composites, with foam insulation between two structural layers that look like wood, brick, or whatever the buyer fancies. Water pipes, electric lines, security systems, and data fibers will be molded in place, with many appliances set permanently into the walls. They will be smaller than today's homes, because families are smaller. Expect one large bedroom; a California bath with whirlpool, stereo, video, and telephone; kitchen; and two general-purpose rooms with beds, entertainment electronics, computers, and so on all disappearing into the walls when not in use. The one uncertainty in this is how long it will take Federal authorities to impose a uniform national housing code to replace conflicting local standards. But by the turn of the century, assembly-line housing should be the single largest market for advanced plastics and composites in the United States.

HAZARDOUS-WASTE DISPOSAL. Ill-used technology caused many waste problems, and technology will cure them. But in large part, the force behind this growing field is political. The pattern was set at New York State's famed Love Canal, where deposits of toxic industrial waste created a ghost town where a neighborhood once stood. Across the country, the Environmental Protection Administration has identified well over 100 similar sites in dire need of immediate cleanup. In Massachusetts, waste products leaking into the local water supply from one chemical plant have been blamed for a high incidence of cancer in the surrounding community. Schools across the country have been closed for months while technicians removed cancer-causing asbestos insulation from the ceilings. And stately granite homes, and those built over deposits of granite and other rock, have been found to contain dangerous quantities of radioactive, cancer-causing radon gas. Citizens in all these regions have been clamoring for government help to protect them from these menaces, and the resulting legislation has spawned a host of new opportunities.

Removing hazardous materials and disposing of them safely is destined to be one of the largest new industries of the 1990s. Just how quickly it will grow depends too much on government action, or inaction, for accurate forecasts to be possible. Long ago, Congress appropriated a $1 billion "superfund" to clean up the most dangerous industrial-waste sites; in 1984, it passed new taxes on the oil and chemical industries meant to bring that fund to more than $10 billion by 1990. Yet the Reagan Administration has refused to spend more than a tiny fraction of the sum available, and only one of the dumps cited as intolerably polluted has actually been decontaminated. But government health regulations have also forced school districts and industrial companies to remove the asbestos from their facilities, and that market alone is expected to be worth $65 billion during the next fifteen years.

Hazardous-waste technicians. These are the hardy souls who plan, manage, and carry out the cleanup of land, air, and water which the rest of us find too dangerous to tolerate. At least 400,000 of them will be needed by the end of the next decade; if the government's superfund program ever goes into practical operation, that could climb to well over 1 million. Training for these positions is both necessary and, at the moment, nearly impossible to find. Look for programs that turn out Certified Industrial Hygienists, and then try to locate courses in the specialties that most interest you. Salaries still begin at less than $20,000 per year, and seldom top $30,000 unless you work your way into a management position. They should rise sharply when the national cleanup gets properly under way. It will happen in the 1990s.

New technologies are not the only force capable of creating jobs. Though computer programming and computer science, engineering, and the basic sciences are among the fastest-growing segments of the labor market, as late as 1995 only one job in eight will be in high-tech fields. Many other high-opportunity areas are about as far from the technological cutting edge as it is possible to get. According to the U.S. Department of Labor's Division of Occupational Outlook, some of the fastest-growing opportunities in the 1990s will be for nurses, teachers, lawyers and legal assistants, accountants and book-keepers, bankers and financial-services salespeople, personnel administrators, and public relations specialists. Other hot fields include food service and hotel management and recreation.

In many of these professions, demographic changes are the job market's prime mover. As the American population ages, more and more people find themselves in the high-risk years, when failing health requires ever-greater medical attention. Thus, the demand for nurses, nurse practitioners, nutritionists, and geriatric social workers is soaring. Older people, on average, have more money and fewer living expenses than the young; hence the fast-growing demand for financial planners and portfolio managers. And the children of the Baby Boom generation are now flooding the nation's school system; thus where the educational job market shrank dramatically in the 1970s and early '80s, teachers once more are finding themselves highly sought after.

Legal and regulatory changes also are fueling growth in some of these employment areas. Americans remain by far the most litigious people in the world, and hardly a suit can be tried without at least one lawyer on each side. Corporations need attorneys by the score to help them cope with the dense web of regulations that surrounds every business today, "deregulation" notwithstanding. Those attorneys are hiring legal assistants in ever-greater numbers. Tax laws regularly stimulate the demand for accountants and bookkeepers. And relaxation of banking laws has opened thousands of new opportunities for loan officers, bank managers, auditors, and financial personnel of all descriptions. In recent years, Sears, GM, and even K-Mart have opened retail financial-service departments; Sears even has its own general-market credit card competing with Visa and MasterCard.

Let's look at a few of these career areas more closely.

Teachers. After a decade of shrinking school enrollments, communities across the country are again finding themselves short of teachers. So far, the demand is acute only in a few specialties; it is strongest in mathematics, engineering, and the sciences, and in such languages as Japanese and Russian. And despite a new, but growing, commitment to core curricula emphasizing—among other subjects—basic English skills, the continuing growth of the Spanish-speaking population in this country will stimulate demand for bilingual teachers, particularly at the elementary and high school levels, throughout the South and West, and in some Northern inner cities. Starting salaries in many communities remain low, so new teachers with families to support will find it hard to get by. This should pass as the decade progresses and the dearth of specialized educators makes itself felt.

Accountants. For the precise, detail-oriented personalities among us, there is no better profession than accounting. By the mid-1980s, there was already a shortage of qualified personnel in this fast-growing field; that deficit is growing quickly. According to the American Institute of Certified Public Accountants, in 1985 and '86 the nation added some 1,500 new workers with college degrees in accounting, bringing the total supply to nearly 60,000. That is a growth rate of 2.6 percent per year. But in that same period, demand rose by more than 6 percent. The Tax Reform Act of 1986, billed by politicians as a massive simplification of the Internal Revenue Code, was so complex that accountants will be kept busy trying to understand it for years to come. And the proliferation of small businesses in the last five years has added still more demand for people capable of setting up and maintaining their corporate books. As a result, major accounting firms now plan to increase their hiring of entry-level employees by 15 percent. By the year 2000, there will be more than 1 million accountants tapping their calculators in the United States.

Hotel managers and travel agents. For business and pleasure, the prosperity of the mid-1980s made travel an indispensable part of many American lives, and the booming hotel and travel industries show it. For travel agents, chances for advancement are relatively limited, but high demand makes this one of the easier industries to enter, and income is limited only by your skill and willingness to work. Career hotel workers may have more to look forward to. Cornell University's School of Hotel Administration reports that graduates with a bachelor's degree now leave school with four or five job offers carrying starting salaries of $20,000 or more. In major chains, advancement is rapid, even for those without a degree. Most hotels maintain a tradition of internal promotion, and outstanding workers often rise from small hotels to larger ones, and even into management positions.

· · ·

Legal assistants. God knows, it isn't that there are not enough lawyers in this country. But after all, they're expensive to hire, and there are a lot of legal tasks that really don't require three years of law school. That is where legal assistants, or paralegals, come in. According to the Bureau of Labor Statistics, this is the single fastest-growing job category in the nation and will remain so at least through 1995. There were 61,000 legal assistants in 1986, up by 15 percent in two years. By the year 2000, legal assistants will number at least 125,000. Five years ago, you could become a paralegal virtually without training. But you would have been likely to find yourself working as a glorified secretary. Today, law offices are hiring college graduates almost exclusively, and the profession has changed dramatically. Become a paralegal, and you can find yourself performing real estate title searches, drafting corporate benefit plans, and even working with clients, though only attorneys can actually dispense legal advice. Many find their way into specialized practices; in large law firms, the majority of legal assistants work in preparing cases for court. Starting salaries average just over $16,000 and are rising rapidly. Those with a specialty or in managerial positions regularly earn up to $40,000.

And one overwhelming industry:

HEALTH CARE. Already, it's one of the nation's largest industries— and, next to government, the most recessionproof. Already, we spend fully 11 percent of our Gross National Product on medicine, and our yearly doctor bill is growing rapidly. We will need about 3 million new health professionals by the year 2000, and nothing short of nuclear war will reduce that demand. In good economic times and bad, we all are willing to spend whatever it takes to remain alive and well.

A wide variety of factors is acting to raise the number of health-care workers needed in the United States.

One obvious factor is simple population growth. Though the national birthrate has dropped in recent years, more than 3.7 new Americans are born each year, while fewer than 2.1 million of us die —an overall increase of roughly 1.6 million per year. Add to this some 270,000 legal immigrants each year, all the law allows, and an unknown number of undocumented aliens. In all, we need about 4,300 new doctors and 12,000 new hospital beds in this country each year.

More importantly, as a society we are quickly growing older. The huge Baby Boom generation born after World War II is now reaching its 40s, when our need for medical care begins to grow inexorably. Their parents are entering the illness-prone years, and the advances in medicine during the last two decades have given them a good chance to live many years longer. People over age seventy now form America's fastest-growing population group. Already, television personality Willard Scott has had to give up saluting viewers on their hundredth birthday; listing them all ate up too much costly airtime. Only twelve years from now, the number of living Americans who have passed their century mark will have tripled, to more than 100,000. They will need not only doctors and nurses, but geriatric social workers, physical therapists, and rehabilitation specialists to aid in recovering from a stroke or broken bone, home health aides, nursing-home staff, and a variety of other medical personnel.

Technology has been creating new jobs in the health-care industry for decades. The development of kidney dialysis, for example, brought with it whole clinics, each with its own personnel, from nurses and technicians to secretaries and receptionists. And in the last fifteen years, more than 5,000 CAT scanners have entered American hospitals and clinics, each employing at least one technician per job shift. Today, new diagnostic and therapeutic techniques add new demands for trained personnel almost daily. Among the developments now either on the horizon or spreading through the nation's hospitals are genetic counseling; prosthetic limbs, which must be custom-made and fitted by trained technicians; and storage of transplantable organs, which will require its own specialists. By themselves, few technologies make a large contribution to the medical labor market; but each specialized new machine or technique creates its increment of jobs. They add up to a major demand for new medical personnel.

Social and political changes add still more employment opportunities. One more reason we will need more services for the elderly is the decline of smoking and the growing awareness of the need for exercise in the last decade or so. The political decision to save on psychiatric costs by "deinstitutionalizing" the mentally ill will, in the long run, create a wide variety of jobs for social workers and psychiatric counselors, as TV news broadcasts of the rag-clad people trying to survive winter nights on snow-covered streets raise the demand for government-sponsored programs to deal with the problems of the homeless. Similar attempts to reduce the cost of health care are slowing the demand for doctors and transferring some of their day-to-day duties to paramedics. And the demand for "holistic," home-oriented medical care is creating jobs for some 15,000 midwives, once an obsolescent, and almost a vanished, profession.

Among the hundreds of specialized medical professions, a few stand out as high-growth fields:

Nurses. The demand for nurses in the 1990s will be little short of staggering. At the end of 1987, there were roughly 1.4 million registered nurses in the United States and 631,000 licensed practical nurses. Just two years from now, according to the Federal Department of Health and Human Services, we will already face a shortage of nearly 400,000 registered nurses. By the year 2000, we will need a full 2 million RNs and nearly 870,000 LPNs. Only 40 percent of these professionals will work in hospitals, compared with nearly 70 percent today. The rest will find jobs in corporate medical offices, neighborhood clinics, nursing homes, and health-maintenance organizations. An ever-greater number will be self-employed. Because there are too few young people—read young women—to fill the need, many older women are making nursing a second career; expect this trend to accelerate rapidly. In major urban areas, experienced RNs can earn up to $40,000 per year, LPNs more than $25,000.

Geriatric social workers. A decade ago, this profession hardly existed. By the year 2000, an estimated 700,000 trained people will be needed to care for the nation's aging population. Geriatric social workers are called on for a wide variety of duties, from simple companionship to guiding the elderly through the maze of America's growing health-care bureaucracy. Starting salaries are still in the mid-teens, mid-career salaries in the under-$30,000 range. They are sure to grow with the demand for this specialty and as geriatric social work becomes increasingly professionalized. However, this is one field best entered for the love of working with people who need you, not in hopes of eventual wealth.

Biomedical engineers and technicians. Someone has to turn new medical techniques discovered in the laboratory into practical hardware ready for clinical use. That is the task of biomedical engineers, a specialty that appeared only twenty years ago. An estimated 50,000 biomedical engineers will be required in the coming decade—vastly more than our projected supply. Another 90,000 technicians will find jobs maintaining and repairing the machines the engineers design.

Paramedics and emergency medical technicians. Fifteen years ago, paramedics needed no special professional training. Most had spent time as battlefield medics in Viet Nam. Today that supply of experienced personnel has long since found its way into civilian health care, and new paramedics receive much the same premed courses as doctors-to-be. The shortage of doctors and nurses in some rural areas and the continuing development of big-city emergency medical services have added to the demand for paramedics. By the end of this century, there will be jobs for some 400,000 of these journeyman primary-care providers.

5

MAKING YOUR OWN WAY

AT LEAST 95 percent of us probably should be working for someone else; some experienced entrepreneurs put it closer to 99 percent. It's a rare employee who combines the skills of production and marketing, personnel administration and finance that it takes to run a business. And it isn't just a matter of experience. Most of us need the security of job and paycheck, of knowing exactly where our next meal is coming from; cut us off from those foundations, and panic sets in quickly. Few of us are willing and able to endure the grueling schedule that starting a business requires. And though we might prefer to believe otherwise, most of us simply aren't self-starters; without the structure of a job to give direction to our efforts, we soon lose our drive and sense of organization.

Our big-business economy was built by and for that great majority of us who can't or don't care to hack it on our own. In the 1950s and early '60s, the American Dream was a corporate dream: Find a responsible position with a major company, and you could count on a house in Levittown, an all-American wife and children, and a pension when your "Golden Years" were at hand. In forty years of working life, you would never have to face the insecurity of making your own way through a hostile world. (Or find out just what you could achieve outside the protective corporate shell.) Your own company's founders might be honored, but their modern counterparts were strange, even suspect. They couldn't be team players.

Yet in the turbulent economy of the late 1980s, corporate America is looking as dated as the crew cut, while those oddball entrepreneurs are business heroes. Even President Reagan has heaped praise on them for supplying virtually all the new jobs created in the 1980s (though at the same time he was trying to disband the Small Business

Administration, which has given many entrepreneurs their start). By 1990, companies with fewer than 200 employees will provide jobs for 80 percent of American workers. Most of the people who flourish in the next ten years will be the entrepreneurs who start new businesses in their mold.

Big business itself may have done the most to change our attitudes. It used to be that only blue-collar workers faced layoffs due to automation and shifts in the business climate; if managers were fired, it meant that something was wrong with their job performance. But the recent wave of takeovers and "downsizing" of corporate staffs has destroyed millions of executive jobs. In the last five years, so many white-collar employees have been fired that joblessness has lost its stigma. And for many people, corporations have lost their image as a secure route to the top.

Today's high-tech success stories have also helped to alter the business climate. Everyone has heard of the two Steves, Jobs and Wozniak, who—with a lot of help from more experienced businessmen— took Apple Computer from Jobs's garage to the Fortune 500. And what about Mitch Kapor, whose Lotus Development Corporation blossomed overnight into the nation's third-largest software firm?

So more and more people have decided that the only route to real success—and real job security—is to own the company. As recently as 1985, only 7 percent of executives who lost their jobs fought back by starting their own businesses. According to Challenger, Gray & Christmas, Inc., an international outplacement firm based in Chicago, the figure is now close to one in five. In 1988, Americans will set up about 1.3 million new businesses, including 700,000 corporations, 500,000 sole proprietorships, and 100,000 partnerships.

One of them could be yours.

In the 1990s, starting your own business may be more than fashionable. If the economy falls apart, it may be your only route to a decent income. When no one else wants to hire you—or can afford to—you can always hire yourself.

But hire yourself to do what? In a recession, companies always cut back. Some of them go under. What business could be so hot that it makes sense to enter it when the economy is at its worst? A lot of businesses. They all fit into one of two categories: Either they deal in necessities, or they save people money.

The list of necessities is longer than you might think, and the list of opportunities even longer. Each product needs manufacturers, wholesalers, retailers, probably repairmen, and—increasingly often in today's high-tech marketplace—consultants to help select and explain them. You could find your niche in any of these markets.

Food, clothing, shelter, and health care just begin the catalog of things that people today can't—or won't—do without. Pricey health clubs could be in for hard times when their members are forced to recall how much food their annual dues would buy, but some other businesses that seem frivolous may be surprisingly resistant to economic pressures. People may buy fewer pedigreed Shih Tzus and Burmese cats when exports dry up and the stock market plunges again, but parents will find some way to keep their kids supplied with hamsters and goldfish. Most pet shops will survive a recession. Fast-food restaurants are a natural when money for more elegant meals is hard to find. And, of course, liquor stores do more business during bad times, not less.

Services that help their customers keep extra money in their pockets will flourish when the rest of the economy fails. Some of them are obvious, others less so. Used-car lots boom whenever habitual new-car buyers suddenly can't afford to trade up to the latest status machine. The new-home market may collapse and leave developers wondering where their customers went, but local carpenters, plumbers, and electricians will be busy putting up needed additions for homeowners who in good times would have gone looking for a bigger house. Cash registers will jingle, too, at lumberyards and hardware stores that pitch their merchandise toward do-it-yourselfers. Tax-preparation offices that promise big refunds are big business even in good years; when people are feeling the pinch, they are even more likely to take time for a visit to their local H&R Block.

But the biggest winners in an economic crunch may be companies that save money not for individuals, but for other companies. Even in the prosperous mid-'80s, major corporations all over the country saved money by cutting back on home-office staff. Transamerica Corp. managed sales of over $7 billion in 1986 with 100 headquarters employees; Burlington Northern, with nearly $7 billion in sales, made do with only 77. General Foods fired nearly all of the 2,000 people once employed at the company's headquarters. Some have been hired by divisional presidents; the rest are gone. What makes this possible is the decision to hire service companies to perform many of the traditional corporate functions. This has created a boom for accounting firms, investment bankers (not tied to Wall Street), computer service bureaus, management consultants of all kinds. And the mass firings have meant a bonanza for outplacement firms to help displaced workers find new employment. As the economy turns down and more companies find it necessary to cut their in-house overhead, all these businesses will flourish.

With enough imagination, it is possible to make a spectacular success even in fields that well-established competitors seem to have sewed up. Look at just two examples:

In Phoenix, the First Business Bank of Arizona has come from nowhere and grown into the 22nd-largest of the state's banks in less than three years—without a single branch office, or even a teller. First Business sends bonded couriers door-to-door to handle transactions for its business clients. Couriers cost a lot, but not nearly as much as the personnel and real estate that most banks require; that keeps the bank's profits high. And how many banks make house calls? For executives with no time to waste in a line that creeps toward the teller's window, banking with First Business is an instant sale.

Then there is Michael Dell and his Dell Computer Corp., founded in 1984, when the entrepreneur was a nineteen-year-old premed student at the University of Texas at Austin. In those days, IBM still had the business market for desktop computers almost to itself. Dell chose to build high-quality IBM-compatible machines at bargain-basement prices. His unique price-slashing method: Keep his company's costs down by marketing only through magazine ads and taking orders over the telephone. By early 1988, he was doing $159 million in revenues, with profits of $9 million. A substantial portion of those sales are made to corporations that once would not have thought of buying from anyone but IBM.

Where will you find a business that can carry you through the 1990s in comfort? The best place to look may be where you work now. One of the surest ways to start a profitable company is to find some part of your employer's operation that you can do better, faster, cheaper. Then talk him into letting you do it under contract. It won't be a hard sell if you can prove that using a supplier—you—will save money over handling it in-house. Soon you'll be doing it for your old employer's competitors as well. At that point, with a stable cash flow, it should be relatively easy to branch out into other markets. It isn't quite instant success, but it's about as close as you can come.

Where else should you look? Try Chapter 4. All those fast-growing industries offer as many opportunities for the budding entre-preneur as for the job hunter. Computerized business services, health-care products, high-tech in all its forms—a new career is wait-ing for you. And you won't ever have to worry about being fired.

Are you convinced now that even the darkest night of the world economy is a good time to strike off on your own? If not, you have two choices: Either think about going into business now, before a crash strikes, so that you will be prepared when the time comes—or skip to the next chapter.

But before deciding to start your own business, or take over some-one else's, you will have a lot of thinking to do. Just why do you want your own business? What strengths and weaknesses will you bring to it? Which businesses best fit your talents, skills, and personal needs?

Let's start where you should begin when you actually sit down to make your decisions—with motivation. Chances are that just needing a job won't be enough to drive you through the grueling process of building a company.

Most successful entrepreneurs share a need to be their own boss, even when given their pick of easier ways to make a living. In part, it's a matter of freedom. If you work for yourself and see that some-thing needs doing, you do it. Working for others, you have to justify every project, to get other people's permission, no matter how ob-viously right the idea. Apple Computer exists only because Steve Wozniak's bosses at Hewlett-Packard couldn't see the point of build-ing a computer for the masses.

Most entrepreneurs also share a need to test themselves, to do their best without help or interference. For these people, no success is so sweet as the one you've made with your own mind and hands, and even failure is more tolerable when there is no one else to blame. If that sounds familiar, it could be time to think about going your own way, even if your current job won't fall out from under you when the economy falls out from under your employer.

A taste for money wouldn't hurt. For some business builders, dol-lars are just a good way to keep score; they get their satisfaction from the game itself. For many more, they give the final push needed to break with the stifling security of a job. And for still others, the trappings of conspicuous wealth—a huge house, fast cars, a yacht in the America's Cup, or whatever fits your taste—seize the imagination so strongly that the rigors of life in the business jungle seem a small price to pay. Whichever pattern fits you, money can be one more reason to keep going when success seems all too far away.

It doesn't really matter what moves you to build your own business. What matters is that your motives be strong and durable. Get them straight in your own mind before committing your time and money to a business. They will have to carry you through days when nothing seems more important than seeing your much-neglected family, escaping the tension, or just getting some sleep.

Then think about what you have to offer a business. It's no good going into personal sales if you are so shy that meeting someone new leaves you literally speechless. Or setting up a bookkeeping service if you incessantly transpose digits. But you probably know about your weaknesses already; it is people's strengths that most often slip their notice.

While you are weighing your strengths and weaknesses, take a close look at your health. It sounds silly, but one of the best things you can do now for your future business is start eating right and getting some exercise. Even if you are not planning to start a furniture-moving company, being physically fit is a big help when you're building a business. In the early days, your scarcest asset is likely to be money. Above all, money to hire a staff. That means that nothing will get done unless you do it yourself. And that means working until you crash on the cot in your office, day in and day out, until you can afford to pay for help. We know one small-scale publisher who, when the time came each year to revise the business directory that was his major product, put in seven 18-hour days each week for seven months at a stretch. (In his slow season, he settled for putting in only 45 hours a week.) He repeated that grind each year for twelve years, until he sold the company to a larger firm. Another acquaintance became president of a major university at age 34, founded a Fortune 500 company at 36, and retired with a substantial fortune at 40. Without question, he was a brilliant man; but he credited much of his success to his ability to work comfortably for days on end, taking only an occasional twenty-minute nap. Few of us will ever come close to matching his achievements, even under the best of circumstances. But how much we accomplish in life will depend in part on how much energy we have available to spend on our chosen tasks. Your chances of business success will be that much better if you get into shape.

Think about your family as well. They can make or break your business. There is no way to start a business without putting enormous demands on those around you. Do you spend your Saturdays mowing the lawn and taking care of household chores? Or are you a homemaker, with all the duties that entails? Who will take care of them while you are busy trying to build your company? If your spouse or children won't pick up the load, everyone had better get used to tall grass or dirty dishes. Get ready for some jealous anger, too, if they are not fully behind your business ambitions; you are not going to be giving them the attention they probably expect. On the positive side, no one can help your new business more than a spouse willing to pitch in. Even if he/she is not qualified to handle your business itself, you will probably need someone to answer the phone and keep the books. If your spouse can do it, that is one less person you will have to hire—or one less job you will have to fit into your own day. Finally, there are times when a few words of encouragement will keep you going when you really want to give up. You won't get them from a spouse who resents all the hours you devote to your work. Make sure your family is on your side!

Finally, sharpen a few pencils and figure out what you are worth. You can start a bookkeeping or typing service without much money, but unless you plan to depend on word-of-mouth, even those businesses will require advertising in the local newspapers and Yellow Pages—before you start to show a profit. In most states, starting a real estate or travel agency will require you to pay for an approved training program, followed by a year's apprenticeship in an established agency. Any manufacturing business calls for a serious investment in machines and raw materials, and it could be a long time before that money comes back in sales. Services tend to be less capital-intensive, but you will still need enough money to survive and keep your business going until it shows a profit. Depending on your field, that could be several years.

So: How much do you have in your bank accounts? How much in stocks and bonds, corporate or Treasury? How much can you borrow against your life-insurance policy? Have you any hard assets you could cash in? Balance that off against outstanding bills and other immediate debts, and you will begin to see what is left in start-up capital.

No, we didn't mention your car and house. It was not an oversight. It's true that you can sell your car or borrow against your equity in your house. In fact, so-called "home-equity loans"—second mort-gages renamed for the '80s—are now one of the most popular forms of borrowing. But what are you going to drive after selling your car? Where will you live after starting your new business leaves you so starved for cash that you can't make the payments on your loan? No matter what anyone tells you, your house is not the kind of asset that should be turned into start-up capital.

If you've completed the self-assessment prescribed above, it's time to begin thinking about one of the most important decisions you will ever make: What kind of business do you want to own? Even if you're sure you know a business that suits you, make a systematic search for alternatives. You might find a business that fits your needs even better than the one you have in mind. Your choice will change your life more than any decision since marriage and children. Right or wrong, it is one you will have to live with for a long time. And you can see the penalty for being wrong in the boarded-up shopwindows of almost any inner city.

But put the question another way: What is it you want out of a business? Most entrepreneurs share a few obvious goals: indepen-dence, at least enough money to live comfortably through bad times, and perhaps a chance for wealth and status in your community when the economic climate improves. But how much money is enough? And what sort of life do you want to live while earning it? The answers should have at least as much influence on your choice of a business as your talents and training. If your ambition is to become a concert pianist, nothing will make up for being tone-deaf; short of that, it is much easier to get the training you need in a field that suits you than it is to make a success of a business you understand but don't like.

Take money first. How much do you need to support your family? How much more do you want for vacations, entertainment, and sav-ings? Is $30,000 a year enough? $50,000? $100,000? Or are you aiming to build a company that someone else will buy in five or ten years, turning you into one of those "instant millionaires"? The more money you want, the fewer the businesses that will meet your criteria.

You will rule out many businesses at this stage, even if they seem to offer the income you need. Just ask yourself how well those fields will fare in a severe recession. Would people still pay for your product or service when money is tight? If the answer is no, or even uncertain, move on to something else.

Have you goals other than money? A few successful companies got their start because the founder wanted to create work, not so much for himself as for unemployed neighbors in a depressed city. Others have aimed at helping the handicapped. If that is your motive, you will have to look at labor-intensive businesses, such as light manufacturing, not at bookkeeping or mail-order sales.

Be honest, now. Wouldn't you like your neighbors to look up to you? Most of us would. Status within the community is one more thing that owning your own business can bring, and you should give at least a little thought to it, no matter how firmly you believe you're only in it for the money. There are few businesses more lucrative than buying up junk cars for $25 or so—or getting them free for the towing—and selling off the parts for several hundred dollars. All it takes is a knowledge of cars and some land where the neighbors won't complain about the mess. But it's not going to give you the social standing of the local neurosurgeon. Picture yourself getting rich as you and your helpers strip the useful parts from dead cars and sell them at an exorbitant markup. If there's a scratchy discomfort somewhere in the back of your brain, you want something out of your business beyond mere profits. It could be the kind of status enjoyed by doctors, lawyers, and the heads of some high-tech manufacturing companies.

What kind of work do you enjoy? Are you the kind of natural craftsman who spends his off hours building model airplanes or full-sized furniture? There are dozens of businesses that would let you use those skills, from setting up a hobby or crafts shop to light manufacturing. Do you get a thrill from getting people to do what you want? You could have a bright future in your own sales organization. From helping them overcome difficulties? Day-care services, employment agencies, accounting, and a dozen other businesses could fit your needs. Or would you prefer to work outdoors? You could become a landscaper or building contractor, or run a marina or camp-ground. Remember, you are going to be at this for long hours, quite possibly for the rest of your working life. It doesn't matter how much you like the money a business might bring in if you can't stand the work.

How comfortable are you with people? If you are the relaxed, confident type, meeting new customers can be the high point of your day. For others, it can be a dreaded invitation to put your foot in your mouth and freeze in that uncomfortable position. For many of us, the question of personal contact may be the most important factor in choosing a business—next to money, of course.

Almost anyone can deal with his or her own employees. Even if you are not a great manager, at least you can have the confidence that comes from knowing you're the boss. But someone has to buy your product or service, and many people find it difficult to deal with those customers. In that relationship, you are no longer the boss, but your company's salesman, facing the threat of being told "No." Just how often you will have to endure that role varies widely from one busi-ness to the next. You will be dealing with customers every day if you start a real estate or travel agency or go into any kind of personal sales. On the other hand, if you decide to repair automobiles, you will barely have to talk with anyone but your own employees.

If you find it difficult to meet people, you might consider taking on a more gregarious partner. In a manufacturing firm, someone has to talk with customers and bring in new orders, and someone has to run the factory and make sure the work gets done correctly and on time. If your business can support more than one owner, they need not be the same person.

Think hard about what a business is going to do to your lifestyle. Do you hope to work normal hours—9 to 5, Monday through Friday? Forget about real estate, then, and any other business where you will have to see customers on evenings and weekends. A homemaker may look for a part-time career that can grow into full-time employment once the kids are old enough to fend for themselves. Others may want just the opposite pattern, working long hours now for the priv-ilege of eventually becoming a part-time manager or absentee owner. If you are still single, constant travel could be an exciting fringe benefit of a new business; if you are not, it may place an intolerable strain on your family life. Whatever business you enter, in small ways and large it is going to change the way you live. Those changes are predictable, and they should be one of your prime considerations in picking a business.

As you go through the list of businesses that capture your attention, measure them against your desired income, working conditions, and lifestyle. Do this systematically, writing down your criteria and your best estimate of how well each business fits each need. Could you earn enough money at it? Do you enjoy the kind of work involved? Would it give you enough travel? Too much? Would it subject you to odd working hours? This first inspection will rule out most of the possibilities immediately.

At this stage, you will probably find two or three that seem to meet your standards. If not, review your criteria. Are you asking for a high income from a part-time job? A chance to work outdoors *and* meet lots of people? Some conflicts can be hard to spot. If all is well there, it may just be that you haven't scanned enough possibilities.

Now comes the hard part: winnowing your alternatives down to a final choice—the single best business for you. Pick one of your possibilities, and start looking for more information, as much of it as you can get. A good place to begin is the *Encyclopedia of Associations,* available at most libraries. In it, you will find all the trade organizations in your business area. Call or write to them, explain your purpose, and ask for whatever they can supply in the way of market research and general information about the business. The Small Business Administration offers several hundred booklets about starting and operating your own company, including specialized information about many specific businesses. Subscribe to trade magazines. There are few better ways to find out what is going on in the business. Finally, talk to other people in the field. Half an hour chatting with someone who actually runs a print shop will tell you more about the business of printing than all the reading you can do. And five out of ten businessmen will be willing to talk at length once they know you are not about to set up shop in their market area.

You are looking for the same basic information as before, and a lot more as well, from people with firsthand experience. How often will you have to make long-distance trips as a manufacturer of small-engine accessories? Will you have to do your own marketing? How much chance is there that you'll regularly make it home by 7:00? And don't be afraid to ask how much your contact makes from his business. Some people may not tell you—but some will, and one firm answer is worth more than all your guesses.

Try for all the details you can get about the business itself. How hard is it to break into the market? How much special training or experience will you need to begin? How much competition is there? How difficult is it to get skilled help? Are the Japanese automating American firms out of existence? What kind of future does your expert see for the industry? Above all, how well will this trade endure a recession? His guess may be no better than yours, but by the time you have talked to half a dozen people you should have a pretty clear picture of what you are getting into.

Unless you are lucky, the first business you study will prove unsuitable when you get enough detail about it. Just go on to the next. And, if need be, another after that. But if you find yourself rejecting more than two or three possibilities, it may be time to rethink your criteria again. If you have laid out reasonable requirements, there should be few unpleasant surprises.

When you start thinking about building a new business, a few questions may come to mind—questions whose answers might save you from a costly failure, or at least make success that much closer to certain. Which businesses face the most competition from other entrepreneurs with the same idea? Which are most likely to survive? Which have the best chance of growing into a major company? And where should you locate to give your new firm the best chance of prospering?

Fortunately, MIT Professor David L. Birch, director of the institute's Program on Neighborhood and Regional Change, has worked hard to provide just that information. Birch recently surveyed 236 industries—all that had at least three hundred start-ups in the United States between 1978 and 1982—to see which were most popular among entrepreneurs and which had the best chances for success. Alas, there was not much overlap between the two groups.

To answer an obvious question first: There is only one business that makes the top 50 in all three categories: highest frequency of start-ups, best survival rate, and best chances of growth. If you are an engineer or architect, congratulations. Engineering and architectural services come closer than any other business to having a guarantee of success. Even that is not very close, however. They may rate in the top 50 on all three lists, but they do not make the top 10 on any of them.

Which businesses do people start most often? A catchall category heads the list: "miscellaneous business services." After that, there are few surprises. Bars and restaurants take second place. Then come "miscellaneous shopping goods," auto-repair shops, home builders, machinery and equipment wholesalers, real estate operators, miscellaneous retail stores, furniture and furnishings retailers, and computer and data-processing services. As you might expect, all that competition cuts into your chances of success in these fields. Only three of these businesses make it into the top-100 survival rank: real estate operators (number 38 on the list), auto-repair shops (78), and miscellaneous retail stores (100). And just one business, computer and data-processing services, made it into the top 100 in the growth category; it placed 34th on that list.

Not one of the most frequent start-ups makes it onto the list of businesses most likely to survive. Here professionals and high-investment companies dominate the top 10. Veterinary services, funeral services, and dentists' offices take the top 3 positions. Commercial savings banks are 4th. Hotels and motels come next, followed by campgrounds and trailer parks, physicians' offices, barbershops, bowling alleys and billiard parlors, and—surprisingly—farms producing cash grain crops. Of these, only commercial banks make it into the top 150 growth industries.

In fact, commercial savings banks top the list of growth industries. And the other 9/10 of the top 10? Every one of them is a manufacturing industry. Their products: electronic components, paperboard containers, computers and office machines, miscellaneous paper products, miscellaneous plastic products, basic steel, pharmaceuticals, communications equipment, and partitions and fixtures for offices and the like. Not one of these businesses is easy to break into. Makers of miscellaneous plastic products ranked 84th on the list of frequent start-ups, commercial savings banks 93rd; after that, it was all downhill. Nor do they rate high on the list of survivors (with the sole exception of commercial savings banks). Makers of paper products and paperboard containers came in at 68th and 72nd place, respectively. None of the other broke 100.

What should all this tell you about your chances of making it in business? Well, perhaps not that much. People fail in business for a variety of reasons: because they entered a field where there was already too much competition; because they were undercapitalized; because they could not adapt to changing conditions; because they gave up too easily; because they simply didn't take the time to know what they were doing. People make a success in those same fields by carefully analyzing possible markets, picking a business that suits their talents and investment capacity, and adapting to whatever changes come their way. The 1990s will be a decade of change. If you can adapt to it, you can make it even as your competitors are falling by the wayside.

6

FAVORABLE TERRAIN

How WELL you'll survive the coming downturn depends in part on where you live. Many will be caught in home territories where their skills are no longer needed, while other areas might be more hospitable, even to workers whose specialties are generally in decline. For some people, moving could mean the difference between bare survival and prosperity; for others, it may be the only way to endure.

In the 1990s, we do not expect to see the kind of wholesale dislocation that struck Oklahoma almost sixty years ago, when unrelenting drought turned the entire region into the Dust Bowl and sent thousands of "Okies" on the long trek to California. More likely is a repetition of the early 1980s, when skilled industrial workers from the North-Central States moved to the then-booming areas of Texas in search of work.

In general, big cities will be in the deepest trouble, because they concentrate all the defects that make a place unlivable. Where land is scarce and expansion occurs vertically rather than horizontally, the cost of living also aims for the sky. Massive overcrowding degrades the quality of life. Costly, inefficient mass-transit systems turn the ride to work into daily torture. School systems decay. Businesses have no reason to put up with high taxes and union problems now that most of their work can be conducted by telephone. So they leave, as Mobil Oil, American Airlines, and many others have fled New York City. So urban employment opportunities sink, and there is less and less reason to stay and compete for the jobs that remain. The suburbs, meanwhile, have added new jobs and developed shopping centers and cultural attractions that more than make up for the assets that once drew people to the cities. Thus, for more than thirty years, middle-class city dwellers have been fleeing to the suburbs, leaving behind only the rich and the very poor. The recession of the 1990s will make it even more difficult for the middle class to hold their place in major cities. Urban flight is one trend that can only continue to grow.

You can see the losers of the next depression in crude population statistics from the last few decades. In 1950, New York City had nearly 7.9 million inhabitants; by 1984, there were fewer than 7.2 million New Yorkers. In Chicago, the population has dropped from 3.6 million to under 3 million over the same period. Detroit, hard hit by the Rust Belt blights of automation and foreign competition for car and heavy-equipment sales, was home to 1.85 million people in 1950; by 1984, 750,000 of them were gone. Even lush, inviting San Francisco, with just over 700,000 people in 1984, had lost more than 60,000. Many more will follow these departed city dwellers.

The people who remain can expect more of what they are used to: high prices, overcrowding, crime, grime, and a generally poor quality of life. As the economy sinks, so will their income, leaving them less able to fend off the inevitable urban insults. And as the population base shrinks, the fixed costs of operating city services must be shared by fewer people; taxes will rise. Jobs will be harder to find, not only because companies stop hiring in a recession, but because more of them will head for more hospitable and less costly environs. Lose your job, and there will be ever-fewer places to turn.

Some other cities will fare much better. Again, the key is direction. Cities that grow horizontally, tied together by an efficient network of high-speed, limited-access highways, attract new people and new businesses. Thus, while New York, Chicago, and Detroit were slowly wasting away, Los Angeles grew in its broad valley from fewer than 2 million inhabitants to more than 3 million. Houston, spreading across the flat Texas prairie, nearly tripled in size, to 1.7 million. If you absolutely must live in a big city during the 1990s, search out one of these.

Most comfortable of all will be the smallest cities, with populations of 100,000 or fewer. City services, and therefore taxes, are at their cheapest in such places, and delivery is at its best. Crime rates are low, traffic jams unknown. Generally lower prices will make it easier to endure loss of income. If it becomes necessary to live through a depression, you might as well do it where the living is easiest. There are exceptions, however. Look for a diversified economy. Where the local job market depends on a single employer, there is too much risk that a downturn in that company's fortunes will reduce a small prosperous city to an even smaller, impoverished one. Many of the small urban communities in the industrialized Midwest met this fate in the last major recession. They will face it again in the next.

Where will migrant job hunters find a welcome in the next decade? It depends on just how bad the downturn is. In the worst-case scenario, the answer is probably nowhere. In a general economic collapse, even today's pockets of prosperity will be doing well just to hold their own. But regions that are growing fastest today will feel the pressure last and least. Look for areas with a high proportion of jobs in high-tech service industries. You'll find most of them in states with an ocean view, clustered around major universities. Farm states will also be hospitable in bad times, if you can find some niche in the local economy; there will be no more money to spare than in the most blighted industrial centers, but what farmers can't sell, they and their neighbors can always eat. Try to avoid heavily unionized industrial regions and those with high taxes. The first plants closed will be those where doing business costs the most.

If you can, it's best to prepare for a move now, before the economy takes the plunge. Owners of travel trailers and self-contained recreational vehicles will find it easier to change job markets when the time comes. If your circumstances seem likely to require a move, this may be the time to buy one, particularly if you are not tied down by a house and mortgage—or if you can face abandoning them, as many former homeowners have done in the hard-pressed oil states. In a pinch, a good RV can serve as a home for a small family almost indefinitely.

In 1986, the National Planning Association published a study of job creation in the United States from 1985 through the year 2000. Though the organization assumed that the economy would remain in a period of stable, restrained growth throughout these fifteen years, their report gives at least a rough indication of where jobs may be found in the 1990s.

Overall, the NPA foresees a gain of 26.1 million jobs during the last fifteen years of this century, to 140.1 million—a total increase of 18 percent. A severe recession or depression will cut that gain dramatically.

The association noted two trends that it expected to continue through the period: the prolonged shift of business to the South and West, and the revitalization of older industrial centers in the Northeast and North-Central states. The first of those trends will continue even during a recession; the second will run into a brick wall. Thus, the NPA's forecast of new jobs in such places as Detroit and Newark should be viewed with skepticism.

Table I gives the association's growth estimates for the 30 largest expanding metropolitan job markets, along with Forecasting International's assessment of each community's ability to withstand a recession. Note that these are not necessarily the fastest-growing job markets in the country. Many smaller cities are growing faster than the ones on this list. But because these urban areas are far larger, and still expanding at respectable rates, they will add more jobs than small, fast-growing communities.

In many cases, the regional economies of the 1990s can be seen in their performance during the 1980s. The "Rust Belt" and farm states were hit hard during the recession of the early '80s; they will again be good places to leave. Cheap oil will block any quick or substantial recovery for Oklahoma, Louisiana, and much of Texas. As technical and information-service centers, California and the Northeast will fare better than the rest of the country; the unemployed of other regions will look to them for jobs.

Some states and major cities have unique strengths and weaknesses, so let's look at each region more closely.

Pacific Region: Alaska, California, Hawaii, Oregon, Washington

California is doing well as we approach the 1990s. Citrus fruit, vegetables, and computer products are all in high demand abroad, so as long as the lower dollar continues to boost exports, the state's economy will do well. Semiconductor manufacturers are also finding it easier to sell here at home because products sold by foreign rivals cost more as the dollar comes down.

Jobs are growing tremendously as a result. Throughout the Pacific region, jobs went up 4 percent in 1987; in 1988, it will be 3 percent to 3.5 percent if the dollar stays low.

Toward the end of the decade, the fertile San Joaquin Valley will become a regional trouble spot. For decades, large-scale irrigation

TABLE I. METROPOLITAN JOB GROWTH

METRO AREA	TOTAL JOBS IN YEAR 2000	CHANGE, 1985–2000	PERCENT CHANGE	IMPACT OF A RECESSION
Los Angeles	5,306,000	1,032,000	19.0	Low
Boston	3,056,800	754,700	24.6	Medium
Anaheim	1,849,900	701,500	37.9	Low
San Jose	1,453,600	539,200	37.0	Low
Phoenix	1,453,700	537,000	36.9	Medium
Washington	2,622,100	509,000	19.4	Low
Houston	2,191,500	497,700	22.7	Low
Chicago	3,627,700	493,500	13.6	High
Dallas	1,853,700	485,000	26.1	Medium
Atlanta	1,875,900	462,700	24.6	Low
San Diego	1,438,200	422,400	29.3	Low
Tampa	1,245,400	421,500	33.8	Low
Philadelphia	2,700,000	406,100	15.0	High
New York	4,700,800	383,600	8.1	High
San Francisco	1,435,700	360,400	25.1	Medium
Denver	1,283,700	354,800	27.6	Medium
Minneapolis–St. Paul	1,652,800	352,000	21.2	High
Detroit	2,177,300	328,500	15.0	High
Long Island, NY	1,498,500	318,500	21.2	Medium
Orlando	773,700	308,600	39.0	Low
Ft. Lauderdale	796,400	299,400	37.0	Low
Miami	1,198,400	284,100	23.7	Low
Oakland	1,149,000	277,700	24.1	Medium
Seattle	1,202,500	268,400	22.3	Medium
Baltimore	1,445,800	249,000	17.2	Medium
Middlesex County, NJ	736,000	206,100	28.0	High
Riverside, CA	816,500	200,500	24.0	Low
West Palm Beach	534,200	196,400	36.0	Low
Newark	1,232,300	195,300	15.8	Very High
Hartford, CT	844,800	190,200	22.0	Medium

has made this one of the most productive farming areas in the world, but that will soon come to an end. The water that gives life to San Joaquin crops both deposits large quantities of salt in the soil and depletes the aquifers from which it is drawn. By 1995 or so, the salt will have built up to toxic levels, and water for the area will be running out. At that point, crop yields, farm profits, and job opportunities will all drop sharply. Unemployed farm workers will soon begin competing for scarce positions in other parts of the state. California agriculture will not recover until the development of fusion power around the year 2015 makes desalination of seawater cheap enough for it to be used in irrigation.

Oregon and Washington have excellent export prospects from their paper and lumber industry and thriving aircraft plants. Boeing specifically should prosper. All are benefiting from today's low dollar.

The two remaining Pacific states are also in for tremendous short-term growth. In 1987, 1.8 million free-spending Japanese tourists visited the United States, many of them enjoying their vacations in Hawaii. The dollar is lower now, so foreign tourism will be up even further. In addition, there are a lot more American tourists visiting Hawaii these days. It's a lot cheaper now than any of the overseas destinations that were popular two or three years ago, when the dollar was at its peak.

Alaska will also benefit from this low-buck bonanza for the next couple of years. Here the fountain of profits and jobs is the adventure-type cruise. For the next few years, people who like to rough it will visit Alaska; those who don't will vacation in Hawaii. This burst of growth in the tourist trade has gone surprisingly far in making up for the loss of jobs in Alaska's oil industry, which has been hit as hard by low prices as those of Texas and Oklahoma. Oil remains a drag on Alaska's economy, however. This state will not repeat the massive job growth seen in the late 1970s and early '80s.

This entire region will feel the crunch when export markets slow their buying, either because the dollar recovers on the currency exchanges or because the United States is in recession and can no longer afford to buy *their* products. Despite that, it will remain one of the most promising destinations for job seekers. With its massive internal economy, dominant service sector, and many university-based hotbeds of high tech, California is likely to survive a contraction better than its neighboring states.

Mountain Region: Arizona, Colorado, Idaho, Montana, New Mexico, Nevada, Utah, Wyoming

Even in a growing economy, this entire region would be in for a period of minimal job growth. Arizona, Colorado, and to a lesser extent New Mexico have all managed to diversify their economies in recent years, and this has protected them from the widespread joblessness that has struck the purely agricultural and purely industrial regions in the nation's midsection. It will not keep them going when growth elsewhere slows.

Phoenix, Tucson, and especially Denver all have enjoyed a construction boom in recent years, both in housing and in commercial property. Arizona has become a low-cost alternative for electronics companies fleeing land prices in Silicon Valley. Demand has not kept pace with supply, however, and building has now slowed throughout the region. Construction jobs will be relatively scarce until the homes and offices now standing empty are filled. Even in a good economy, that will take several years.

The tourist business has also been good to Arizona, with a host of new resorts springing up in the Phoenix area. This trend was slowed in 1987 and early '88 by the ugly spectacle of political scandal and the impeachment of former Governor Evan Meacham, but should soon recover for as long as the national economy holds out.

The energy and mining industries, which are important in Colorado, Montana, and Wyoming, should pick up at least into 1990. Mining generates relatively few jobs, however.

In sum, the new high-tech businesses in Arizona will still require a few trained computer and electronics specialists, come what may. Loss of construction jobs will cancel them out in crude employment rates, however. The rest of the region will have little to offer.

West North-Central Region: Iowa, Kansas, Missouri, Minnesota, Nebraska, North Dakota, South Dakota

This entire region has lagged behind the rest of the country during last five or six years of economic expansion. In 1988, this will work to its advantage. Unlike some areas that already are near full employment, these states can expect continued growth of a service economy. Des Moines, Minneapolis, and other major cities will benefit most. The farm economy will benefit as the weaker dollar spurs farm exports from Nebraska, Kansas, and Iowa.

This farm boom will produce fewer new jobs than might be hoped.

The real beneficiaries of the export market will be the giant agribusinesses, not small farmers, and huge corporate farms are so mechanized that they need relatively few workers. Farmers with gross incomes less than $500,000 are the major employers, and they will continue to have problems.

Unfortunately, any gains will be short-lived. So long as the dollar stays down, American farmers can compete for business anywhere in the world; they can be counted on to grow all they can and profit while the sun shines. But price supports and indirect government aid accounted for roughly $26 billion in farm income in 1987. Farmers are not going to get that support if the American economy sours. When the dollar rises again or farm subsidies are cut, unemployed farm workers will again take to their cars in search of work.

Even in this heavily agricultural region, a few small areas are relatively independent of the farm economy; they should survive better than the rest. Minneapolis will be one such local hot spot, thanks to such companies as Honeywell, 3M, and Control Data, all closely tied to technology and the information industry. Though not Silicon Valley, this metropolitan area has developed a manufacturing sector that specializes in building equipment for the information-service industry itself. It should do relatively well, even in a downturn.

East North-Central Region: Illinois, Indiana, Michigan, Ohio, Wisconsin

For the moment, this area is recovering from the decay that struck it in the early 1980s. With the dollar down, American cars, heavy equipment, and other manufactured goods are at last recapturing sales from the imports, and products from this region are flowing into the export market at a rate not seen in years. Profits are up. Employment is up. Even land values have surged. Detroit, where not long ago would-be home sellers could hardly give their houses away, now has the fastest growth in home prices in the United States—an astonishing 37 percent leap in 1987. The prestigious National Planning Association predicts that this bubble is the first stage in a permanent recovery for the downtrodden "Rust Belt." Alas, Forecasting International does not believe it.

For one thing, the grand rebirth of manufacturing has done far less for local employment than local boosters would like to believe. Region-wide, only 1 in 15 of the lost manufacturing jobs has been regained. Illinois, Indiana, and Wisconsin have all made up some of their losses, but in Michigan and Ohio factory employment is still dropping.

For another, much of the area's economy is built on a very frail foundation. In overall terms, how well this region does in the 1990s will depend largely on one company: General Motors. And low-dollar sales are a benefit GM has thrown away in the past; when the dollar falls, raising the price of imported autos, GM's traditional response has been to raise its prices as well, taking a quick profit instead of rebuilding its sagging market share. The company's other policies have been similarly perverse, with predictable results. Five or six years ago, General Motors owned 47 percent of the car market; last year, its share had fallen to 37 percent. That represents $100 billion in sales lost mostly to foreign competition. Put it another way: GM's inept management is single-handedly responsible for about one-fifth of the U.S. trade deficit. And some of that is money that should have been paid out as salaries and supported this region's economy.

Even without that worry, the odds are stacked against a major leap in employment here. Though manufacturing production has gone up in 1987 and '88, relatively few workers have been hired. The reason is automation. U.S. manufacturing has experienced its highest productivity gains in history these last eighteen months or so, thanks largely to the replacement of men by machines. And if factories produce more product per worker, fewer people are needed, even when sales aim for the sky. Even if the economy remains stable, at least 20 percent of heavy-manufacturing workers in this area can look forward to being replaced by automated machines in the next ten years or so. A major contraction would slow new-equipment purchases, but lost sales would eliminate jobs nonetheless.

Add to this a sharp slowdown in travel and consumer spending. Demand has been slow within the region for several years, because many people laid off from manufacturing jobs in the mid-'80s never did get back to work. High unemployment, renewed inflation, and lower incomes in relation to the cost of living can only cut back spending throughout most of the United States. This will kill demand for the automobiles and big-ticket items on which this region's economy depends.

Two cities in this area will be particularly hard hit: Detroit, as we noted earlier, and Chicago. Detroit's fortunes are linked so inextricably with those of the auto industry that it will be many years before the city can survive comfortably even a minor decline in car sales—if that day ever comes. And Chicago is the region's primary financial center. It is already suffering the same post–Black Monday loss of jobs that has struck New York, a trend that will accelerate as financial services further automate their operations in an attempt to boost sagging profits.

In all, the East North-Central region should be able to squeak by without losing many jobs in the last of the 1980s. But neither will it create many new openings. And when the 1990s strike, the sales that brought at least some workers home to the plants will decline, and the Rust Bowl will sink back into its long-term decay.

West South-Central Region: Arkansas, Louisiana, Oklahoma, Texas

The decline of oil prices has brought most of this once-booming area to its knees. Those prices are expected to be slightly lower in '88. In fact, they will decline even farther than most energy-industry forecasters believe, because the Middle Eastern petro-nations have been pumping oil into the market as fast as they can. In the 1990s, tight budgets will drastically reduce both personal and business travel, depressing prices from the demand side as well.

However, throughout this region there are pockets of well-being where local businessmen have managed to diversify their economy away from oil. So long as they last, today's strong exports will help such port cities as Houston and New Orleans. Dallas and Houston are quickly building local biotechnology industries. Austin, one of the region's major educational centers, is building the kind of high-tech growth industries that sprouted in the 1960s around Boston and in the 1970s near Berkeley, CA. Microelectronics is particularly strong in this area. Forecasting International predicts job growth of 2 percent per year in Texas, significantly above the national average.

Oklahoma also has a growing technological-service area to help make up for lost oil revenues. The state is largely nonunion, a major advantage in attracting new business. Good high-tech vocational-education programs assure those companies of a skilled work force. On the scale of high technology, Oklahoma is a step below Silicon Valley and the Berkeley biotechnology center. And for job hunters, that may be an advantage. This state has specialized in building electrical and electronic equipment and appliances, and in servicing those products. This is a more labor-intensive market than such more glamorous fields as bioengineering, bionics, and enzyme research and should provide more jobs than the higher technologies can. This is a relatively small labor market, easily saturated, but laid-off manufacturing workers from other areas could find Oklahoma their best bet for a new job if they are among the first to apply.

For the rest of this region, the outlook is bleak. The port of New Orleans is Louisiana's only major asset, and that will decline once the surge in exports has passed. Arkansas lacks even that temporary advantage.

East South-Central Region: Alabama, Kentucky, Mississippi, Tennessee

The nonmetropolitan areas were this area's shining stars in 1987, thanks to the resurgent farm economy, and particularly to cotton farming. Rural unemployment was running at 8.5 percent as the year began; by December 31, it had fallen to only 5 percent. That improvement will continue in '88, but will die out in the following year. Overall employment growth will be slow, along the lines of the rest of the nation.

One manufacturing industry that should do very well for this region is auto parts. Consumers have been putting the brakes on new-car sales, so owners have had to make their old autos last longer. That means a fat payoff for the industrial centers of this region; the profit on auto parts is six times what it is when you sell the original car.

Health care is a surprisingly large industry in this region, and may be the single most productive creator of new jobs. Nashville and Louisville are the two major centers, Nashville because of its university, Louisville because it is home to Humana Hospital Corp.

Both these industries are relatively recessionproof. Industrial and medical opportunities should hold up relatively well in a downturn.

South Atlantic Region: Delaware, Florida, Georgia, Maryland, North Carolina, South Carolina, Virginia, Washington, DC, West Virginia

Two parts of this nation are virtually recessionproof, and both are in this region. Their advantage over the rest of us: Their chief economic assets endure from day to day, year to year, with little visible interest in the national economy. Those assets are the weather in Florida and the government in Washington.

If a mere depression could slow the growth of government, it might almost be worth having one every decade or two in order to accomplish the pruning that Capitol Hill is unable to face. But, of course, the government grows whether the country does or not. So Washington, DC, Maryland, and northern Virginia will continue to benefit from the strong service economy needed to support all those politicians and bureaucrats. Defense-related spending, a major source of jobs and income in this area, is safe only for this year, however. In the 1990s, cuts in the defense budget will slow the region's economy. At that point, job creation will continue, but at a slower pace.

North Carolina offers one of the most diverse economies in the Southeast. A large and prosperous farm sector centers on tobacco and soybeans. Manufacturing supplies jobs for nearly 30 percent of the state's nonfarm workers, more than in any other state. Just east of the Raleigh-Durham area is the Research Triangle, built around Duke University and the University of North Carolina. Many of the Fortune 500 companies have established R&D divisions there, bringing the state a large supply of scientists and engineers.

Georgia and Maryland are also home to economic hot spots that should resist the drag of a national slowdown. Atlanta benefits from active, well-respected universities, served by one of the country's most efficient regional transportation networks. Like North Carolina's Research Triangle, it has been able to build a base of small high-tech R&D firms, service businesses, and regional offices of national companies. In Maryland, the fertile centers are the National Institutes of Health, in Bethesda, and Johns Hopkins University, in Baltimore. Between them, these academic institutions have spawned a plethora of new biotechnology companies second only to the concentration around Berkeley, CA. Though not labor-intensive, biotechnology will draw new, highly skilled workers to the area, even when other employers have slowed.

Florida is the fastest-growing state in the nation, and likely to remain so for the rest of this century. Obviously, hot sun and sandy beaches get the credit.

For Florida, that weather forms a paid-up insurance policy against depression. Not even a national disaster will stop retired Yankees from seeking a warm haven after a lifetime of snow. And unlike too many others, they will be able to afford the move, no matter what happens to the economy. Their secret: the fixed incomes—Social Security and pensions—that many now complain are hopelessly inadequate. Fixed incomes may not rise as quickly as prices during periods of high inflation; but neither will they vanish in hard times, like a laid-off factory worker's salary. Fixed-income retirees will be the new rich of the next recession.

These new Floridians need an unending supply of service workers to tend their needs: carpenters and masons, plumbers and painters to build their houses; realtors to sell them their new homes; laborers to tend their yards; bank tellers to open new accounts and bank officers to process loans; cooks and waiters and waitresses to staff restaurants. The list is virtually endless.

Florida has other assets as well. On the Atlantic coast, technical professionals attracted by the Kennedy Space Center at Cape Canaveral have created a flourishing electronics industry. Inland, Walt Disney World draws millions of visitors each year. And Miami's large population of Cuban émigrés probably form the most concentrated fund of entrepreneurial energy in the country.

With all this going for it, Florida may be the single most depressionproof state in the nation. Many of the jobs offer low wages, and many are dead ends. But at least they are available. They will continue to be available long after the rest of the country has succumbed.

In a major slump, however, one city could turn out to be a local trouble spot. Jacksonville, FL, is one of the country's most active port cities. Through it pass more than 500,000 foreign cars each year, to be distributed to dealers all over the East. If trade with Japan collapses, or if Americans lose the ability to buy even inexpensive new cars, that flow of labor for local dock workers will collapse, and unemployment in this city will leap abruptly.

Tiny Delaware is one of the nation's leaders in two disparate industries: manufacturing and finance. The original E. I. du Pont set the course of business in Delaware when he founded the American chemical industry. Chemicals and other manufactured products remain the most important products. Since 1981, however, carefully aimed tax incentives have brought more than 9,000 banking jobs to the state, many of them in processing centers for national credit-card operations. The chemical industry is getting a boost from higher exports and will maintain its strength as long as dollar values remain low. When the economy turns down, consumer purchasing will dry up, and local banking will slow.

The best that can be said of West Virginia is that the economy won't collapse any further. Coal mining is the state's only significant industry, and coal prices are already as low as they can get. West Virginia is one of those states which people move from, not to, and there is no prospect that this will change in our lifetimes.

Middle Atlantic Region: New Jersey, New York, Pennsylvania

More than most other regions, the Middle Atlantic States mirror the strengths and weaknesses of the entire nation. Almost any industry important in the United States as a whole plays a significant role in this area's economy. Each state has large areas of farming, heavy manufacturing is important in Pennsylvania and New Jersey, and New York is the financial capital of the world. So whatever is good or bad for the country is soon felt here.

This diversification adds up to a very average future for these three states. Steel, chemicals, and other basic industries in Pennsylvania and New Jersey will continue to perform well as long as the dollar remains down and American manufacturing is selling overseas. New Jersey's pharmaceutical manufacturers also get a boost from higher exports. As in the North Central region, automation is reducing the number of jobs that this temporary trend would otherwise create.

As in the country at large, lower consumer spending already threatens the health of the area's manufacturing. Most immediately at risk are parts suppliers for the auto industry; like Kentucky and Tennessee, these states will lose manufacturing jobs unless carmakers are uncharacteristically smart enough to keep prices low.

Financial services in the New York area already have been hit very, very hard. The best estimates hold that 35,000 to 40,000 people will eventually lose their jobs as a result of 1987's Black Monday massacre; the toll is nearing that already. From now on, all those business-school finance graduates will have to make their money the old fashioned way—by working for a living. That means new competition for white-collar jobs in all industries

Partly because so many high-spending Wall Street executives have suddenly become low-spending job hunters, this region's service sector will not grow as quickly as in years past, particularly in downstate New York and suburban New Jersey. Restaurants, financial services, retailers, and the like have already felt the pinch. Many more will do so as the region's economy lags.

New York, of course, remains one the nation's busiest ports. This industry too will decline rapidly in any downturn. Sagging international trade is one reason; there is little need for a port when there are no products being shipped. But the main reason is the heavy union influence here. New York may well be the most unionized port in the country. This translates to higher costs and more labor problems. As a result, more and more shippers are opting to move their merchandise through ports in the South; this trend can only grow as profits become even smaller and harder to find.

Elsewhere in this region, prospects for the 1990s vary widely from place to place. Urban industrial areas will be hard hit when export sales drop; rural areas will suffer less, but there are fewer jobs there to begin with. Nowhere will there be the relative prosperity found in California and the deep South. There is no reason to expect the same kind of mass flight from the Middle Atlantic States that struck the Rust Belt in the last recession, and will in the next, but job hunters can expect to face a long, hard search until the national economy picks up again.

New England: Connecticut, Maine, Massachusetts, New Hampshire, Rhode Island, Vermont

When one looks at bare job forecasts, the future seems pretty bleak for much of this region, and especially so for Massachusetts and New Hampshire. Job growth will slow dramatically in those states in the coming years. Look closer, and it turns out that the downturn is good news. Growth in New England has soared uninterruptedly for more than five years. The jobless rate in Massachusetts is only 3.2 percent, though edging upward. In New Hampshire, it's stable at 2.6 percent. There will be few new jobs here in the coming years only because there is hardly anyone left to hire.

One major driver of this prosperity is the high concentration of technical skill in and around Boston. Since 1980, a single square mile of Cambridge centered on the Massachusetts Institute of Technology has created more new jobs than each of thirteen states. Nearby New Hampshire has proved a magnet for people seeking a largely rural environment where income and sales taxes are yet unknown.

For the moment, the low dollar has brought New England the same export boom that has revitalized manufacturing elsewhere. Foreign sales of computers and medical technology—major employers here —were not hurt as badly by the high dollar as those in other industries; the change has helped fuel demand for skilled workers. When the boom is over, it will be missed, even here. This is particularly true in Connecticut, Massachusetts, and Rhode Island, which combine strong manufacturing and service economies. Connecticut will also feel the decline of New York, particularly in its southwestern corner, where much of the population commutes to the city each day.

Northern New England should face fewer problems. New Hampshire, with a unique combination of strong high-tech industry, large rural areas, and very small governmental establishment, should resist a recession better than its more urban neighbors. Vermont and Maine are almost entirely rural. Their greatest loss will be in the tourist dollars now brought by visitors from areas that will be hurt more directly; tourism now brings more than $1 billion per year into each state.

More than other parts of the United States, New England will get a strong boost from the recent free-trade agreement with Canada. The first restriction to be eliminated under the treaty is Canada's 3.9 percent tariff on computers and related products. Canada has already been New England's best customer, importing $1.46 billion in merchandise from the region in 1986; fully 40 percent of that was in computers and telecommunications equipment. This trade is expected to soar as Canadian tariffs on computers are eliminated in 1989 and those on telecommunications hardware—regulated separately—are phased out by 1994. Restrictions on some lesser trade markets will be eliminated more slowly. Canadian tariffs on precision instruments and scientific equipment, for example, will remain in place until 1999; this trade makes up about 10 percent of New England's exports north of the border. This gradual lowering of trade barriers will provide a small continuing impetus for New England manufacturers.

Service industries may not do as well, however, and they are as important to this region's major cities as they are to New York and Chicago. The slowdown expected in financial services will cost jobs in the insurance business as well; it's a leading employer of white-collar workers in Boston, Hartford, and Providence. Most other service industries in this area will also suffer from the next recession.

A number of cities have strengths beyond those of their general region. These are the hot spots where entrepreneurs congregate to make fortunes for themselves and new jobs for others. In many of these favored places, it is a major university or research center that propels the local economy. In others, it is a major government institution. MIT professor David L. Birch, whose study of business start-ups was quoted in the last chapter, has also looked at places around the United States with the highest frequency of new businesses and at places where they have the best chance to grow and prosper. Here are the most interesting cities noted in the study, along with Forecasting International's observations about them and about several other promising communities:

Albuquerque, NM, not on the Birch lists, has several strikes against it, including a high crime rate and high power costs. Businesses wishing to settle in the Southwest will find some strong assets as well, however. Corporate taxes are low, and the state offers many tax incentives to companies locating in New Mexico. Perhaps most compelling of all, in a region of water-starved cities, Albuquerque is believed to have water enough to support at least twice its current population. As neighboring cities run out of water and are forced to curb their growth, this could be a crucial advantage for Albuquerque.

Atlanta, GA, ranked sixth in start-ups and seventh in growth prospects for new businesses at the beginning of the 1980s. It can only have improved since then. Time was when the biggest employer in town was Coca-Cola. Today, the city has become the Southeastern headquarters for virtually all of the Fortune 200 companies, and many small service businesses have sprung up to tend their needs. Credit for this goes to Atlanta's central location, excellent transportation system, and very high quality of life. Added benefits for business include low business and personal tax rates and relatively little union activity.

Austin, TX. In the four years from 1978 through 1982, Austin had more new business start-ups than any other city in the country. It also ranked tenth on the list of places that offered the best chances for business growth. At mid-decade, Forecasting International rated it the most attractive city for business among a dozen fast-growing communities and predicted that it would remain so through the year 2000. The reason: Texas imposes virtually no taxes on business and very low personal taxes, living costs are low, and unions are largely unknown. A sunny climate, the complete absence of air pollution, and a strong school system are other compelling assets.

Despite the oil-soaked economy that burdens much of the rest of the state, Austin remains a haven for entrepreneurs. As in many such communities, the driving force is a major university, the University of Texas at Austin. Though lacking the prestige of MIT or Stanford, this is one of the most productive and fast-growing research centers in the West, particularly in such bankable fields as microelectronics and biotechnology. In 1987, Austin added one more high-tech facility: Sematech, an ultrasophisticated microchip research center operated by fourteen of the country's major chip makers. A host of new computer-business start-ups can be expected to form around the institute.

Boston, MA. Throughout the 1960s, '70s, and most of the '80s, Boston has been one of the hottest growth centers in the country. The Boston area's growth began with the fabled Route 128 complex, the first of the great high-tech corporate incubators to spring up around a major educational center. Company start-ups surged mightily in the late '70s (despite state and local taxes that were then among the highest in the nation) following a cut in defense spending that left many of the area's scientists and engineers scrambling for a new way to earn their living. Computer and medical-instrument manufacturers, and recently a few biotechnology companies, have all found homes in this densely populated region. At this point, an estimated 700 high-tech firms within 30 miles of Boston employ more than 250,000 people.

The highly skilled labor force that has colonized this region for more than two decades is likely to keep the entire metropolitan area growing for some time to come. However, Forecasting International believes that Boston's day of high-tech glory are largely over. The city and its suburbs grew so quickly, for so long, that the area now is saturated with people. In Boston suburbs, an average home costs $180,000; in the city itself, prices run far higher. Route 128, once an efficient bypass highway that kept commuters out of city traffic, is so congested that home-bound workers routinely face two-hour traffic jams. Despite large and innovative urban-renewal programs, the inner city continues to decay, and Boston schools are in the same decline that plagues major urban educational systems throughout the country. And though taxes in Massachusetts generally, and Boston specifically, have come down in recent years, they remain higher than in many faster-growing areas.

Boston's cultural environment is among the most pleasant in the country. Its universities remain among the best in the world. But there are many other attractive educational and cultural centers, and it seems likely that companies will focus their attention on some of them.

Dallas, TX. During the period covered by Dr. Birch's study, Dallas' fortunes rose with the price of oil in the 1970s; that growing economy put the city on the list for new-business start-ups. Now that oil prices have fallen sharply, you might expect that Dallas has collapsed with them. But like Austin, and unlike too many other oil-field cities, Dallas has managed to build a generally diversified economy with a strong and growing manufacturing base. Many high-technology companies have located there, particularly in the electronics industry. This city has also built itself into one of the leading convention centers west of the Mississippi. Though Forecasting International will be surprised if Dallas is in the top ten start-up centers of the 1990s, its future looks relatively bright.

· · ·

Huntsville, AL, third on the start-up list, has the government to thank for much of its prosperity. NASA's Huntsville Space Center is home to many of the space agency's major research programs. Even with the starvation budgets NASA has endured since the early 1970s, it has drawn a host of high-tech industries to this area. Many of these small companies provide services used by the Space Center itself. Many have been founded by departing NASA researchers, who could see no future in a space program where projects die with each wave of bureaucratic pens at the General Accounting Office.

Huntsville's future looks generally bright. At this point, the concentration of growth industries here has reached a self-sustaining level. Whatever happens to NASA, the companies it attracted here should survive. The new emphasis on regaining America's leadership in space brings at least some hope that NASA itself will soon regain its power to stimulate Huntsville's economy. By 1991, the expanding military space program will begin to subcontract lucrative research programs to NASA; no doubt many of them will be based here. If the civilian space program receives the funding requested for the programs announced by President Reagan early in 1988, the area should experience a boom such as has not been seen since the days of the race to put American astronauts on the moon.

Manchester-Nashua, NH. Set in semirural southern New Hampshire, this high-tech center tops Birch's list of places where newborn companies have the best chance of growing large. It is one of the fastest-growing locales in the country. For several years, Nashua has had the lowest unemployment rate in the nation—around 1.6 percent! Small manufacturers of computer accessories, medical equipment, and related hardware abound, and large companies from Massachusetts' Route 128 area are rapidly finding their way here. Local construction companies are kept busy building new factories and offices for new arrivals, and machine shops and business services have flourished by serving prosperous larger firms.

There are reasons. In part, Boston and Cambridge are to thank for the region's prosperity. The state's strong scientific base is only about 50 miles away, close enough for easy transfer of technical skills along a well-developed highway network. Yet New Hampshire avoids all the crowding and crime endemic to big cities. Route 128's fabled traffic jams are unknown here.

And New Hampshire has merits of its own: no personal income tax, no sales tax, low business taxes, relatively low cost of living, and the comfort of a rural life combined with easy access to cultural centers and other big-city attractions. In a nationwide survey several years ago, nearby Peterborough was picked as one of the ten best places to live in the United States; the rest of the region is not far behind. Despite low educational budgets, New Hampshire also has one of the most successful school systems in the United States. SAT scores for New Hampshire high school students are the highest in the nation. For business, this offers a substantial pool of well-trained, adaptable workers. And perhaps because salaries in northern New England lagged until recently behind those of more populous regions, the tradition of "an honest day's work for an honest day's pay" remains strong here. Union shops are hard to find.

Growth is likely to slow here only because there are few people left to hire. Local construction firms needing extra hands have begun to import workers from as far away as Louisiana for the peak summer building months. For anyone needing a job, this area should be an irresistible magnet.

Nashville, TN, also makes both of Dr. Birch's lists, coming in just after Atlanta in business start-ups and taking third place in growth opportunities. Like all state capitals, it is made relatively recession-proof by government spending, an advantage strengthened by the recent shift of many responsibilities downward from the Federal level. The University of Tennessee has a major campus and medical center here, and Tennessee State University is also located in Nashville. The two institutions are responsible for many small high-tech manufacturers and medical-service companies which have set up for business in this city. Nashville also has a thriving tourist industry, driven primarily by Opryland and the city's other famed country-music attractions.

Orlando, FL. Not just this city, but the entire Route 4 complex from Orlando more than 100 miles south and west to Tampa and St. Petersburg has been in a continuous boom throughout the 1980s. Orlando ranked fourth on the Birch list of start-up areas and ninth in growth opportunities. At the other end of this moneyed axis, Tampa and St. Petersburg found their way to tenth place on the start-up list on their own merits.

Tourism is one major growth industry here. Disney World's giant entertainment complex just southwest of Orlando has spread prosperity for miles around as hotel and restaurant operators struggle to acommodate visitors drawn to the area.

The entire region also has become one of the country's leading centers for research and development in robotics, computer-aided design and manufacturing, and flexible manufacturing systems. Such major corporations as IBM and Westinghouse pioneered the area, attracted largely by Florida's excellent vocational-education program. Since then, all the other major players in industrial automation have followed, drawn there by the large base of skilled technical personnel.

Tampa and St. Petersburg have attractions even beyond this foundation in high-tech industry. Both are major ports and popular retirement centers. St. Petersburg also benefits from defense spending at McDill Air Force Base, located in Tampa.

A recession may slow this region's boom slightly, but nothing will stop it during this century.

Raleigh-Durham, NC, comes in second on Birch's list of places where small companies have the best chance of growing large. Forecasting International rates it one of the four best research and high-tech areas in the country. The reason: Duke University, the University of North Carolina, and North Carolina State are all located within the metropolitan area. Nearby, the Research Triangle has become a major center of industrial research and development, with divisions of many of the Fortune 500 companies. Added to this are a large supply of technically skilled, nonunion labor and one of the most comfortable lifestyles in the East. Both cities offer excellent school systems for children of well-educated workers, and Durham is home to the North Carolina School of Science and Mathematics, which accepts only the most gifted eleventh- and twelfth-graders from around the state. In addition to high-tech industry, Raleigh-Durham has developed a very strong service sector, geared to the needs of retirees moving into the area.

San Antonio, TX. Though lacking the strength of Austin or Dallas, San Antonio managed to place fourth on the list of fertile corporate birthplaces. Thanks largely to the Alamo, tourism is one of the area's largest industries, and the city has capitalized on this to build itself into a major convention center. A large helping of Federal funds also nourishes this city. Both giant Kelly Air Force Base and the Army's Fort Sam Houston are located here. Small service businesses seem to do particularly well here, but San Antonio has yet to develop the broad-based economy needed to make it an economic leader during the 1990s.

Washington, DC. No surprises here. Everyone knows what drives this city. New law offices, new business services, new real estate developers set up shop almost daily. Close behind them come retailers, restaurants, and entertainment services for the thousands of well-heeled bureaucrats and functionaries for whom Washington is, at least temporarily, home. The constant flow of government largess has meant prosperity not only for the capital itself, but for many of the small cities surrounding it. Arlington and Alexandria, just across the Virginia border, are two of the fastest-growing forests of office buildings in the country.

Despite what passes for austerity in Washington, the steady flow of government money has also brought continuing prosperity to the ever-growing ranks of the "Beltway Bandits," the hundreds of small consulting firms dotted thickly along the bypass highway that surrounds Washington itself. In the early 1980s, Washington, DC, ranked fifth on the list of places where new companies have the best chance of growth. There is no reason to believe that the future will be any less bright for capital-area start-ups.

7

FINDING ALLIES ABROAD

WHAT DO YOU DO if you can't find work at home, and the rest of your native land seems equally short of opportunity for someone with your skills, assets, and interests? The time-honored answer is to emigrate to a country that offers greater promise. In the past, the United States has been the favorite destination of the displaced the world over. American expatriates have tended to be retired people looking to make the most of fixed incomes; writers and artists huddled in their own enclaves; employees of multinational corporations, who maintain their ties here and carry much of our culture abroad with them; and a few rootless adventurers with little reason to come home. In the next depression, the economic tides may carry Americans to other lands in record numbers.

There is not a single developed nation in the world that will completely escape the impact of recession in the United States. The old saying that "when the U.S. sneezes, everyone else catches pneumonia" is substantially true, because the United States is by far the world's largest market for imported goods. To the extent that a country depends on exports for its prosperity, it depends on a healthy American economy.

Yet there are several reasons to think that some foreign countries, for some people, at least, may be more hospitable than the United States during a major downturn. One is our ample supply of technical professionals and skilled labor; within limits, practical knowledge is generally most welcome and best rewarded where it is hardest to find. Another is the relative simplicity of some economies; the nations likely to survive a crunch best are those that do not depend for their survival on international trade. And agrarian lands may be short on amenities, but they tend to have plenty to eat, even in bad times.

The question is, what are you going to do there? In Japan, and to a lesser extent South Korea, almost anyone who speaks English can earn a tolerable living teaching English to executives bound for America—particularly anyone with the good fortune to be young, blond, and female—but that job market could dry up quickly in a severe decline of trade. While the world economy remains strong, the import/export trade is a natural for anyone with a good market sense. Farming may be the most transferable skill; a number of farmers hit by hard times in the American Midwest have managed to resettle in Central America with much less difficulty than a manufacturer would have encountered. But even for those best suited to life abroad, finding a niche in another land will mean carefully weighing your personal assets, gathering information about possible destinations, and preferably making several trips to scout the territory before making a final commitment.

One thing that will probably ease your move is plenty of ready cash. U.S. immigration policies are remarkably fair-minded; they take into account the applicant's political status in his home country, the presence of relatives and promised employment in the United States, and a variety of other factors—but not the would-be immigrant's bank balance. Many other countries put their own interests first; they welcome people who promise to create jobs for their citizens. And it isn't just Third World nations. If you have business skills and $250,000 to invest ($190,000 U.S.), Canada will be happy to give you permanent resident status, which grants all the benefits of citizenship save the right to vote. In Australia, the price is $360,000. By far the easiest route into many nations is paved with gold.

Working for a major company also can ease the transition into another country: Simply apply for a transfer to an overseas division or subsidiary. You can scout out local opportunities, make contacts, and find out whether your potential new home has what you need. If so, you can either stay with your employer or set off on your own as the impulse strikes and good sense dictates. Plan well, however: Many Americans working overseas and paid in U.S. currency found themselves badly short of money when the dollar dropped from its 1985 high and local prices, measured in dolllars, suddenly skyrocketed. Though the worst of the decline should be over, make sure either that you are extremely well paid or that your contract provides for a cost-of-living adjustment geared to local conditions. And if you decide to make your move permanent, try to put some money aside. There is every chance that your division will get the ax if foreign trade dries up and your company finds itself with too little profit to justify overseas operations.

Finally, one piece of all-too-obvious advice about a lesson that American ambassadors never seem to learn: If you are going to a country where English is not the native tongue, learn at least the basics of the local language before you move. You can pick up the subtleties once you are there, but you'll do business only with other expatriates until you can make yourself understood. Learn as much as you can of local customs and courtesies as well. American businessmen trying to open foreign markets have often lost potentially profitable opportunities by inadvertently offending their hosts. The rigid, formalized customs of Japan are an extreme example, but similar pitfalls can be found in almost every culture.

Forecasting International continuously updates a database of information about foreign countries of interest to government agencies and corporate clients. This wealth of hard facts has made it possible to forecast such seemingly unpredictable occurrences as the Arab oil embargoes of 1973, the fundamentalist Moslem revolution in Iran, the rise of Solidarity in Poland, and the Republican landslide in 1980. For the national profiles below, this resource has been augmented by data from other sources and distilled to the essential information needed by someone so hard-pressed at home that he must weigh his chances of prospering in another land. It is as up-to-date as possible.

Each of the national profiles that follow begins with a capsule summary that may let you decide at a glance whether or not the country would be a good place to live. Most of the statistics in the capsules are easily understood, but two items may need some explanation. The stability rating is a unique development of Forecasting International, based on computer analysis of our database, designed to provide a convenient measure of the nation's politics, economy, and culture. The higher our stability rating, the less likely the country is to experience a revolution or other major upheaval. This is one good measure of how confortable life there is likely to be.

So far, we have studied more than 40 nations thoroughly enough to provide a stability rating. The rating is expressed as the nation's position within that group. The higher the rating, the more stable the country. For example. Argentina now ranks 20th; it is less stable than the United States, at number 1, but more stable than Egypt, at 32. We offer both the current rating and a forecast of the nation's rank in the last five years of this century.

The second, complementary, rating is the useful income, adapted from the purchasing-power-parity index of economists Alan Heston and Robert Summers of the University of Pennsylvania. Useful income measures the average economic well-being of each nation's citizens, compared with conditions here in the United States, rather as per capita income does. But where per capita income tells how much money people have, useful income tells roughly how far it stretches. In two countries with the same per capita income but different consumer price levels, the country with lower prices has a higher useful income; people live better there. Because useful income is based in part on exchange rates, a country's standing can shift dramatically whenever it revalues its currency. Naturally, it can also change rapidly during periods of high inflation or recession. By definition, the United States has a useful income of 100; other countries' are calculated as percentages of the U.S. rating. At the moment, the United States has the world's highest useful income.

Please remember that these profiles are only brief and general guides to the countries they describe. They should help you to rule out destinations that clearly would not fit your needs; they should help you pick out nations that deserve further research. But it is possible that exactly the opportunity you need lies hidden in some obscure corner of a country you have not considered. Finding it will take the kind of personal digging that only you can handle.

ARGENTINA

Current Stability Rating: 20
Per Capita Income: $2,331
Population: 31,168,000
Urban Pop.: 80%
Life Expectancy: 66.8 male;
  73.2 female
Govt.: Republic

Projected Stability Rating: 15
Useful Income: 26
Pop. Density: 27.8 per sq. mi.
Literacy: 94%
Language(s): Spanish
GNP: $65.4 billion

Labor Force: 19% farm, 36% commerce & industry, 20% services
Major Industries: automobiles, chemicals, machinery, meat
  processing, mining, textiles
Comments: Maybe—if you speak Spanish fluently and have a
  high-tech specialty.

After years of military rule, Argentina returned to civilian government with the election of President Raúl Alfonsín in 1983. That change did not bring as much in the way of stability as one might have hoped, however. Two major political parties and numerous minor ones are locked in what seems to be an endless struggle for power, complicated by the agitation of corrupt, violent, and highly politicized labor unions. Add to this the ever-present Army, which remains ready to overthrow the civilian government and resume control over the country; in the last year, two major revolts by middle-ranking officers have been ended by negotiation, largely because it seemed doubtful that Argentine soldiers would act against even treasonous comrades. While the government has managed to keep this stew from boiling over for five years now, the combination makes it difficult to be sure from one year to the next who will lead the country or what their policies will be.

Economically, Argentina should be the garden spot of South America. It is blessed with huge, fertile agricultural regions that make it self-sufficient in food; abundant hydroelectric power that provides all its energy needs; and a variety of natural resources. There is a large urban population with a substantial middle class to serve as an internal market for manufactured goods. A well-educated labor force has helped to build large steel, textile, chemical, and construction industries. Substantial exports of food, chemicals, and other products give the country a positive balance of trade. Luxury items for the wealthy make up a significant part of the country's imports. In all, it's a diversified, well-balanced economy that most neighboring countries can only envy.

What Argentina has always lacked is good leadership, and incompetent economic policies have long undermined the country's natural advantages. When Alfonsín took power, he inherited an inflation rate of 434 percent. It peaked in 1985 at more than 1,000 percent; unemployment may have totaled one-fourth of the work force; foreign debt was $43 billion; and manufacturing capacity had vastly outgrown demand. A wage–price freeze in 1985 temporarily halted inflation, but the rate had returned to 90 percent a year later and today has again risen above the 100 percent level. Thus, during the 1980s the nation's standard of living has plummeted, particularly among the middle class. Argentina's contentious politics make it difficult to hope that the situation will soon improve.

Foreign-debt payments are a constant drain on Argentina's economy, despite frequent refinancing and debt-restructuring plans. How quickly those debts will be repaid, and even whether they will be repaid, depends on the nation's balance of trade. It doesn't look good. In 1987, that balance was expected to be $3 billion, up a bit from the year before, but well below 1985's record of $4.6 billion. In fact, declining exports and a sharp rise in imports reduced the balance to only $800 million. The government is being pressured to follow Brazil in suspending interest payments on its national debt and is expected to do so within the year.

In sum, Argentina seems a poor prospect for immigration. Save in a very few high-tech areas, the country needs few skills from outside, and this independence can only grow in the next decade. A depression would very likely cut into Argentina's exports as other nations find it difficult to sell the finished products now made from Argentine steel and chemicals and their beef imports give way to home-grown meat products. This can only worsen existing economic and political difficulties, bringing a return of uncontrolled inflation and labor unrest. Continued inflation will be no kinder to the standard of living of resident aliens than to that of natives. It is a good bet that the military will eventually retake control of the country, bringing a return to the inept and inconsistent policies that have so badly damaged what should have been a strong economy.

Lightly settled, with some 85 percent of its people in the coastal

---

AUSTRALIA

Current Stability Rating: 4
Per Capita Income: $10,282
Population: 15,763,000
Urban Pop.: 85%
Life Expectancy: 72.6 male,
  79.1 female
Govt.: Democratic, federal

Projected Stability Rating: 1
Useful Income: 72
Pop. Density: 5.4 per sq. mi.
Literacy: 98%
Language(s): English
GNP: $184 billion

Labor Force: 6% farm, 21% mining & mfg., 22% govt., 51%
  services
Major Industries: aircraft, automobiles, chemicals, electrical
  equipment, iron and steel, machinery, mining, ships, textiles
Comments: If you really want to leave the United States, book
  passage. This will soon be the world's most stable country, with
  one of its strongest economies—and they speak English.

---

cities, this vast country is one of the most comfortable in the world. Ruled by a strong democracy, it has a very homogeneous population, largely of British descent. The literacy rate, at 98 percent, is one of the highest in the world. Medical care is excellent in the cities, though rural residents may have to travel long distances to find health services. All this makes Australia one of the most stable countries in the world; by the year 2000, it may be *the* most stable country, ranking even ahead of the United States.

A decade ago, Australia's economy was so weak that currency speculators referred to its dollar as the "Pacific peso." In those days, the island continent managed to combine a Western culture with a Third World industrial base. Exports were limited to farm crops and minerals. But things have changed since then. Since 1983, the Australian growth rate has been a healthy 5 percent to 6 percent per year. Though most of its exports are still made up of agricultural products and a vast array of mineral resources, manufacturing has grown rapidly, and limited oil production is adding to foreign income. If all goes well, the 1990s should see rapid growth in the computer and telecommunications industries, oil-field equipment and services, health care, and modern agricultural equipment. Even traditional raw-materials exports could grow explosively if Japanese manufacturers notice the advantages of buying from their closest supplier. Australia's internal demand for consumer goods should rise as the economy continues to grow.

All that said, the picture is not without its flaws. A generation of postwar British immigrants infected Australia with the brand of trade unionism that helped to destroy the economy of the United Kingdom. Strikes, slowdowns, and other job actions are constant and unending. Cradle-to-grave social programs in the British style are a major drain on the economy. Worst of all, there is some doubt about how long Australia's vast growth will continue. According to many critics inside the country, Australian workers have become so accustomed to their comfortable life that the idea of doing any work has been forgotten by all but Asian immigrants. Leisure services make up the fastest-growing sector of the economy, while manufacturing, though growing in real terms, has fallen from one-fifth of the GNP to 12 percent in only five years. Unemployment is slowly moving upward, and exports have run into competition from South Korea, Taiwan, and the other fast-growing Asian powers.

Yet this country is well fixed to ride out an economic downturn. Though loss of export sales could cut into its economic growth as long as a depression lasted, Australia is nearly self-sufficient in food and will soon be capable of providing for all its own needs. When prosperity returns, they will be poised to make the most of it.

For would-be immigrants, this had become one of the most hospitable destinations in the world. A long-standing "White Australia" policy was dropped fifteen years ago, and though it still helps a little to be Caucasian, the country has accepted a substantial number of Indochinese refugees in the last decade; by the year 2000, they will make up 8 percent of the population. Despite the abundance of well-educated workers here, Australia is so large and so many industries are still in the development phase that skilled labor is often in short supply. In any but the worst of times, anyone from high-iron construction workers to computer programmers should find a welcome. If you can make your move before the bottom drops out, so much the better.

BRAZIL

Current Stability Rating: 28
Per Capita Income: $1,523
Population: 143,277,000
Urban Pop.: 72%
Life Expectancy: 60.9 male,
   66 female
Govt.: Federal republic

Projected Stability Rating: 20
Useful Income: 25
Pop. Density: 43 per sq. mi.
Literacy: 76%
Language(s): Portuguese
GNP: $218 billion

Labor Force: 35% farm, 25% industry, 40% services
Major Industries: appliances, automobiles, chemicals, machinery, petroleum products, ships, steel
Comments: Even if you speak Portuguese, moving here is asking for trouble. The income gap between the upper tenth of the population and the bottom tenth is so great that violent civil unrest is all but inevitable.

The largest country in South America returned to democratic government in 1985, after twenty-one years of military dictatorship. Its economy is diverse, well balanced, and growing at a rate of 3.2 percent per year, thanks to a strong work ethic. All this is backed by huge mineral deposits that offer the prospect of a strong foreign trade. With a stable, growing world economy, Brazil could become one of the most prosperous nations in this hemisphere.

So much for the good news. Twenty years of rapid growth in the 1960s, '70s, and early '80s has collapsed into severe recession, leaving behind it inflation that totaled 350 percent in 1987—it briefly touched 800 percent—and may average 400 percent during 1988. The government spends more than it takes in, to the tune of 5.5 percent of the Gross National Product. Brazil's growth years were propelled by easy borrowing overseas and massive spending on public-works projects; all that is left today is a foreign debt of $113 billion, second among the world's debtor nations only to our own. Early in 1987, the government suspended interest payments on $68 billion of its debt to foreign banks and called a halt to all major investments; unlike other Third World debtors, it continues to hold out against repaying its loans. Strong labor unions agitate almost constantly for pay increases to offset the continuous loss of real income to inflation, adding to the country's economic woes.

The one positive aspect of Brazil's economy has been the trade balance, which in 1987 reached nearly $11 billion. Despite the existence of a significant manufacturing sector, minerals and farm products continue to be by far the most important export items. Brazil's major economic partners are the United States and the Common Market nations, which enforce tariffs and other trade restrictions on nearly half of the country's export products.

Brazil has largely pinned its hopes of curing its economic ills on development of the vast Amazon region, which occupies more than half the country. The area already is home to the world's largest iron mine, copper, precious metals, diamonds, and oil and gas deposits. Centerpiece of this development scheme is the city of Manaus, halfway up the Amazon. Aided by tax breaks and shielded from tariffs that virtually ban foreign capital equipment from the rest of the country, Manaus has grown from jungle to nearly 1 million people and 300 manufacturing companies in a decade. The incentives expire in 2007, however, and the consensus outside the government is that the city on the river will be a ghost town soon thereafter. The jungle will regain its hold on the resources it has long owned.

With almost no investment capital available inside the country, Brazil is desperate for money from outside. As in many developing countries, however, the Brazilian government owns two of the largest, most significant industries: oil and steel. In 1987, they lost $4 billion. Outside Manaus and one other development region, Brazil requires that local companies be at least 51 percent native-owned, so foreign investors who might otherwise help the economy are forced to take on Brazilian partners. In addition, the government attempts to protect developing industries against outside competition and influence; often sorely needed foreign investment is restricted. Imports of steel, and even desperately needed computers, are banned. Few outsiders have seen any reason to cope with such problems. With the suspension of interest payments on foreign debt, outside investment has dropped from $2 billion per year to only $300 million.

Despite a racially mixed society, ethnic conflict is at a minimum in Brazil; the real problems are all socioeconomic. There are no unemployment programs. There are no schools for the poor; some 6 million of the country's 28 million school-age children have never attended a class. In short, there are no significant social services beyond the charities run by the Catholic Church. The result is a vast gulf between the rich and the poor. The relatively small urban upper classes live in Western-style comfort, while some 60 percent of the workers earn less than $100 per month. Only a few miles away from the privileged neighborhoods, vast numbers of unemployed barely manage to survive. Some of the largest slums in this hemisphere, inhabited by millions of people, are the shantytowns built in the city dumps of Rio de Janeiro and São Paulo. In this environment, violent crime has prospered in recent years.

In 1984, Forecasting International gave Brazil a stability rating of 28 among the world's nations and predicted that it would rise to the 20th position during the 1990s. Unfortunately, that view assumed that the country's vast natural resources and growing manufacturing sector would be translated into foreign trade, fueled by greater foreign investment in the national economy. Among Brazilians, that hope flourished after the return to democracy in 1985; in the last three years, it has died. According to one poll, two-thirds of the middle class now hopes only to leave Brazil.

The nation seems ripe for large-scale civil unrest, a return to military government, and an economy that will remain dead in the water for many years to come. Look elsewhere for a new home.

CANADA

Current Stability Rating: 9
Per Capita Income: $13,000
Population: 25,625,000
Urban Pop.: 75.9%
Life Expectancy: 69 male,
  76 female
Govt.: Parliamentary democracy
Labor Force: 3% farm, 52% commerce
  & industry, 28% services
Major Industries: automobiles, mining, timber

Projected Stability Rating: 3
Useful Income: 91
Pop. Density: 7 per sq. mi.
Literacy: 99%
Language(s): English, French
GNP: $367 billion

Comments: Almost as good as Australia, and closer to home. If
  you have money, it will work for you in Canada. But it's cold!

Just beyond our northern border lies one of the most desirable destinations for the transplanted American. One writer characterized Canada as a part of the United States where the people are so smart they don't even pay taxes to Washington. It isn't a description that most Canadians would appreciate, and it is not entirely accurate. Still, there is an element of truth in it; the British tradition that dominates most of Canada gives the country a homey feel for visitors from the United States.

Yet there is at least one profound difference between the two countries. Where the United States manages to be relatively homogeneous, despite the varied heritages of its citizens and diverse local economies, Canada suffers intense competition between its provinces. In the lightly populated West lie the great forests and mines that once gave the country nearly all of its export products. On the Atlantic coast, Newfoundland and Prince Edward Island depend largely on fishing and suffer unemployment rates of 20 percent or more. And between them, in Ontario, live the majority of Canadians, with strong, rapidly growing manufacturing and service industries and the political power to dominate the country. As a result, the standard of living in Ontario is considerably better than that of its neighboring provinces; government services are plentiful in Ontario, hard to find in the West and the Atlantic provinces. Though the separatist movement in French-speaking Quebec appears to have withered, there is no clear consensus among the provinces that they have any reason to belong to a single country.

Canada's economy is large and varied, with rich mineral resources;

significant deposits of oil, gas, and coal; highly productive farmlands; and a robust manufacturing sector. High-tech industries have been very successful in the last decade. A large pool of skilled labor—paid at rates 30 percent below those of their U.S. counterparts—makes Canada relatively self-sufficient in the job market. In Ontario and Quebec, manufacturing is growing so rapidly that in recent years it has accounted for about 80 percent of the growth in the country's economy. Yet there are weaknesses as well. Overall unemployment has seldom fallen much below 10 percent in recent years, the government runs at a sizable deficit, inflation tends to remain several points over that in the United States, and the balance of trade has often fallen into the red.

Some 80 percent of Canada's exports are sold to the United States, a trade that is growing rapidly, in part because the Canadian dollar is worth only about 75 percent as much as the U.S. currency. For many years, fear that the United States would completely dominate the Canadian economy led the government to restrict foreign investment. The recent agreement discarding such barriers between the United States and Canada should result in a much quicker growth rate.

Any recession in the United States will sharply reduce Canada's export income, making for hard times. Yet this is less a problem for Canada than for almost any major trading nation. During whatever lean years are to come, Canada should remain relatively comfortable, if only because of its large supply of productive farmland. For potential immigrants from the United States, the simple fact that English is a native language makes Canada an attractive destination. Those with a strong business sense and enough money to invest will find a warm welcome. For others, the best way to move there may be as an employee of a U.S. firm.

EGYPT

Current Stability Rating: 32
Per Capita Income: $686
Population: 50,525,000
Urban Pop.: 48.8%
Life Expectancy: 55.9 male,
  58.4 female
Govt.: Republic

Projected Stability Rating: 21
Useful Income: 10
Pop. Density: 124 per sq. mi.
Literacy: 44%
Languages(s): Arabic
GNP: $33 billion

Labor Force: 50% farm, 28% services
Major Industries: cement, chemicals, petroleum products, textiles
Comments: If you really want to move to the Middle East, this is
  the place. But why would you?

Two thousand years ago, virtually all of Egypt's population lived jammed into the fertile Nile Valley, only 4 percent of the land area that now lies within its borders. That remains true today. Some 96 percent of the country's 50 million people live within ten miles of the great river. Nearly one-fourth of Egypt's population lives in Cairo, a city of 12 million people, with a sewage system designed for 2 million; crowding is so intense that several hundred thousand live among, and even in, the tombs of a huge graveyard known as the City of the Dead. For several years, Egypt's population has been growing at a startling 3 percent per year—roughly 1.5 million more mouths to feed each year.

Their government is rigidly authoritarian. Though there are several small opposition parties, well over half of the National Assembly's 492 seats are filled by members of the National Democratic Party, founded by Anwar Sadat and led by President Hosni Mubarak. Yet a strong, covert element of Moslem extremists makes the nation less stable than it appears.

Egypt's economy remains primitive. Half the nation's people are subsistence farmers, yet 70 percent of the country's food must be imported. Massive subsidies for food, energy, transportation, utilities —virtually all the needs of its citizens—consume one-third of the national budget, leaving too little capital to sustain economic-development projects. In years past, hundreds of thousands fled to find work in the Gulf States; falling oil prices have cut more than $3 billion per year from the money they manage to send home. Exports of cotton, sugar, and oil combine with tourism to bring in about $3 billion per year in foreign exchange, but until recently, when the government imposed import quotas, food and other imports drained nearly twice that. As a result, Egypt is heavily in debt and depends on foreign aid for at least 25 percent of its budget; the United States alone contributes about $2.3 billion per year. Foreign debt now totals $40 billion.

Because its oil reserves are relatively small, Egypt is attempting to build up its natural-resource and manufacturing industries. Iron, manganese, phosphate, salt, and even uranium are mined. Manufactured products include textiles, chemicals, and metallurgical products, and there is a rapidly growing arms trade. Low oil prices have reduced the national income in the last year and will continue to do so, slowing overall economic and social progress in this country.

Egypt is one of the easier nations of the Middle East for Westerners to emigrate to. In an effort to attract development capital, it offers to ease taxes and import duties for foreign companies willing to do business there (though business regulations remain needlessly complex, and the government has found no way to ease the chore of wringing the necessary approvals from its stodgy bureaucracy). In addition, Egypt shares with other Arab nations a need for foreign teachers specializing in scientific and technical disciplines.

Why anyone would wish to emigrate to any of the Middle Eastern countries is another question. Moslem lands have of late proved themselves relatively inhospitable toward Western residents; they could quickly grow even less so if a large-scale recession further reduces their standard of living and encourages extremist ideologies. Though Egypt is probably the most stable nation in the Middle East, a strong fundamentalist movement is working to bring Egypt under traditional Moslem law, such as rules in Iran. And until the other Arab states accept some permanent settlement with Israel, the threat that Egypt will be dragged into another war will never be far away. The added risk of an Iranian victory in the long-running Iran–Iraq war makes the entire region too unstable for one to consider moving there.

WEST GERMANY

Current Stability Rating: 2
Per Capita Income: $9,450
Population: 60,734,000
Life Expectancy: 67.2 male, 73.4
  female
Govt.: Federal republic

Projected Stability Rating: 6
Useful Income: 84
Pop. Density: 635 per sq. mi.
Literacy: 99%
Language(s): German
GNP: $678 billion

Labor Force: 6% farm, 42% commerce & industry, 42% services
Major Industries: automobiles, cement, chemicals, coal, machinery,
  ships, steel
Comments: Wait at least until 1995, when the picture should be
  clearer.

If you look closely enough, staid, stable West Germany turns out to be the wild card of Europe. On the surface, there is no reason to expect any great change from the conservative, prosperous pillar of the Common Market. Yet the 1990s could alter German business and politics to a degree not seen in all the forty-plus years since World War II. What this transformation will mean for Americans seeking relief from depression at home you will have to judge for yourself.

Germany has the largest economy in Europe, and probably still the strongest, but the 1980s have not been kind to it. Exports make up an astonishing 34 percent of the country's Gross National Product, compared with only 16 percent in Japan, and those exports are in trouble. Throughout this period, Germany has lost heavily to competition from Japan in fields where it once was a major force: consumer electronics, optics, automobiles, and computers. Since 1986, the speedy decline of the dollar has meant a growing loss of export sales to the United States. Economic growth has suffered as a result; expansion ran less than 2 percent in 1987 and is expected to improve little in 1988.

So far, this decline has had less impact on Germany than on its Common Market trading partners. Economists estimate that the slow German economy has cost France up to 2 percent per year in lost growth, and Italy is almost equally sensitive to decisions made in Bonn. Both countries have been prodding Germany to stimulate its economy. But German planners remember too well that runaway inflation that nearly destroyed the country after World War I, and the return of 10 percent inflation due to oil price hikes in 1983 has made their fear of a recurrence downright obsessive. The current inflation rate of under 1 percent—prices actually *dropped* in 1985—is all the encouragement they need to keep a tight rein on the money supply. Current plans call for a $10 billion tax cut this year and another $12 billion cut in 1990. There is no sign that any greater stimulus will be forthcoming.

Several other problems also burden the German economy. Thanks to a large, costly welfare system and relatively high defense budget, the government runs at a deficit. Though less than 2 percent of the Gross National Product, it still amounts to $16 billion per year. In an effort to reduce costs and modernize their companies, German employers have been laying off workers throughout the 1980s. Thus, national unemployment has hovered around 9 percent since 1983; in certain regions, it is far worse. And the remaining workers receive an average of more than $18 per hour in wages and fringe benefits, compared with only $13.67 for American workers and just over $12 for Japanese.

As things stand, Germany would suffer as badly as anyone in Europe from a recession that harmed its export market in the United States. But changes are coming.

One, perhaps the less significant, is the opening of Common Market borders to products from other member countries. By 1992, if all goes according to plan, the maze of conflicting product standards that have hindered European commerce will be replaced by a single unified code, so that virtually any product salable in one Common Market country can be sold in them all. As things stand, for example, one television factory is forced to spend an extra $2 million per year on more than a dozen different electric plugs needed to customize its products for European customers. Getting rid of this burden will mean instant savings of billions of dollars for European exporters, and vast new markets in their neighboring countries. German exporters, with a reputation for quality, can expect to clean up.

The second change, which will lead to others, is a pipeline that will bring in natural gas from the Soviet Union. Scheduled to open in 1990, the pipeline is expected to supply up to 70 percent of West Germany's energy needs, freeing the country from the threat of future oil-price shocks. It will also give the Soviet government an unprecedented level of influence in Bonn.

As this occurs, the relationship between the two Germanys is also changing. For thirty years, East and West Germany were almost at war with each other. There were no significant diplomatic ties. There was little or no trade. Travel across the border was alternately restricted and cut off completely. Today things are different. Retired people can visit freely between the Germanys; in 1986, more than 575,000 East Germans below age sixty-five visited the West, three times as many as the year before. Even East German Chairman Erich Honecker has visited West Germany. And trade between the two nations is growing rapidly. Volkswagen now makes auto parts in both East and West Germany, and its cars are sold widely in East Germany. This trend can only continue.

As it does, an old, seldom-mentioned goal will reemerge. For several years now, the two countries have been working toward *"Zusammengehörigkeitsgefühl,"* or togetherness. West German leaders admit, when asked, that they would like to see their country reunited. East German rulers rule that out, but privately the wistful yearning is not forgotten. Already, there is talk of such cooperative projects as an environmental-protection treaty, rejoining the countries' electric-power grids, and building a high-speed train from West Germany to West Berlin. Objections by the Soviet Union to a unified Germany will vanish when it gains control over West Germany's energy supply. So travel between East and West Germany will continue to ease. Trade will grow. Little by little, the ties that join one part of a nation with the rest will be rebuilt. The ugly symbol of the Berlin wall will come down. And one day it will happen. Before the end of the 1990s, there will again be one Germany.

There will be a price, of course: Germany's membership in NATO. It is a price that West Germany will be willing to pay. Bonn will withdraw from the European defense pact, and the new/old nation will come to resemble Finland, a country with a Western economy and government, but taking enormous care to avoid offending the Soviet Union.

More than nationalism is at stake. Reunion will soon give today's East Germans a Western standard of living, while companies in the West will find a vast new domestic market waiting for them. Abandoning its alignment with the United States will turn Germany into a Third World nation—the only one with a truly modern economy and strong political influence in the West. Within a decade, the reunited Germany will be not merely a European leader, but one of the world's richest, most powerful countries.

At this point, there is no way to be sure how long the process of reunion will take. If a deep recession strikes before most of the barriers have come down, West Germany will be so preoccupied with solving its economic problems that other goals will be temporarily forgotten. A return to Cold War could also delay Germany's restoration, particularly if it results from some incident in Europe. But the mid- to late '90s seems a reasonable target date.

Would you wish to live in West Germany during the changes to come? It depends on how quickly recession strikes. If the world economy turns decisively down within the next two or three years, as looks all too possible, a move seems pointless. But if Western leaders manage to muddle through until the mid-1990s, it will be an interesting, prosperous decade in which to be there.

FRANCE

Current Stability Rating: 6
Per Capita Income: $10,260
Population: 55,239,000
Urban Pop.: 77.2%
Life Expectancy: 70.2 male, 78.5 female
Govt.: Republic

Projected Stability Rating: 8
Useful Income: 77
Pop. Density: 263 per sq. mi.
Literacy: 99%
Language(s): French
GNP: $563 billion

Labor Force: 9% farm, 45% commerce & industry, 46% services
Major Industries: aerospace, automobiles, chemicals, electronic equipment, munitions, perfume, ships, steel, telecommunications, textiles, wine
Comments: This may eventually be a good place to live, if you speak French well enough. But they must get their house in order.

More than most other countries, France is in the midst of a crucial transition. If it can make the necessary changes in time, its future will be bright; if they are not completed before the next major recession, the French economy will remain mired for many years to come. At this point, the issue remains in doubt.

In the past decade or so, France has made some of the right moves. To escape dependence on foreign oil, it has built one of the world's largest, most modern nuclear power systems; reactors now supply 40 percent of its national energy needs. To wean the economy away from flagging industries, France has also made a strong commitment to high-tech markets. Its computer and telecommunications industries are now rated behind only those of the United States and Japan. Collaborating with other Common Market countries, it has backed Arianespace, the Free World's only commercial satellite launch service outside NASA, and Airbus Industrie, the most successful new manufacturer of airliners established in decades. And the land of Brie and Dom Perignon has become one of the world's most aggressive and successful munitions dealers, supplying everything from small arms to advanced fighters to any nation with money to spend.

Yet other policies have undermined the benefits of these decisions. Many of the problems that France is now trying to solve grew out of mistakes made in 1981, when the Socialist government of François Mitterrand nationalized more than 50 large manufacturing firms and commercial banks. At the same time, in an effort to create new jobs and hold down inflation, it shaped its policies to stimulate the economy. The result was a sharp drop in productivity on the one hand, and growing demand for imports on the other. But that demand was out of step with economic policies in the other Common Market countries, and French export markets remained flat. By 1982, both inflation and the French trade deficit had begun to soar.

Mitterrand then reversed his economic policies, cutting government spending, raising taxes, and tightening the money supply. The franc was devalued three times in 1983. Inflation dropped below 5 percent by the end of 1985.

From 1986 through early 1988, France was led by the unlikely coalition of Socialist President Mitterrand and Conservative Prime Minister Jacques Chirac. Under this team, many of the restrictive regulations that have plagued French productivity have been repealed; for the first time, businesses have the right to discharge unneeded or incompetent employees who previously would have remained on the payroll. In addition, some $10 billion worth of the companies nationalized in 1981 were sold back to private investors in 1987; another $15 billion worth were scheduled to go on the block by 1988. By luck, France also benefited from the world drop in oil prices, which cut the country's energy-import bill in half.

None of this has had an overwhelming impact on the French economy. Growth in 1988 is still expected to total barely more than 1 percent of the GNP, unemployment is near 11 percent and rising, and the country's trade deficit climbs at a rate of some $5 billion per year. Recession is easy to forecast. Industrial competitiveness has been declining since mid-decade. And whether sales of government-owned companies will continue is now in doubt; unfortunately, privatization quadrupled the number of French shareholders just in time for them to lose half their investment on Black Monday. All this leaves the French bureaucracy, with its roots in the time of Louis XIV, in charge of 48 percent of the national economy.

If the next recession is mild and limited to the United States, or if it is delayed into the mid-1900s, France should be in a relatively good position to endure. The delay should give it enough time to modernize much of its industrial plant and move into more promising markets. Already, more than half its export revenues come from trade with its Common Market partners. This proportion should rise dramatically in 1992, when the EEOC nations are scheduled to abandon the archaic network of standards and regulations that have always inhibited trade between them. And France is one of the leading producers of wheat and dairy products and is virtually self-sufficient in food products. Its farms produce virtually everything needed to survive in comfort.

More likely, the French modernization program will be delayed by the need to find investment capital in a slow economy. Odds are, also, that any recession in the United States will arrive before the Common Market can forge a unified economy, and it will be deep enough to cost the EEOC countries much of their American export market. In that case, layoffs will begin, unemployed workers will cut their spending, demand within the Common Market will fall, and the recessionary spiral will begin.

GREAT BRITAIN

Current Stability Rating: 5
Per Capita Income: $7,216
Population: 56,548,000
Urban Pop.: 92.5%
Life Expectancy: 70.2 male,
   76.2 female

Projected Stability Rating: 4
Useful Income: 68
Pop. Density: 601 per sq. mi.
Literacy: 99%
Language(s): English
GNP: $453 billion

Govt.: Constitutional monarchy
Labor Force: 1.7% farm, 26% manufacturing, 64% services
Major Industries: airplanes, automobiles, banking, chemicals, distilling, electronics, finance, insurance, shipping, steel
Comments: You don't want to depend on the local economy, but if you have money this is one of the best places to go. They even speak a form of English.

According to an old story, no doubt apocryphal, the British government once commissioned an eminent but crotchety academic to figure out how to repair the sagging national economy. He labored mightily for two years, then announced that he had the answer. At the conference where he was to present his solution, he strode to the podium, glowered at the assembled dignitaries, and demanded, "Make the workers do some work!" Then he stalked off the stage.

In reality, Britain's economic problems were more complicated than that, and still are. But as the island nation approached the 1980s, industrial productivity was low, GNP growth even lower, inflation rising, unemployment growing almost as fast as the budget and trade deficits. The decades-old welfare program soaked up nearly 50 percent of the GNP, money sorely needed to spur economic redevelopment. In all, Britain had one of the most sluggish economies in the Western world and showed little sign of recovery.

The turning point came when Prime Minister Margaret Thatcher took office and administered a nearly toxic dose of right-wing capitalism. In 1979, the new Conservative government cut income taxes to a maximum of 60 percent—from a peak of 98 percent!—lowered corporate taxes, offered further tax breaks to promote investment in small business, and tightened the money supply to curb inflation. Government subsidies for uncompetitive industries were cut, and protesting labor unions were fought to a standstill. For the last few years, the British government has been selling its many state-owned industries back to private investors; yet to come as this is written are "privatizations" of British Petroleum, the nation's electric and water utilities, and the government's near–50 percent of British Telecommunications. Most difficult were attempts to cut the giant welfare system.

To a surprising extent, it worked. Unemployment soared through the mid-'80s but, though still high, has dropped back to around 10 percent. The moribund shipping and coal industries have largely been replaced by high technology and finance, which now employs fully 10 percent of the work force. The privatization program and sales of North Sea oil helped bail out the budget, and trade deficits have eased as a decline in the value of the pound makes it easier to export British goods. Productivity grew by 40 percent between 1981 and 1987 (though British workers still produce little more than half what their American cousins do), while corporate profits have climbed by 150 percent. GNP growth has consistently topped that of Britain's European neighbors, while inflation has dropped from more than 20 percent per year in 1980 to less than 4 percent. And the number of British start-up companies receiving venture capital rose from only 500 or so in 1982 to 2,500 in 1987. In that year, the government even found it necessary to raise interest rates in order to slow an economic boom that, it was feared, might soon drive up the country's 4.5 percent inflation.

Keeping that improvement going will not be easy. The October 1987 stock crash pared growth estimates for 1988 to less than 2 percent. Production of North Sea oil is now well past its peak, and sharply lower oil prices have cut into export income. If all goes according to plan, the government will run out of companies to sell early in the next decade, eliminating one more source of nontax income. Attempts at welfare reform largely disappeared under the sheer vastness of the task; government programs still absorb more than 42 percent of the GNP, about $10,000 per year for each household in the country. Continuing to pay for them will mean a return to higher taxes and further slowing of the economy.

And hidden by Britain's remarkable economic comeback are some nagging social problems. The big-government welfare programs that have dominated the country's social policy since World War II are strained almost to the breaking point. The national health service copes with more patients every year despite flat budgets, but there is a growing consensus that the quality of that care is slipping. Graduates of the state school system are little if any better educated than their counterparts in the United States. A massive influx of nonwhite immigrants from former British colonies in the 1970s and '80s gave birth to racial tensions that have yet to be resolved. Worst of all, new jobs in growing industries have gone primarily to new workers; blue-collar workers who lost their jobs when the Thatcher government cut subsidies to dying industries form an underclass of the permanently unemployed throughout Scotland, Wales, and the North of England.

In a stable world economy, all these problems might be manageable. In a worldwide recession, however, Britain's national income will drop sharply, while government expenditures will not. A rapid regrowth of deficit spending and a drop in the standard of living seem all but inevitable. Unemployment jumped as the financial industry, which was facing layoffs already, reacted to the stock crash of Black

Monday; in any significant contraction, more jobs will be lost throughout the economy. When the worst has passed, it will again take Britain a decade of hard work even to begin putting its house back in order.

For American expatriates, the world offers few more comfortable, charming havens than Great Britain. But these days even New Yorkers are startled by the cost of living well in London. Paying your way can only become harder if your life there depends on finding a job in a recession. Either make your move while the world economy is relatively well off, and find a well-paid, bombproof niche for yourself, or don't go.

INDIA

Current Stability Rating: 30
Per Capita Income: $150
Population: 783,940,000
Urban Pop.: 21.5%
Life Expectancy: 52 male,
  50 female
Govt.: Federal republic

Projected Stability Rating: 41
Useful Income: 7
Pop. Density: 612 per sq. mi.
Literacy: 36%
Language(s): Hindi, English
GNP: $190 billion

Labor Force: 70% farm, 19% commerce & industry
Major Industries: appliances, autos, cement, chemicals, fertilizers, processed foods, steel, textiles
Comments: The income difference between the upper tenth of the population and the lower tenth is more than 4,000 percent, one of the highest in the world. Trouble is inevitable. Do not move there!

The world's largest, most populous English-speaking nation is clearly on the way up in some crucial ways. Where the country once survived on American grain, it now is a significant exporter of foodstuffs. Manufacturing hardly existed at the end of World War II; cotton and jute textiles remain the most important products, but government support has built steel, chemical, and other heavy industries. Substantial reserves of coal, iron ore, bauxite, manganese, and even oil remain to be developed. Growth-inhibiting import controls on high-tech equipment and capital goods have been eased and tax rates are down. Perhaps most important, compulsory education has brought basic literacy to roughly half of the country's 800 billion or so people.

Yet most of India's problems remain unsolved. While the economy has grown steadily for many years, its rate is slow; though industry expands at more than 7 percent annually, growth in the economy as a whole is not over 3 percent per year. The population rises by more than 2 percent per year, so per capita income has hardly improved in the last two decades. Perhaps 75 percent of the people still live in the countryside, and nearly all who live outside the major cities exist at subsistence levels. Well over half the population survives by agriculture and faces severe privation whenever the monsoon season fails to bring needed rain. Industries by and large are far less efficient than in more developed nations, so manufactured goods are needlessly expensive. Unemployment is a way of life for many. And foreign aid remains an indispensable part of the economy.

Perhaps worst of all, the potential for ethnic conflict is worse in India than in almost any other country this side of South Africa. The strong, sometimes violent, Sikh separatist movement in Punjab is opposed by an equally violent anti-Sikh faction among the Hindu majority. Conflict between the Hindus and the large Moslem minority, though relatively quiet for several years, remains an ever-present threat. And the peacekeeping force now fighting the Tamil Tigers in Sri Lanka risks eventually provoking a violent protest from the far more numerous Tamils of southern India.

Its problems notwithstanding, India can be an attractive place for would-be traders, particularly those interested in traditional handicrafts. There are whole towns that specialize in working fine leather, dying a particular kind of textile, or making a characteristic style of jewelry. For many years, a few Westerners have made an annual journey to India, buying, for example, fabric in one city, having it stitched into men's shirts or women's skirts in another, and returning home to market the finished clothing in the United States or Europe. How well this trade would survive a depression in the buying countries is open to question.

Relocating to India permanently can be more difficult, particularly if you hope to set up a business of your own. Entrepreneurs there suffer from heavy taxes, frequent political meddling in commercial matters, and an enormous, slow-moving, and corrupt bureaucracy. Frequent power failures plague manufacturers; most hospitals and industrial plants maintain their own generators to protect their power supply. And an outdated, breakdown-prone rail system makes long-distance travel more a matter of luck than a practical business tool.

Should you emigrate to India? More than most countries, India will make it difficult to decide. While consumers in the developed countries of the West retain their buying power, it will be relatively easy to establish a trading business there. And the decaying remnants of the British Empire can still be comfortable places to live for those with a little money and a (questionable) taste for playing pukka sahib. But the Indian economy is nearer to disaster than most. If the world markets slow and the monsoons fail once more, India could yet find itself faced with unemployment and starvation on a scale not seen anywhere else in the world.

ISRAEL

Current Stability Rating: 24
Per Capita Income: $5,609
Population: 4,208,000
Urban Pop.: 86%
Life Expectancy: 72.1 male, 75.1 female (Jewish population only)
Govt.: Parliamentary democracy

Projected Stability Rating: 33
Useful Income: 51
Pop. Density: 548 per sq. mi.
Literacy: 88% Jewish, 48% Arab
Language(s): Hebrew, Arabic
GNP: $21 billion

Labor Force: 6% farm, 23% industry, 30% public services
Major Industries: aircraft, arms, diamond-cutting, electronics, machinery, pharmaceuticals, plastics, textiles
Comments: If Israel manages to trade land for peace with the Palestinians, Jewish Americans may want to consider moving there. Not otherwise. (Take your car and appliances when you move; they are fantastically expensive in Israel.)

When the state of Israel was founded, most of its territory closely resembled the rest of the Middle East; and that in turn resembled an enormous pan of Kitty Litter. In the forty years since then, though surrounded by enemies and almost constantly at war, Israel has become by far the most modern, productive country in the region—and it still threatens to sink back into the sand from which it grew.

Overwhelming security problems are only one threat to Israel's future, and may not be the most important. In effect, the country cannot be defeated by military means; its covert, but widely known, possession of atomic weapons means that any nation which threatened to destroy Israel might well die with it; the 2,000-year-old lesson of Masada, where a handful of Jews stood off an overwhelming enemy army for months and then committed suicide rather than submit, remains ever fresh in Israeli minds.

Economically, Israel's never-ending war is a smaller handicap than it appears. Though defense costs the country about $7 billion per year, or one-fourth of the Gross National Product, American aid pays 75 percent of the bill. With that assistance factored in, defense costs only about 6 percent of Israel's GNP, roughly as much as in the United States or Korea, and only a little above Great Britain.

The real problem has been the Israeli government itself. Some 30 percent of the nation's work force—400,000 people—hold patronage jobs, nearly half again as many people as work in industry. Despite a halfhearted program of "privatization," the government owns more than 200 companies with sales of $7 billion, one-fourth of the country's Gross National Product. Manpower shortages for private-sector jobs are acute and chronic.

Most of the remaining industry in Israel is owned by three major banks and the Labor Federation's holding company. The banks suffer liquidity problems severe enough to threaten their investments. Similar difficulties plague many government-owned companies and the Labor-affiliated farm co-ops.

Taxation hits Israelis harder than almost anyone else in the world. Though the top income-tax rate has been chopped from 60 percent to 45 percent, taxes on goods and services bring the government's cut of the official Gross National Product to well over 50 percent. The result is rampant tax evasion and a vibrant underground economy, which adds an estimated $3 billion per year to the GNP.

Add one more hazard to the list: Israel has virtually no resources of its own. Raw materials are almost all imported, and most of its energy needs are met by oil imported from Egypt and Mexico. Loss of those supplies would mean instant disaster.

With all these problems, Israel has become one of the most heavily polarized of the world's nations. The powerful, militant right wing and war-weary left battle constantly for control of foreign policy; at the moment, the right has the upper hand. And with 90 percent of jobs unionized, labor unrest is an intermittent, but often damaging, feature of Israeli life.

Yet the Israeli economy is improving. Inflation in 1984 was running at 450 percent. Then the government ordered a stringent austerity program: Wages and prices were frozen, the shekel was devalued by 25 percent and exchange rates fixed, and fat government ministries were put on strict budgets. Within a year, inflation dropped to 20 percent. (In part, that can be credited to the drop in oil prices, rather than to government action.) Other changes have cut business subsidies from $1.1 billion per year to $400 million. Aided by grants and tax benefits, corporate start-ups are running at an all-time high, and many American firms have established subsidiaries around Jerusalem and Tel Aviv.

Foreign trade also is picking up; after many years of deficits, Israel saw its first trade surplus in 1984. Trade should expand further as tariffs on goods from the Common Market are abandoned in 1988 and on those from the United States—Israel's largest civilian trading partner—are phased out by 1995.

If Israel can find some way to cope with its remaining troubles, it could become one of the world's most prosperous nations. Agricultural exports, particularly of citrus fruit, bring in substantial trade profits. A high level of education and a commitment to technology— made because of the constant need for sophisticated weaponry—have made Israel's manufacturers world-class competitors in computers, telecommunications, medical diagnostic equipment, avionics, and of course the arms trade. Given such assets, a nation at peace could bring economic stability in short order.

American Jews, like others from the world over, are always welcome in Israel. Whether many would wish to go there during an economic collapse is another question. The current labor shortage makes it relatively easy to resettle there, but that could end quickly; whenever the government decides that a healthy economy is as important as buying loyal voters, its first move must be to fire most of the useless functionaries now on its payroll. And with trade so critical to the nation's progress, any significant reduction in buying by the United States and Common Market countries could cause a sharp contraction at home.

If Israel can solve its Palestinian problem, it could soon become one of the best destinations for (Jewish) Americans fleeing poverty at home. If not, moving there will remain a matter of ethnic loyalty, not economic good sense.

ITALY

Current Stability Rating: 12
Per Capita Income: $6,447
Population: 57,226,000
Urban Pop.: 71%
Life Expectancy: 73 male,
   79.1 female
Govt.: Republic

Projected Stability Rating: 34
Useful Income: 57
Pop. Density: 492 per sq. mi.
Literacy: 97%
Language(s): Italian
GNP: $368 billion

Labor Force: 10% farm, 30% commerce & industry, 60% services
   & govt.
Major Industries: automobiles, chemicals, machine tools, shoes,
   steel, textiles, wine
Comments: If you are retiring with cash, a pension, and relatives
   in Italy, this could be a pleasant place to live. Otherwise, go to
   Australia or Canada.

Once the center of Western civilization, Italy still seems in some ways a favored place. The sun and sea that attracted British expatriates in the early 1800s still remain; the cities where Percy and Mary Shelley lived and John Keats died are just as beautiful. More important, many small, entrepreneurial companies regularly create new jobs and generate modest economic growth each year, and a host of American companies have branches there where you might find a job to ease your move. If you are thinking casually about leaving the United States, Italy could top your list of places to go. The moment you grow serious enough to look at the details, however, the decision becomes harder.

It's always been as easy to make jokes about the Italian economy as it is about the Italian army. Outside observers have wondered for years how Italy avoids complete collapse; it probably mystifies even Italian economists. In the next decade, that mystery will almost surely come to an end as Italy's standard of living declines rapidly below those of Nigeria and Zimbabwe, roughly to the level of Iran.

If a country were run by the U.S. Postal Service, Italy is what you'd get:

• The country imports 70 percent of its energy and most of its raw materials. Plans to develop nuclear energy and other alternative sources have never been put into practice. Offshore oil deposits discovered in the early '80s have yet to be tapped in any quantity, in part because the money to develop them is not available and in part because lower oil prices have temporarily eased the problem. In any case, there is not enough oil there to keep Italy alive for long.

• Because of these imports, trade deficits usually approach $5 billion per year, despite Italy's well-known exports of high-quality clothing, textiles, jewelry, leather goods, and of course, wine. And though Italy is home to hundreds of small exporters, the real profits are funneled into a very narrow segment of the economy; more than 80 percent of Italy's exports are sold by just ten large companies.

• Inflation tends to fluctuate wildly, soaring out of control and then crashing as the Bank of Italy panics, restricts credit, and devalues the lira yet again. (In the latest cycle, inflation fell from 21 percent in 1980 to about 4 percent in 1986; it is now headed up again.) When the lira is high, other countries cut back their imports, and Italian trading profits drop sharply. Then, when the lira is devalued, energy imports become more expensive and the trade deficit worsens. Until recently, under an indexing scheme called the *scala mobile,* wages promptly went up by an amount equal to half the inflation rate, further aggravating the situation.

• Labor costs are enormous, but industrial productivity is among the lowest in the developed nations. Unemployment has risen to nearly 12 percent nationwide, but for some regions and groups it is far worse; more than twice as many are jobless in southern Italy as in the north, and one in three Italians under age twenty-five is out of work. Labor unrest, once under control, is growing strong again. Nearly 20 percent of the workers receive either private or public pensions. All this further raises the cost of Italian exports.

• No discussion of Italy would be complete without mention of the black market, estimated at 15 percent of the official GNP. Taxation is so heavy that tax evasion is to Italy what baseball is to the United States.

• Worst of all, government spending is so far out of control that not even the the most blatant wastrels in Washington can dream of matching it. Pensions for government employees are among the world's most generous. Such huge industries as energy, shipbuilding, and the telephone system are state-owned, mismanaged, and almost always in the red. In an average year, fully 60 percent of the Gross National Product goes to feed government programs, leaving an annual budget deficit equal to about 15 percent of the GNP. By the end of 1986, the national debt had reached some 793 trillion lire, or $612 billion. (By contrast, the U.S. national debt, widely regarded as far beyond tolerable levels, still totals less than 30 percent of the GNP.)

A strong, competent government with the support of its citizens could eventually solve Italy's problems, bad as they are. Whipping the state-owned industries into line, or turning them back to the private sector, would cut the budget deficit. Adopting nuclear energy after so many years of procrastination would cut the trade deficit. The remains of the *scala mobile* must go. That is just a start, but there is nothing inherently impossible about the list.

Yet a strong, competent, well-supported government is exactly what the country lacks. Most of Italy's administrations have been fragile center-leftist coalitions that survive only as long as they buy votes with government handouts. As this is written, the latest, led by Prime Minister Giovanni Goria, is falling after less than a year in office. But then, similar things could have been said at almost any time in the last forty years. Since the end of World War II, Italian governments have survived, on average, for barely a year. Under these conditions, there seems no chance that Italy will be able to cure its ills.

There is one circumstance in which you might consider moving to Italy: if you are ready to retire and have a guaranteed income large enough to support you in comfort, no matter what happens to the country around you. Otherwise, steer clear.

JAPAN

Current Stability Rating: 3
Per Capita Income: $10,266
Population: 121,402,000
Urban Pop.: 76.2%
Life Expectancy: 74.5 male,
  80.2 female
Govt.: Parliamentary democracy

Projected Stability Rating: 30
Useful Income: 77
Pop. Density: 833 per sq. mi.
Literacy: 99%
Language(s): Japanese
GNP: $1.3 trillion

Labor Force: 9% farming, 34% manufacturing, 48% services
Major Industries: automobiles, chemicals, electrical and electronic equipment, machinery, steel—and almost everything else!
Comments: Even if you could afford to live in Japan, there is no good reason to move there.

Among Washington politicians these days, Japan bashing is a sport that trails in popularity behind only baseball and lying about why voters should return them to office. And no wonder. When it comes to promoting national prosperity, Japan's leaders have been making them look sick for years. But soon Republicans and Democrats alike will have to seek a new scapegoat, for Japan's long climb from post-war devastation to economic triumph is nearing its end.

Japan has a long way to fall. With virtually no natural resources, Japan has climbed in forty years from a Gross National Product that was barely worth measuring to more than $1.3 trillion. Of that, nearly one-seventh—$174 billion—is exported to other countries, more than one-third of it to the United States. (The U.S. trade deficit with Japan totaled more than $58 billion in 1987; by 1992, our total debt to Japan is expected to reach $1 trillion.) Japanese workers, once as poor as any in the world, now receive, on average, $17,000 per year, nearly as much as American workers; in Tokyo, the average household income totals $42,500 per year.

The sources of this prosperity are easy to find. Japanese workers are among the best-educated, hardest-working, thriftiest people in the world. The school year is 240 days, compared with an average of 180 in the United States, and students supplement long hours of homework with longer hours in private academic coaching clinics. When Japanese manufacturers adopt statistical quality-control methods in their factories at home, high school graduates handle the complex mathematical procedures; in their U.S. factories, they are forced to hire people with master's and doctoral degrees. Once on the job, the Japanese work about 2,200 hours per year; in the United States, the work year is only 1,800 hours. And when they get their paychecks, Japanese workers bank nearly 14 percent of their money—down from nearly one-fourth a few years ago! Americans save barely 3 percent. Bank depositors receive less than 2 percent interest, and their money is used to fund corporations, which pay the banks less than 5 percent for it. This gives Japan a powerful advantage in world markets, even without the maze of product regulations that greet foreign companies seeking Japanese profits.

Yet Japan's biggest asset may be its social structure, which has fostered modern prosperity while changing its ancient character hardly at all. In the 13th century, Japan was a feudal society, divided into fiefdoms that made war on each other. In the 20th, it is still a feudal society, divided into corporate fiefdoms that make economic war on the rest of the world. Just 13 huge trading conglomerates dominate all of Japanese manufacturing—Mitsubishi, Fuji, Mitsui, Sumitomi, and the rest. With the exceptions of Honda and Sony, the only postwar independents comparable to the old-line trading firms, or *zaibatsu*, virtually all other manufacturing companies are second- and third-tier firms that live by supplying parts to the giants. These conglomerates have their own banks, their own vassal companies, their own government sponsors. When a vassal company needs money to promote its business—on average, Japanese companies borrow nearly 80 percent of their net worth; in small concerns, the proportion is often larger—the *zaibatsu* arranges the matter with its parent bank. When the giant itself needs a favor, its friends in government are always ready to help.

This multi-tier structure carries over into the employee's life. Pay scales among the multinational giants equal those of American companies. A young man joining NEC or Nissan can still hope for lifetime employment, followed by comfortable retirement. But such benefits are strictly for the elite. Workers in the second and third tier make far less than in the leading firms. At the bottom end of the scale, manufacturing employees may earn one-third as much as their counterparts at Honda or Mitsubishi. And at small companies, job security and pension plans are unknown. Thanks to its small firms, Japan has led the world in corporate bankruptcies for thirty years. Japanese workers are world-champion savers in large part because they have no choice. Even with unemployment compensation, job loss is a devastating and inescapable threat. This enormous source of cheap, hardworking, throwaway labor accounts for much of Japan's success.

Yet behind all the hard work and exploitation, the Japanese really aren't in business for the money. And the workers are not really being exploited. We Westerners define success as a matter of raising our personal standard of living; they do not. In the tight-knit, still semi-feudal society of Japan, success means building a productive, secure place in the social structure for all its members. That is the purpose of the trade restrictions which infuriate American politicians.

This ultimate full-employment policy will be difficult to change, no matter how badly American companies want to open Japanese markets, because it has the unquestioning support of the Japanese people, from the top of society to the bottom. Rice farmers, for example, receive a government subsidy of $1,200 per ton so that they can continue working tiny plots of land, even within metropolitan Tokyo, where property values are three times those in midtown Manhattan. This subsidized inefficiency makes the price of rice in Japan six to ten times that in other countries. Yet when the Japanese government proposed cutting the subsidy recently, the leading coalition of consumer groups took to the streets, demanding that rice farmers never be exposed to free-market competition.

In the long run—within the next decade—not even this self-sacrificing unanimity of purpose will protect Japan from collapse. The causes of economic decline are already visible.

For one thing, Japan is now losing its markets. In part, the falling value of the dollar is to blame. In less than two years, Japan's currency has become twice as expensive as when the dollar was strongest. Export sales have fallen sharply as a result, and profit margins have shrunk even more. At the same time, Japan has lost sales to cheaper competitors as Korea, Taiwan, and other developing nations have entered the world economy. This trend is hitting hardest at the heavy industries Japan once called its own. Under severe competition from South Korea and Brazil, steel exports fell by more than 9 percent in 1986 and have continued to slide. Shipyards that once drove Britain and the United States out of shipbuilding have virtually closed down. Even the coal-mining industry, Japan's only substantial native energy source, survived only because of government price supports, which have been cut drastically in the last two years. Between 1980 and 1985, Japan's economy grew at an average rate of more than 4 percent per year; since 1986, it has not reached 3 percent.

All this has meant growing unemployment. In 1987, steelmakers announced plans to lay off 42,000 workers. Shipyards will cut another 20,000. Even the auto industry has begun to lay off manufacturing personnel. So far, Japanese employers have managed to compensate for all but 20,000 of these losses. The booming service sector has hired many of those displaced from manufacturing and heavy industries. Some old-line companies have moved into new, less vulnerable businesses to give their unneeded employees somewhere to go; Japan National Railways has built chains of bookstores, hotels, and fast-food restaurants staffed by former track workers. Yet according to one government estimate, there are 1.6 million unemployed in Japan, and 900,000 more will join them by 1991. In just five years, unemployment will have jumped from little over 1 percent to more than 4 percent. These statistics are worse than they appear. In Japan, someone who works an hour a day is considered employed. And women are not counted at all. By American standards, Japan's condition today counts as full employment; in Japan, it represents a breakdown of the social system.

Japan has fought back in several ways. In an effort to spread existing work among more workers, the government recently ordered the workweek cut from 44 hours to 40; employers have largely ignored the measure. Attempts to stimulate domestic demand have met with considerably more short-term success. Late in 1987, the government passed a retroactive tax cut that put more than $8 billion back into consumers' pockets and announced a $40 billion public-works program. Tax breaks for savings were reduced, and new deductions offered for mortgage loans. Consumer spending soared, and housing starts rose by 30 percent. Yet this was just a brief respite in what will soon become a plunge into permanent recession.

Like the American population, Japan's is growing older. Today, 70 percent of Japanese are in their working years. That will soon fall to 60 percent. The retirement age in Japan was 55 for many years; to ease the strain on pension systems, that has been raised to age 60. Yet by the year 1990, more than one-fifth of the Japanese people working in 1985 will have retired at 80 percent of their salaries. The pace will not slow in the decade that follows, and Japan's social-security fund is already in the red.

Thus for the rest of this century, Japan will have more and more retired people, living ever longer, supported by fewer and fewer workers. Automation could help compensate for the loss of work force, but the stronger yen and growing competition from abroad will continue to eat away at the nation's earnings. Unemployment will climb higher with each passing year, leaving still fewer working people to support the rest.

This leaves Japan with two ugly alternatives: Either they can continue as they are, and watch their standard of living plummet. Or they can reduce the subsidies and trade barriers that now keep prices high, use the savings to support their retired and unemployed, and accept the social chaos that will result; the standard of living will drop nonetheless.

Either way, Japan loses. In 1984, Forecasting International gave

Japan a stability rating of 3. In all the world, only the United States and West Germany enjoyed more peace and prosperity. By the year 2000, Japan will have fallen into 30th place, below such garden spots as Zimbabwe and El Salvador.

By now, you have the idea. Even if Westerners could easily fit themselves into comfortable roles within Japanese society, Japan will soon be a place to flee, not to seek. Even a slight recession can only make the fall quicker and more harrowing.

MEXICO

Current Stability Rating: 18
Per Capita Income: $2,082
Population: 81,709,000
Urban Pop.: 70%
Govt.: Federal republic

Projected Stability Rating: 27
Useful Income: 29
Pop. Density: 106 per sq. mi.
Literacy: 74%
Language(s): Spanish
GNP: $158 billion

Labor Force: 41% farming, 18% manufacturing
Major Industries: chemicals, electrical equipment, handicrafts, light manufacturing, oil, rubber, textiles, steel
Comments:The gap between rich and poor is much too great to allow stability. It's a nice place to visit, but . . .

Little more than a decade ago, the heads of Mexican leaders danced with visions of a future as the Saudi Arabia of the Western Hemisphere, awash with oil money that would bring a rich new life to their people. And rather than wait, they ran up a $103 billion debt, most of it owed to American banks. Some of that went to finance long-term investments, but much was squandered on short-term price subsidies. Then the price of oil dropped from $39 per barrel to $12, and Mexican oil exports reached a plateau. As a result, the economy, though not quite in a recession, is growing at only 1 percent per year. Mexico still earns much of its foreign exchange through oil sales, but rapidly growing exports of cars and car parts, cement, and even beer brought in $9.7 billion in 1987. Exports gave Mexico more than $14 billion in foreign-currency reserves that year.

Yet it is not nearly enough. Interest on foreign loans is costing the country about $10 billion per year, more than 45 percent of the Federal budget goes to pay off domestic debt, and the government still operates at a deficit equal to more than 18 percent of the GNP.

Inflation ran around 150 percent in 1987 and is expected to hit 200 percent in '88. Inevitably, the already low standard of living is dropping rapidly; the minimum wage now equals about $3 per day.

A high national birthrate makes these problems even harder to solve. The Mexican population is about 80 million and growing by more than 2 million per year; 42 percent of the population is under age fifteen. The country's agricultural output does not grow quickly enough to feed the extra mouths it acquires each year. Another 1 million young men and women need jobs each year, and do not find them. Already, some 40 percent of the work force is unemployed.

Mexico does have potential revenue sources other than oil. There are deposits of nickel, silver, zinc, and lead to exploit; a petrochemical industry could be developed; the government would like to expand the local auto industry; and high-tech companies north of the border have recently noticed that Mexican assembly workers are cheaper to hire than Americans and a lot closer than those in the Far East. But the money to develop these assets must come from outside the country, and foreign financiers have been less than eager to put their cash into such questionable investments. And roughly 90 percent of Mexico's non-oil exports go to the United States; any recession in the U.S. would hit that trade hard.

So far, Mexico has remained politically stable. In the latest austerity plan designed to curb inflation and help pay off foreign debt, announced in December 1987, business, labor, and farm leaders all signed on for budget cuts, pay raises well below losses to inflation, and price hikes that nearly doubled the cost of most government goods and services. How long this cooperation will last in the face of continuing economic problems is anyone's guess.

Mexico still has some compelling advantages for Americans. Prices are low, the climate is good, there are small colonies of American expatriates to provide company, and it's close enough to home to make return visits cheap and easy. But *mañana* won't be good enough for the Mexicans. Move there, and it won't be good enough for you.

PHILIPPINES

Current Stability Rating: 36
Per Capita Income: $598
Population: 58,091,000
Urban Pop.: 36%
Life Expectancy: 61.6 male,
  65.2 female
Govt.: Republic

Projected Stability Rating: 29
Useful Income: 11
Pop. Density: 483 per sq. mi.
Literacy: 88%
Language(s): Filipino, English
GNP: $32.6 billion

Labor Force: 52% farm, 16% commerce & industry, 13% services
Major Industries: appliances, clothing, pharmaceuticals, processed
  foods, textiles, wood products
Comments: The Philippines could be a good place to live once its
  social problems are corrected—say, by the year 2000. For the
  next ten years, steer clear.

By this time, the social and economic problems in this island chain
are so well known that they need hardly be repeated. But to summa-
rize the situation:

Though the Philippine GNP grew creditably in the 1960s and '70s,
the last years of the Marcos regime undermined much of the progress
that had gone before. Both inflation rates and foreign debt are high,
and the standard of living has been dropping for nearly a decade. Six
families out of ten have yearly incomes below the official poverty line
of $1,320 per year for a family of six. Unemployment is probably in
the range of 25 percent, but no accurate figures are available for
agricultural workers, who make up about half of the labor force. With
the notable exception of primary schooling—literacy rates approach
100 percent—delivery of medical care and other welfare services is
poor to nonexistent in most of the country. This poor economic and
social climate has turned the Philippines into fertile ground for the
New People's Army, the local communist insurgency. The refusal of
wealthy landowners to turn even a portion of their property over to
the peasants who work it is winning the NPA further support. Forced
to cope with guerrilla warfare from the left and attempted coups from
the right, the Aquino government has had little chance to cope with
the needs of the people who put it into power, and any remaining
hope that President Aquino will greatly improve the lives of her citizens is rapidly fading. At this point, the country is largely dependent
on foreign aid, primarily from the United States.

For all its problems, the Philippine economy is growing at a respectable rate of 4 percent to 5 percent per year—not bad, given that it actually shrank in 1985. But even respectable growth is not good enough. Philippine economists say that the GNP must grow by at least 6.5 percent per year through 1991, just to restore the nation's standard of living to the level of 1980. To achieve that, $3 billion in private investment will be needed by 1993, at least one-third of it from outside the country. Foreign investors will have to contend with widespread labor unrest, separate wars with an estimated 26,000 communist rebels and 20,000 Moslem separatists, and one of the highest rates of violent crime in the world. It isn't an attractive prospect.

Foreign trade offers little hope of soon paying off overseas debts or adding much to the nation's standard of living. By far the most important Philippine exports are sugar and coconut, and this narrow economy leaves the country vulnerable to any drop in world commodity prices. Manufacturing of textiles, clothing, and even computer chips is growing, but has yet to bring much in the way of export revenue. Though the Philippines have significant deposits of copper, iron, gold, nickel, bauxite, and a variety of other minerals, mining remains largely undeveloped.

In a time of worldwide economic retreat, this gloomy picture is likely to grow far worse. Virtually all of the Philippines' export markets would contract sharply, leaving the country with little foreign income. Imports, made up largely of oil and other energy resources, could not be reduced enough to make up for the loss, and the nation's overseas debt would grow rapidly. The last worldwide recession, in the early 1980s, hit the Philippine economy a lot harder than those of most other nations; much more damage can be expected this time around.

There are too many unanswered questions for anyone to offer more than a good guess about the Philippine future. Will the land reform eventually come to pass? Will the army be able to control the communist insurgents? Or will it someday overthrow the Aquino government instead? Yet if all these uncertainties were settled tomorrow in favor of peace and prosperity, the country's economic problems would still require many years to solve. A depression in the 1990s would arrive long before the Philippines could prepare to weather it.

The average American retiree moving to the Philippines would find himself rich by the standards of most natives. But in a severe economic downturn, only the wealthiest could hope for comfort amid the deepening poverty of the country at large. The added risk of communist-inspired anti-American violence in a time of hardship seems one hazard there is no need to accept. This is one more place not to go.

SOUTH KOREA

Current Stability Rating: 13
Per Capita Income: $3,000
Population: 43,284,000
Urban Pop.: 65%
Life Expectancy: 64.9 male, 76.3 female

Projected Stability Rating: 19
Useful Income: 23
Pop. Density: 1094 per sq. mi.
Literacy: 92%
Language(s): Korean
GNP: $90.6 billion

Govt.: Republic
Labor Force: 30% farm, 22% mining & manufacturing, 47% services
Major Industries: clothing, electronics, light manufacturing, motor vehicles, ships, steel, textiles
Comments: A better choice than Japan for those who feel some irresistible compulsion to live in the mysterious East, but the standard of living remains relatively low and social stability is even lower.

Compress most of the economic changes America has gone through in the 20th century into two brief decades, and you would have a fair approximation of what Korea has managed to accomplish in the 1970s and '80s. When that period began, fully one-third of the country's 32 million people were subsistence farmers; textiles, clothing, and other light manufacturing were the only industries with significant foreign markets. Per capita income in 1967 was only $160 per year.

Yet by the mid-1980s, nearly 60 percent of the country's 37.5 million people lived in cities. Steel, shipbuilding, chemical, and overseas construction industries were booming, and per capita income had risen to $1,900 per year.

Today strong computer, consumer-electronics, and other high-tech industries are beginning to replace heavy manufacturing; the Korean Hyundai has been the most successful new car introduced into the United States in decades; and per capita income may have reached $3,000. In 1986 alone, exports rose by more than 28 percent, driving the Gross National Product up by 12.5 percent. In 1987, its balance-of-trade surplus doubled to $6.6 billion. Only slightly larger than Indiana, with a total economy only 6 percent as large as that of Japan, South Korea ranks 17th in GNP and is number 12 on the list of the world's largest trading nations.

What makes this even more remarkable is that Korea has virtually no raw materials of its own and no native energy resources. All the steel in its cars, the feedstocks for its plastics and chemicals, and the oil to power the factories that process them must be imported. Yet during the years of high-priced oil, the Korean economy marked up steady growth of 10 percent per year. Even the small recession during the early 1980s, which should have stifled its export market, barely slowed its progress.

Korea has been able to accomplish all this in part because it has learned from Japan. The government carefully targets growing industries in which its country's manufacturers can score huge profits. Then it offers tax incentives and favorable credit policies to help those sectors grow. The cash to support that policy came from abroad; South Korea's foreign debt totals $45 billion. Like Japan, Korea vigorously defends its favored industries against outside competition. The United States, too, has helped by reducing or waiving tariffs on goods from South Korea and some other countries with developing economies.

The real key to Korea's success, however, is its work force. Korea's workweek is about 55 hours, the longest in the world. (When visiting Korea, Marvin Cetron asked one worker about holidays. "We have fifty-four holidays a year," came the reply: "Christmas, Easter, and fifty-two Sundays.") Pay scales may average $3,000 per year, but many earn far less. Sweatshop workers are lucky to bring in $150 for a month of 10-hour days, including overtime and bonuses; it adds up to 62 cents an hour.

Korean business has not had things all its way, however. Something like 40 percent of the parts in Korean products are made in Japan; so are the machines that Korean factories use to assemble them. Thus, Korea runs a large, chronic trade deficit with Japan. Much of the export income that Korean workers would like to share flows quickly across the Sea of Japan.

There are signs that Korea's productive business environment will not last. Even before political riots filled the streets of Seoul in mid-

1987, the country experienced its first labor riots. Nearly three out of four Korean workers are under thirty and unwilling to live in the poverty their parents knew. According to Korea's Trade Ministry, strikes and other labor stoppages cost the country more than $1 billion in lost production and exports between July and mid-September alone. According to economists, a new minimum-wage law that took effect in January 1988 will almost surely drive Korea's clothing, textile, and other light manufacturing industries to Thailand, the Philippines, and other countries where wages are even lower.

South Korea's political stability remains open to question. General Roh has made at least a start at a reconciliation with his former competitors, and three factors should improve his chances of success: His victory last year over Kim Young Sam, his closest rival, amounted to 2 million votes out of 23 million cast—large enough to convince even his enemies that the voters had put him fairly in office, even if a little fraud tainted the ballot count. Kim Dae Jung, formerly the country's most powerful dissident and still the most hostile to Roh, reportedly is not well enough to consider running for office again. And there is a strong consensus that nothing should be allowed to mar the upcoming Olympic festivities. Whether Roh can translate those short-term advantages into lasting peace has yet to be seen.

The question may be less significant here than in most countries. South Korea's dramatic economic progress has been made during a decade of sporadic rioting against a repressive government. However, worldwide recession could do what politics has not. South Korea's economic miracle is based entirely on the country's export trade; 40 percent of its products go to the United States. If other countries suffer a major decline, South Korea will follow quickly.

Even more important, there are few "ecological niches" open to Westerners in Korea. A small country can use only so many English teachers. As in Japan, personal relationships are important in Korea; this is one country where it can really help to arrive as a representative of a major company and make local contacts while securely employed. Emigrés with strong experience in the import and export markets could conceivably set up their own trading businesses—which would then face the same decline in a recession as native-owned companies. But for the rest of us, Korea has little to offer.

SWEDEN

Current Stability Rating: 7
Per Capita Income: $11,989
Population: 8,357,000
Urban Pop.: 85%
Life Expectancy: 73.1 male, 79.1 female

Projected Stability Rating: 5
Useful Income: 80
Pop. Density: 52 per sq. mi.
Literacy: 99%
Language(s): Swedish, Finnish
GNP: $100 billion

Govt.: Constitutional monarchy
Labor Force: 5% farm, 30% industry, 21% commerce & finance, 44% services
Major Industries: automobiles, instruments, machinery, paper, shipbuilding, shipping, steel
Comments: A prime destination that almost guarantees a comfortable life for all who move there, but the cradle-to-grave socialism is likely to grate on the nerves of rugged individualists.

Sweden is a small, cold land of firsts and superlatives. It is the oldest democracy on the European continent; its Riksdag, or parliament, was founded in 1435. With a policy of armed neutrality, it is among the most peaceful nations; the last war it joined in was fought by Napoleon. The cradle-to-grave social-welfare system adopted by the Scandinavian countries after World War II has given it what may be the highest standard of living in the world. And thanks also to welfare, it has the highest taxes in the world, up to 80 percent of income.

Sweden's economy was stagnant through most of the 1970s and early '80s. Since then a devaluation of the krona and lower oil prices have given it a more favorable balance of trade. With a growth rate hovering under 2 percent and admitted unemployment of about 2.5 percent, Sweden has managed to pare its long-standing budget deficit from 13 percent of the Gross National Product to about 9 percent.

The real key to the Swedish economy, however, is that welfare system. A typical and much-beloved program is the *barnbidrag,* under which even the wealthiest parents receive a government subsidy for each child in their home. Other programs subsidize housing for low-income families and provide free medical care, including the cost of transportation from the thinly populated north country to urban hospitals. Committed to the idea of receiving government services, if not paying for them, voters favor both lower taxes and higher spending. They also evade their taxes with typically Italian *brio.*

Sweden's determination to care for its citizens extends to subsidies for such uncompetitive heavy industries as shipbuilding and steel production and to a unique full-employment policy: During a recession, the government buys and stockpiles its manufacturers' products, much as the U.S. government buys grain from farmers. When the economy improves, it sells the merchandise on the export market —if it can. In recent years, the rapid advance of technology has sometimes made stockpiled products obsolete before they could be marketed, at a staggering cost. Growing competition from other exporters, particularly in the Far East, will force the country to reconsider whether it can afford such largess in the 1990s.

New, high-tech businesses may ease this problem. Sweden is a European leader in computers, software, and computer services and in biotechnology. As these industries grow, they should bring in much-needed export profits. Again, however, they will face severe competition from other countries.

Before the turn of the century, it seems inevitable that Sweden and its Scandinavian neighbors will have to cut back their enormous welfare systems. The national standard of living is not likely to fall dramatically, though any reduction will come as a shock to Swedes accustomed to lavish government care.

Any recession will make the transition far worse, however. With a population of only 8 million, Sweden cannot sustain a modern, prosperous economy on its own; export profits are essential. If the United States and the country's other trading partners go into a tailspin, they will not be available.

TAIWAN

Population: 19,601,000
Per Capita Income: $3,000
Life Expectancy: 70.5 male, 75.5 female
Govt.: One-party system
Pop. Density: 1,396 per sq. mi.
Literacy: 91%
Useful Income: 29
Language(s): Mandarin Chinese
GNP: $56.6 billion
Labor Force: 20% farm, 41% commerce & industry, 32% services
Major Industries: chemicals, clothing, electronics, plastics, processed food, textiles
Comments: There is no place for Westerners here.

From a distance, Taiwan resembles a miniature South Korea, growing at better than 10 percent per year, thanks to exports that expand three times faster. Close up, there are significant differences. With a population of less than 20 million, Taiwan has managed to finance virtually all of its growth internally; it has never incurred a significant foreign debt. Unlike Korea's, its growth is not funneled through a handful of giant conglomerates built on capital-intensive heavy industry; three-fourths of its exports are produced by 38,000 modest, single-business companies, often privately owned, in fields where start-up costs are low. And Taiwanese workers live better than their Korean counterparts; in mid-1987, the average Taiwanese wage earner brought in an average of $325 per month, compared with $296 in Korea.

Though a military takeover of Taiwan by mainland China seems a remote possibility at worst, the animosities of forty years ago have not been forgotten. Defense spending drains 9 percent of the country's GNP, more than in any of the developed Free World nations save Israel, South Africa, and, inexplicably, France. Unlike most countries, however, Taiwan can afford the price.

How long Taiwan's prosperity can continue to grow at its current rate is uncertain, for several reasons: Its enviable inflation rate of less than 1 percent in 1986 could soon rise sharply, thanks to a balance-of-trade surplus of more than $15 billion per year (nearly all with the United States) and foreign reserves totaling $62 billion—literally more than they know what to do with. The Taiwan dollar has risen more than 40 percent on world exchange markets in three years, lifting the price of the country's exports. In the last year, the United States has threatened to rescind the liberal trade policies that have promoted development in Taiwan, Korea, and other small, fast-growing nations; the change could mean a slowdown in exports. And in mid-1987, when martial law finally ended after thirty-eight years, Taiwanese workers won the right to strike, always a profit-sapping exercise.

Taiwan seems a poor haven for Westerners in times of economic decline. The national economy is so heavily dependent on exports, half of which come to the United States, that any major slowdown here would cause chaos there.

WALL STREET WEAK—AND
STRONG

IF YOU ARE like too many wage earners, you have probably been relying on others to give you the comfortable retirement you want. Social Security is a lot stronger than the scaremongers would have you believe, right? The politicians would never let it go under. And your company's pension plan should take care of everything else you need.

Well, maybe. But Social Security really won't give you enough to retire on comfortably. Just ask anyone who has tried to live on it. And your pension is a promise that may never be delivered. Most pension plays are well funded, but some—yours?—could be on shaky ground. How much will be left if the stock holdings it's based on go through the floor in a market crash? How many companies will disappear in the next recession, taking their workers' jobs and pensions with them? And how many people do you know who lost their jobs the week before they qualified for retirement?

If you want a secure future, it's up to you; that is what this whole book is about. And the way to make your retirement years secure is to build for them now. Investing is the only way to make the money you earn today support you after your earning days are over. If you have not been investing at least a small part of your income, it's time to give it some serious thought.

Step one is figuring out where to get the money to invest. The average family today saves less than 5 percent of its income. You will have to do better than that. In fact, unless you have enough of a nest egg to keep you going through a major illness or several months of unemployment, you will have to do better even if you decide not to go for stocks, bonds, or whatever. We'll look at this more deeply in a later chapter. For now, just get a small notebook, and keep track of your expenditures for the next few months. You may be surprised at how many of them can be reduced or eliminated. The money you save could keep you comfortable when others are wondering where to find their next meals.

Entering today's financial markets, you will find a bewildering array of investment possibilities. Should you put your money in stocks? Bonds? Commodities futures? Gold? Land? (You know, they're not making it anymore.) Pick well, and your future is secure. Make a mistake, and you could wind up lunching on Kal Kan. We will try to steer you straight. The rest of this chapter is a guide to the investments you are most likely to hear touted as life preservers when the economic waters get rough.

No matter which you choose, we have three pieces of advice:

• Keep it simple. Exotic vehicles like foreign-denominated bonds, naked stock options, and arbitrage are for professionals with nothing to do but manage money. If you know enough to profit from them, you don't need our advice.

Oddly enough, when the Tax Reform Act of 1986 stripped away most of the tax breaks that investors once used to shelter their profits, it made your decisions a good deal easier. Those complex schemes made some investments more appealing than their underlying value could justify, and there was no way to be certain you had used your money wisely until Internal Revenue had finished auditing your tax return. The game today is simply to find good investments. For your purposes, that means investments that will give you an adequate profit with minimal risk. It is a game that even beginners can win.

• Diversify. Cervantes gave some of the best investment advice when, in Don Quixote, he warned against putting all your eggs in one basket. Don't put all your capital into the stock market or into bonds or land. And don't put all the money that goes into stocks into a single company, no matter how good you think its prospects. The key to surviving a crash is to spread your money around, so that if one investment goes under it won't take your future down with it. To prepare for unexpected opportunities—or total disaster—keep some of your capital in cash or cash-equivalents such as Treasury bills, government bonds, certificates of deposit, or money-market mutual funds.

• Take responsibility for your own portfolio. This does not mean picking every investment yourself; for many people, mutual funds managed by skilled professionals can be one of the best routes into the stock market. Others would be better off handing their capital over to professional investment managers and paying them a commission. But it does mean, at the very least, picking your fund or manager carefully and then closely watching your account's performance. We know one widow whose husband, the founder of a Fortune 500 company, left her a very tidy trust fund managed by one of the most reputable bank trust departments in the country. When the stock market ran into the high-inflation years of the 1970s, the managers' traditional-minded investments cost her more than half her net worth before she moved her business to another firm. Don't let it happen to you.

Even if you decide to let someone else handle your portfolio, learn the basics of investing. If things begin to go wrong, at least you will know what alternatives are open to you.

Finally, when you look at the investments below, keep in mind the probable course of the economy through the next dozen years. If we are lucky, things will look pretty good at first. In 1988 and '89, low but relatively stable dollar values should keep exports growing. Interest rates will stay down long enough to avoid starting a recession until significantly after the 1989 Presidential inauguration. But after that, continued economic health requires an unlikely combination of circumstances: Congress and the new Administration must get the Federal budget deficit under control without a major tax hike. The Fed must keep interest rates low enough to avoid provoking a recession. And foreign investors must continue to buy U.S. government debt, even though they make little profit on their investment and may even lose money. If interest rates rise to attract capital from overseas, or if Japan and Germany decide to stop funding American spending, recession is well nigh inevitable. And rising interest rates in 1990 seem all too likely.

Stocks. Chances are that you own at least one stock already, whether you know it or not. Some 40 percent of Americans do. Half of them own just one stock, in the company for which they work. And many of the rest of us own stocks indirectly, through pension funds, profit-sharing plans, and the like.

If you trade actively in the stock market, you probably have already learned the key lesson about making money—or just surviving—during hard times: The trendy, hard-charging tactics that paid off in a hot bull market will leave you wondering what happened to your bank account when the go-go days have gone. As 1987's Black Monday showed, your trading profits can vanish with blinding speed.

So let us begin with the question dearest to the hearts of most investors: Where are stock prices headed?

We don't know. Neither does anyone else, though you will be hard-pressed to find anyone on Wall Street who will admit to ignorance.

But certain basics are clear: Now that we've seen the last of the speculative euphoria that powered the recent bull market, the price of stocks will be tied a lot more closely to the value of the companies that issued them. Investors will be looking at the growth prospects of publicly held companies skeptically and putting a lower price on projected earnings. And if you read our first two chapters, it should be pretty clear that it will not take much to push the American economy down the cellar stairs; stock prices will fall with it.

There is no way to tell how high stock prices will climb in any given market; 1987 proved that. But there is a floor under the market that the Dow seldom penetrates: the book value of the companies whose stocks are included in the average. It is easy to calculate a company's book value, and the information you will need is published in the corporation's annual report. Just add up the firm's assets—cash on hand, accounts receivable, inventories and work in process, market value of any real estate owned, and so on. Then add up the liabilities—debts, accounts payable, and the like. The difference between those two figures is the stockholders' equity, the sum that shareowners theoretically would receive if the company were to cease operations and sell off its assets. Divide that sum by the number of shares outstanding, and you have the firm's book value. Combine the book values of the stocks in the Dow Jones average, and you can begin to see whether the market as a whole is worth what stock buyers are paying for it.

Though there are more popular measures of corporate worth—projected earnings, for example, and the price/earnings ratio—book value turns out to be a very accurate guide to stock value over the long term. Since 1920, the Dow Jones Industrial Average has fallen below book fewer than a dozen times, never by much, and never for more than a few months. And whenever stock prices have reached or exceeded twice book value, they have soon recoiled. For the last sixty years, investors who bought the Dow stocks when prices were near book value and sold them—or, better yet, went short—whenever they neared twice book value might have had to wait out short periods of speculative euphoria and bearish gloom, but on average they would have made large, reliable profits.

Whenever the Dow hits 2000, its stocks are selling at roughly twice their 1987 book value. Historically, it is difficult to see any justification for higher prices. And if we hit a severe bear market, the fundamental floor under the average won't be reached until the Dow sells at 1000. (And that does not include the predictable draining of cash, accounts receivable, and real estate values from the asset side of the companies' ledgers.)

We are not suggesting that you take out a second mortgage on your home, rush to a broker's office, and tell him to short the Dow stocks. Prices may churn wildly before finally turning downward, and you can lose a lot of money by being right about the direction of the market six months before it actually turns. Further, if enough of the politicians and bureaucrats in Washington read Appendix A and bring the budget and trade deficits under control, there is an even chance that we can avoid a major bear market. And this brand of trading is not for the impatient; the cycle from one market low to the next can take twenty years (though prices always fall a lot faster than they rise). But if you are going to invest in stocks, do it very selectively, for long-run profits, and with money that you can afford to leave in the market for several years.

Your stock selections should be as conservative as you can make them. Weed out the speculative issues, and stick to low-risk stocks. Three obvious groups come to mind:

Blue-chips are always in demand. Thus, they fall less than the general market in most downturns and are among the first to recover. And while you are waiting for the price to go up, you'll be receiving better-than-average dividends. Early in 1988, dividends for many of the stocks listed in the Dow Jones Industrial Average actually yielded more than a good bank CD.

Some products hold their demand even in hard times, and companies that deal in them are perennial bear-market favorites. Food, beverages, and tobacco top the traditional list; people don't scratch these off their budget no matter how long they've been looking for work. Utilities also fall in this category. Electricity and telephones are nearly as indispensable as food, and many power companies pay dividends that rival top-quality-bond yields. Add some entertainment stocks to the list. Texas cable TV companies report that subscriber lists keep growing even when the local oil boom went bust; customers kept paying their bills, even when they were about to abandon their mortgages and move to healthier economic climes.

Finally, there are a few companies whose businesses actually get better in a downturn. Look at vocational-school operators and temporary employment agencies. This side of an all-out depression, they will do well as job seekers try to prepare for new careers and companies try to meet their personnel needs without taking on permanent employees.

We hesitate to mention it, but there is one play so unpopular that in the long run it seems almost a sure winner: growth stocks. Growing rapidly, reinvesting their profits, and offering tiny dividends or none at all, these relatively small companies have been so far out of favor for so long that staid investment analysts have been known to giggle at the thought of buying shares in one. That lack of popularity is one of their greatest assets. Their prices are so low in relation to their earnings that is hard to imagine them going down much further. Sentiment about growth stocks could change at any time, though you may have to wait out a recession first. Whenever it happens, their prices should move up quickly. Of late, too, the merger mania that until recently had giant companies competing to take each other over has begun to shift toward smaller companies. Invest in them, and someday an industrial giant may offer well over the market price for your shares. As always, look for companies likely to do well even in an unfavorable economy. Possibilities include manufacturers of prefabricated housing and operators of acute-care facilities, community-based health-care, and day-care centers.

This brand of speculation violates most of what we said about investing conservatively. Try it only if you can afford to guess wrong, and limit it to a small part of your portfolio.

If you are not up to the hassle of picking your own investments, your safest play may be in mutual funds. There is no guarantee that professional investment managers will be any closer to right about the market than you would be. If the market as a whole falls, their stocks will not be spared. But at least they can afford to spend all their time trying to make your money grow, and spreading your capital over many stocks means that if one or two of their picks fall badly, it won't destroy your whole investment. The key to success is to pick funds with histories of profits in good years and bad—or at least minimal losses when nearly everyone runs into trouble—and to avoid putting all your money into a single fund.

A technique that works well with mutual funds, and is worth considering for any stock investment, is dollar-cost averaging. Instead of saving your money and buying all your stock at once, you save up for, say, a month and then buy as many shares as your funds and the current prices allow. Each month you save the same amount and buy as many shares as you can. Thus, when stock prices are down, you buy more shares than when they are high. This reduces the average price of your shares and relieves you from having to guess about where the market is headed. Eventually, stock prices will rise, and you will make your profit. This is a technique for long-term investors, not for speculators with an eye for a quick buck. But then, to survive a recession, part-time investors probably shouldn't be speculating anyway.

Let's end by repeating a message from the last section: Diversify, and avoid being hurt by ugly surprises. For example, food stocks may be a great investment in most recessions, but farm prices have been very low these past few years. What if they go up and the company's profit margin suffers? What if the firm's elderly founder dies and is replaced by his idiot nephew? If it's your only stock, you'll find yourself caught in your own private bear market. The only protection against this too-common fate is to split your capital among several stocks in unrelated market sectors, so that if one stock or group of stocks heads for the basement, they won't take your bank balance with them. Do it.

Bonds. Stock traders used to see the bond market more or less the way Bostonians view Providence, as a backwater where nothing ever happens. If someone had inherited a bundle from his rich uncle and wanted complete freedom from worry, he'd probably put the money into bonds and spend the rest of his life clipping coupons and collecting the quarterly interest.

Those comforting dividends are still available, but everything else has changed. The name of this game today is volatility. In 1987, the price of thirty-year Treasury bonds with a face value of $1,000—one of the most popular vehicles for large bond speculators—swung by a breathtaking $220.

What drives these moves is interest rates. Like most other loans, bonds pay a fixed rate of interest. When interest rates on CDs and other safe investments are low, bonds look good and their prices go up. When the Fed raises interest rates, bonds are suddenly less inviting, and their prices fall. It doesn't take much of a change in interest rates to shift bond values wildly. In the spring of 1987, a relatively small hike in the prime lending rate meant hundreds of millions of dollars in losses for such giant investment bankers as Merrill Lynch and First Boston Corp. Then, after watching the stock-market crash that October, investors frantically searching for safer havens quickly bid the price of bonds back up.

It is still possible to deal in bonds conservatively, of course. If you can find a high-quality bond selling at its face value or less, you can buy it and collect the dividends, secure in the knowledge that, barring disaster, when the bond matures you will get all your money back and, if you bought at a discount, a bit more. But that takes more patience than many traders have. Why make do with the 8 percent or 10 percent interest even a generous bond offers, they reason, when you can make far more by speculating in price changes? The answer, of course, is obvious: You can also lose a lot more by speculating. And for the volatile 1990s, that consideration will be more important than ever. If the economy falls apart, those dividend payments will look awfully good compared with the losses that many in-and-out traders will rack up.

For small investors, the best bet in bonds may be the classic government savings bonds. Hold them for at least five years, and you receive 6 percent interest or more. Guaranteed. You can't lose on this investment unless the government admits it's broke.

For larger investors, Treasury bonds are probably the safest, most liquid choice. Unless Internal Revenue goes out of business, there is no doubt that interest payments will be met and principal returned on time. But Treasuries with distant maturation dates are among the speculators' favorites. When interest rates change, thirty-year Treasuries are among the hardest-hit.

Several bonds issued by Federal agencies are backed by residential mortgages; the most popular are issued by the Government National Mortgage Association and are known as Ginnie Maes. These bonds seem inviting, because they are uncommonly safe and offer relatively high rates of interest, but they hide a disappointing trap for unwary investors. If interest rates go down, and homeowners refinance their mortgages, the bonds can be paid back early, snatching away all the juicy interest you thought had been locked in.

Municipal bonds escaped the bout of Congressional populism that destroyed nearly all other tax loopholes in 1986. Their raw interest rates are slightly lower than those of Treasuries, but the tax exemption means that top-bracket investors will get to keep as much profit from a muni that yields 8 percent as they would from any other debenture yielding 12 percent. (All that and the pure pleasure of knowing that for once you kept Internal Revenue's greasy fingers off your wallet!) There are two kinds of municipals: general-obligation bonds and revenue bonds. General-obligations are paid from state or local taxes, while revenue bonds meet their payments from the proceeds of the project they were used to support—a hospital, toll bridge, or whatever. General-obligations are safer—anyone who can remember a government project that didn't turn a profit, raise your hand—and their interest rates are only about 0.5 percent lower than those paid by revenue bonds. Only a few municipals have been issued since the 1986 tax "reform," so prices have remained strong. If the next Administration in Washington raises taxes, munis will be even more desirable.

Corporate bonds require a bit more evaluation. Fortunately, most of it has already been done for you. Stick to issues with top-quality ratings—AAA if you are using Standard & Poor's, or Aaa from Moody's Investor's Service. In the next recession, so-called "junk bonds" will be thrown out with the trash.

As with stocks, there are any number of funds that are devoted to bond speculation. Some specialize in municipal issues. Others in corporate debt. A few even limit themselves to foreign bonds, hoping that changing currency-exchange rates will add to their profit. (These funds have done very well in the last two years, but they are strictly for the sophisticated investor.)

With all bonds, the key to safety is the time left until the issue matures. The more distant a bond's date of maturity, the more its value will fluctuate with interest rates. That's great if interest rates are falling; long-term, high-rate bonds will soar. But what if interest rates go up? According to one estimate, a bond that matures in thirty years would lose 9 percent of its value for each 1 percent rise in interest rates; a bond maturing in three years would lose only 3 percent of its value. On the other hand, the bond that matures later may well offer more interest. The bond player's challenge is to make the best compromise between yield and safety.

Compulsive traders should probably decide whether the prime will remain relatively low or aim for orbit and choose their investments accordingly. But for longer-term investors, bonds maturing in five to ten years are the middle ground, offering both adequate yields and the chance to make a new choice in the foreseeable future. Then again, if interest rates begin to move, you may find yourself wanting to reevaluate any bond trades, no matter what their expiration date or how conservatively you vowed to hold them to maturity.

Summary: Though bonds have lost their staid image, it is still possible to make a healthy profit on them, even in hard times. Whether you will want to try depends on your level of patience and on how closely you are willing to watch your investments. Either put your money into safe issues that mature in five or ten years—and leave it there—or keep one eye on the interest rates at all times, and be ready to bail out at the first sign of renewed inflation. Conservative, income-oriented bond *owning,* not trading, can be one of your best defenses against recession.

Real estate. Are you tired of reading about how to make a million dollars in real estate in six weeks? Don't worry, you won't find any of that here. It is almost always possible to profit from property because, unlike other investments, real estate is almost strictly a local business. Even when the national market is falling apart, an alert buyer with an eye for a bargain can make money. But it will not be as easy in the 1990s as it was through most of the 1980s.

One reason is the souring of local economies. In Texas, where property values once floated on the rising tide of oil, $250,000 homes abandoned by bankrupt owners can be had at almost any bank for one-fifth of their former prices. The disastrous farm economy of the mid-'80s has built new ghost towns in the grain belt. And in the industrial centers of Michigan and Illinois, boarded-up homes and stores offer silent testimony to the state of local property values.

Throughout the center of the nation, real estate is available at bargain-basement prices, but there are few takers.

The tax changes of 1986 have been another drag on the national real estate market. Owners of rental property can still use up to $25,000 in losses to offset their other income, so long as they make less than $150,000 per year. But the tasty depreciation allowance that once made a second home everyone's best investment has been cut back drastically. Money spent on residential property, formerly depreciated in only nineteen years, must now be written off over thirty-one years. In effect, the amount of income that can be sheltered by depreciation has been cut in half. That may be one factor slowing the growth of formerly buoyant housing prices.

Yet some general advice will hold true wherever you go:

Residential property remains by far the best real estate investment. Prices of single-family housing are still rising by about 6 percent per year throughout most of the country, and that is expected to continue. At that rate, a second house rented out for enough income to pay its own way stands up well when compared with stocks and bonds.

Foreclosed homes are a good bet these days. Where "REOs"—real estate owned by the lender—once tended to be shoddy houses in poor neighborhoods, the economic problems of the last five years have put choice properties into lenders' hands. Prices of foreclosed houses generally run about 15 percent below market, so you start out with a built-in profit.

And don't overlook those run-down, neglected properties. Fixer-uppers can be the best money-makers in real estate. In the low end of the market, it is not difficult to acquire a house for, say, $65,000, put a few thousand into fixing it up, and sell it for twice your investment. Do as much of the work yourself as you can. Contractors' bills can really eat up your profits.

You will find few such opportunities in commercial property. Most major cities are already glutted with office space. In some regions that results from hard times. In cities like Houston and Dallas, where the booming oil economy has collapsed, up to 75 percent of offices have "For Rent" signs on the door. In New York, Boston, and Washington, skyrocketing rents have forced many businesses to move where costs are lower. So far, small strip malls with ten to fifty stores strung along a parking lot have done well. The best traditionally have been anchored by a supermarket or department store that attracts customers to the rest, but discount stores and factory outlets are drawing business to many of the newer malls. But if recession looms, the small shops will close their doors, and the mall operator's profits will dry up.

For a speculative play, several respected money managers have taken to recommending farmland. Bumper crops, rising agricultural exports, and an overall improvement in farm income have eased the hard times that drove more than 100,000 people from their farms in 1986 and '87 alone. And if farmers can make a living again, croplands, which dropped by half in the first six years of the 1980s, can only recover their value. And in fact, the price of farm acreage is expected to go up by about 2 percent in 1988. You may think that if you sink from $50,000 to $125,000 or so in an 80-acre farm, you should eventually reap green, growing profits; and while you are waiting, you can make 6 or 8 percent leasing the land to a good farmer. So the reasoning goes.

Unfortunately, it isn't so. It is true that the decline of the dollar has brought new health to moribund farm exports. True also that farm incomes have risen, so that farmers have managed to pay off more than one-fourth of their debt since 1983. But that new income does not come from crop sales, it comes from Washington. Between 1984 and 1987, the much-maligned Reagan Administration spent more than $86 billion on farm subsidies, more than 2.5 times as much as in the Carter years. There is no way that farmers could live on the earnings from their crops alone. So what happens if the politicians ever get serious about reducing the Federal budget deficit? Chances are those subsidies will be among the first items pruned, and the farmers who are still deep in debt—about one in four—will follow their former neighbors to big-city unemployment lines. And this year's little blip in land values will be forgotten as the price-per-acre heads for new lows.

REITs, or real estate investment trusts, are another good place not to put your money. REITs are like mutual funds that invest in property instead of stocks or bonds. After brief popularity when they appeared during the 1970s, these companies quickly lost favor. Too many of them were too badly managed. That remains true today. It is possible to find existing REITs with records of low vacancies and steady profits; but it is easier to find good investments in other fields.

Don't even think about trusts that are just getting set up. Without a track record, investors are just gambling.

Finally, the bad news. All these forecasts have assumed that the national economy will manage to muddle through more or less as it has for the last few years—no great expansion, but also no collapse. If the worst happens, real estate won't be much safer in the short run than any other speculation. As an investment, land is a lot like a large, immovable bond. Interest rates are a prime factor in the health of the property market. When mortgage rates rise even slightly, it becomes a lot harder to sell a house. When rates go up further, property values sag. Add to that the natural reluctance of people to make large commitments when strapped for cash, and real estate could be in trouble in the next recession. If the next Administration in Washington finds itself forced to raise interest rates to attract foreign investors, not even the market for single-family homes will survive intact. Property values will be down sharply for as long as it takes the economy to recover. They will come up eventually, and unlike most other investments the land will always be there. But the wait could be longer than you want to endure.

Commodities futures. If you already know about commodities futures, skip on to the next section. There is nothing we can tell you about them that should not have been obvious after your first few fumbled trades. What follows is strictly for the uninitiated, the poor innocents who will soon be much poorer if they listen to the brokers —and even a few otherwise sensible business publications—who would like them to believe that futures trading can be a safe haven when the stock market catches a bad case of China Syndrome.

For anyone who has not flipped the page: If you have not yet traded in commodities futures, you are missing the most exciting brand of speculation there is. It costs only a few dollars to get started, and there is no faster way to run a little money into the high six digits. All it takes to succeed in the commodities market is the kind of talent and dedication that would, given other interests, carry you to an Olympic gold. Either that or more dumb luck than you have.

The idea behind futures trading is to protect commodities producers and users from some of the risks inherent in their business. Look at wheat futures, for example. A Kansas wheat farmer knows when he plants his crop how much money he will need to make at harvest time in order to end his growing season with a profit. Unfortunately, wheat prices vary widely, and he has no idea what his grain will bring when he actually has it to sell. Prices are likely to be high at planting time, because last year's crop has begun to run out and buyers are competing for what is left; but by harvest time, with new grain flooding the market, the price could drop so far that our farmer actually loses money. On the other hand, a New Jersey baker needs wheat all year round; but when prices are at their peak, he may not be able to buy. What both these people need is a guarantee today that they won't wind up broke in the future.

Future contracts were invented to give them that guarantee. In a wheat contract, the farmer promises to deliver 5,000 bushels of wheat at a specific date in the future; the buyer promises to buy the wheat. No grain is actually bought or sold, just the promise to deliver and to buy it when the time comes. But the price of the grain is set when the contract is exchanged. In this way, our farmer "locks in" his profit; he might have made even more money if the price of wheat goes up, but at least he knows that he will make enough to pay his costs—or at least that he won't fall any further into the hole. Similarly, the baker who buys the contract knows today what his wheat will cost when it finally arrives.

Brokerage firms and the commodities exchanges make the process easy by matching buyers with sellers and taking care of the messy accounting details. That is how they earn their commissions.

But what if the baker does not want to buy a contract when the farmer wants to sell it? That is where the speculators come in. A speculator buys the farmer's contract, hoping that the price of wheat will rise and let him sell at a profit. In doing so, he accepts the risk that it will drop—the risk that the farmer wanted to avoid. When the time comes to sell the contract, chances are that it will be bought by another speculator, who still hopes that the price will rise from its current level. Speculators can also write their own contracts to buy or sell wheat; in fact, nine out of ten futures contracts traded are made between speculators who never see the commodity itself. When the time comes to yield up the grain, they simply buy another contract and deliver that instead. In the long run, the speculators' contracts to buy and sell cancel each other out, and the baker winds up with the farmer's contract and receives his wheat.

Though futures contracts were invented to help farmers and their customers, they have become enormously popular in many other fields where there are large markets and quick price changes. Today futures are traded not just in wheat, corn, soybeans, cotton, and pork bellies (the raw material for bacon), but in nonagricultural commodities like lumber and crude oil; metals such as gold, silver, and copper; and "financials," including currency exchange rates, Treasury bills, and the Dow Jones Industrial Average.

For speculators who know their business, commodities offer enormous profits. The cost of trading a futures contract is very low, typically around 5 percent of the value of the commodity itself. So for only $750, our wheat speculator gets to profit from the price changes of a commodity worth perhaps $15,000. If the price of wheat rises 10 cents per bushel—in a volatile market, it can happen overnight—the speculator makes $500 on his 5,000-bushel contract.

And for the merely daring, commodities can sing a siren song. How many other investments will give you a 67 percent profit on your money (not counting commissions) in a single day? And in a strong market move, high-profit days can follow each other for a long time. One of the authors (not Dr. Cetron; he knows better) once entered two trades on a sunny Monday morning in spring. By midsummer, the contracts that had cost him less than $2,000 were worth just over $80,000! (Unfortunately, he had chickened out and closed both trades within the first week. Prices for both had moved in the wrong direction at first, and that much excitement soon corrodes the judgment of all but the most nerveless speculators.)

The trouble is, when commodities prices turn against you, your capital can disappear faster than at a Las Vegas craps table. In our hypothetical wheat trade, instead of rising by 10 cents per bushel, the price could as easily have dropped by 15 cents. In that case, our speculator would have lost his entire $750 bet. And it need not stop there. As long as you own a futures contract and the price moves against you, you keep losing money. Under most circumstances, your broker will automatically sell your contract to make sure you don't go broke before paying for your losses; otherwise, his company will be stuck with the debt. But every year fast-moving markets trap unwary, or just unlucky, speculators in losses many times greater than their original trading capital.

Unfortunately, few commodities traders have the knowledge it takes to be successful; for the rest, this brand of speculation is little more than gambling. It shows in their trading records. According to one survey at a major brokerage house, most commodities speculators stay in the game for less than a year. Only one in four breaks even in any given year, and only one in twenty who attempt futures speculation ever learns to take money consistently from this most difficult of all trading markets. Nine out of ten who stick with futures long enough eventually go broke.

If you like excitement and can afford the price, commodities trading may be the game for you. You may even be the one in twenty who masters this harrowing business. But commodities trading is strictly for the rich or reckless. It has no place in preparing to weather a depression.

There is an old speculator's adage that all investors should know: "The surest way to make a small fortune in commodities is to start with a large fortune." Engrave it on your memory, and repeat it like a mantra if you are ever tempted to put your money in this market.

Precious metals. It's true: All that glitters is not gold; there are silver and platinum as well. And for some doomsday theorists, these precious metals are the key to surviving bad times; economist Ravi Batra, author of the popular *The Great Depression of 1990,* would have you put one-third of your capital into gold. Other investments may outperform gold during good times, the argument runs, but when stocks fall and inflation soars, the yellow metal will always hold its value. Since Black Monday, even respected financial planners have taken to including precious metals in their portfolio recommendations. Not much, you understand (no need to look like the "gold bugs" they once ridiculed). Just put 5 to 10 percent of your trading capital into gold to act as a hedge against uncontrolled inflation.

Ten years ago, that would have been a good idea. Remember 1980, when inflation was in double digits? Gold topped $800 an ounce, more than double its price less than two years earlier, and everyone's dotty Aunt Mabel cleaned up in Krugerrands.

We have not seen that kind of move in gold recently. Though gold-mining stocks were Wall Street's top performers in 1987, the metal itself went up only 10 percent from 1982 through the October crash. During that same five-year period, the Dow Jones average doubled. And during the week of Black Monday, when any credible refuge from economic chaos should have drawn money from the New York

Stock Exchange like a giant vacuum cleaner, gold rose less than $1.50 an ounce, while silver and platinum fell by more than 20 percent. By year's end, gold prices had rallied to new highs—and a month later, they had fallen to the $457 range, some $15 an ounce lower than their price on October 19. It's not the performance of a good hedge against economic chaos.

There is a good reason, of course. In 1980, gold was the only place to go when the investment world seemed too dangerous to face. Today, there are many alternatives. With the dollar dropping, many sophisticated investors have made money in currency futures, profiting as the yen and deutschmark rose. (No, we still don't recommend trading in futures, even yen futures, as a hedge against depression.) Others have put their capital into mutual funds with large holdings overseas, where companies dealing in harder currencies than the dollar have stood up well. Why bother with something as quirky as gold when you can trade in hedges that seem comfortably akin to traditional investments?

Well, there is one possible reason. You won't be able to avoid hearing about it if the economy falls apart: If the inflation rate heads decisively up, and the doomsday crowd begins to scream that the sky is falling—and not one minute sooner—you may want to add some gold to your portfolio. Everyone else will be buying it, and you may turn a tidy profit as they bid the price up. But remember, this is no magic defense against hard times. Precious metals are strictly a speculation, to be bought for profit and kept only as long as they move your way. Timing is everything in this trade. Be ready to run when the market turns against you.

For small traders, gold coins are probably the safest, easiest play in precious metals. You can buy and sell them at banks, coin dealers', and many brokerage houses about as easily as trading in stocks. Don't bother taking possession unless you are afraid the dealer may go under in a recession (and in that case, think about buying elsewhere). A bank or broker will hold and insure them for you for about $5 per year per coin. Your best choices are the American Eagle and the Canadian Maple Leaf. You will have to pay about 3 percent more than the spot price of gold itself, but the markup on other coins can reach ten times that.

By contrast, other forms of metals speculation are chancy at best: Gold-mining stocks soared in 1987, and mutual funds that specialize in them rose by 50 percent or more before the October crash—not bad for a nine-month profit. But since the crash they have fluctuated with the general market. No protection there.

Silver used to be the poor man's gold. As gold rose and fell, so did silver. But silver is an industrial metal as well as a supposed hedge against inflation. Making money in it requires a sound fundamental analysis of manufacturing demand, not just inflation psychology. Silver prices these days often move against gold, and their swings make gold prices look downright stable. Bouts of panic buying and selling by small speculators hit this market every few years. You don't want to be caught in the stampede.

Mention platinum, and even hardened commodities traders go pale. Demand for this metal rests primarily on two industries: jewelry and automobiles (for antipollution equipment). Just over 3 million ounces are produced each year, compared with 620 million ounces of gold, and 85 percent of that comes from South African mines. The result is one of the fastest-moving, least predictable speculations you can find. Platinum is strictly for professionals with a perverse taste for danger. If you get the urge to trade in this metal, lie down until it goes away.

Art and collectibles. When a stock price doubles, it's news to warm a speculator's heart. When an investment goes up by more than 100,000 percent . . . well, who cares if it takes forty years? That is what happened with Vincent van Gogh's *Irises*. Bought four decades ago for a mere $47,000, the spectacular painting sold at Sotheby's New York auction house for $53.9 million—this less than three weeks after the October 1987 stock-market crash. And while the owner had it, he enjoyed the rare pleasure of living with one of the world's great pieces of art.

Kind of makes your mouth water, doesn't it?

You can find similar, if less dramatic, tales told in many arts and crafts: antique furniture (have you priced a Chippendale highboy lately?), glass (your grandmother may well have thrown out a Tiffany lamp that today would buy you a summer house in Maine), china, and an endless variety of other artifacts. On a more modest scale, there are "collector's items" from comic books to barbed wire to old Avon cosmetics jars. All are bid ever higher by eager hobbyists.

None of these stories is likely to make you any money, however.

There are four reasons never to think of art objects or collectibles as investments:

Making money in this game requires far more expertise than even the commodities market, and good advisers are hard to find. To profit on the scale of the stories that leave you gasping, you have to get to the item before the crowd. It requires the kind of eye that takes an adult life to develop, and that grows only from pure love of the art for its own sake. Collector's items demand only slightly less knowledge and seldom attain profit margins that could justify studying them solely as investment vehicles.

It is growing harder and harder to find bargains. Too many people already know too much more about their field of interest than you do, and they all have their eyes open for the same profitable items you want.

Dealers' markups on most art and collectibles are horrendous. Buy many of these items on the open market, and sell them at the shop next door an hour later, and you will have lost at least one-third of your investment.

And contrary to popular delusion, art prices sometimes fall, even for good pieces. In fact, they usually drop significantly about six months after the stock market takes a pummeling. In the bear market of the early 1980s, they were down by 25 percent. The value of works by some Old West painters crashed when oil prices plunged and left their New West owners with empty pockets. At this point, trying to recover your investment in the works of secondary Western artists is a lot like trying to sell your share of the national debt.

If you are interested in buying the odd Monet, Ming, or sculptured Jim Beam bottle for its own beauty—knowing in the back of your mind that you may eventually be able to sell it for more than you paid —so be it. But most people find buying art for money about as pleasurable as marrying for it, and a lot less profitable.

PART THREE

PLANNING FOR THE BAD YEARS, AND BEYOND

9

YOUR STRATEGY FOR THE FUTURE

How THEN to cope with the coming bad years? Find some way to keep your current job. Find a new, more secure job. Or start your own recessionproof business. If you need a new job or a new career, you can either search for it where you live today or move to a healthier economic climate. Which path is right for you depends a lot on where are you are going to begin.

After reading the last eight chapters, you may have figured out how well you are prepared to face the 1990s. You know that many once-secure jobs are doomed to disappear, and that life will be grim where the factory is still king and trade unions remain strong. Yet people who have found careers in fast-growing industries, in fast-growing regions, will prosper, no matter what happens to others. Chances are that you have a good idea even without thinking which of these futures is likely to be yours.

But unless you have already made the decision to change careers and move to one of the Sun Belt technology centers, a good idea may not be good enough. If you work for a progressive, technology-oriented company in a generally low-tech business, your job could be safer during a recession than others in your industry. But if you work for, say, a service-oriented computer shop in Michigan that sells accounting systems to local retailers, your job is tied closely to the local economy. When the big factories that employ most of your neighbors start to lay off their workers and retail business collapses, all your computer-oriented expertise won't keep you out of the unemployment lines. In this as in all else, details count.

So it's time for some self-appraisal. To figure out for sure how you can best cope with a recession, you must look carefully at the five basic aspects of your economic life: yourself, your home, your job, your financial position, and your family. If it turns out that you decide to find some new line of work, you must also take a look at the unique set of preferences and abilities that you will bring to your new career. (We will save that step for the next chapter.)

The time to work all this out is NOW! Reorganizing your life is hard enough in good times; if you wait until today's general prosperity fades, it may be impossible.

Before you go much further, pick up a notebook. Figuring out exactly where you stand, how well you can endure a recession, is a long and difficult process. If you find that you need a new way to earn your living, making a good choice will be more demanding still. Taking notes at every step will make sure you do not forget any thoughts or observations that could lead to a promising new career. You will probably find yourself looking at it repeatedly as new information and further thoughts shed new light on material you have already covered.

Let's take each facet of your analysis in order.

• By the time you finish reading Chapter 10, self-analysis will have turned into the single greatest chore in the whole, difficult process of preparing for the coming decade. For now, let's limit it to some relatively general questions: How old are you? If you are within a year or two of retirement, you could be safely on a pension before there is any immediate danger of recession; if you are at the beginning of your working years, you are in an ideal position to aim for one of the fastest-growing careers. How good is your health? If you are not up to the strain of holding down one job while preparing for a new, perhaps entirely different, career, that limits your options; you may want to look for a way to retire early, perhaps for medical reasons, or to limit your career search to relatively safe part-time employment. How practical was your education? With a better grounding in mathematics than most of us possess, even if it needs some refurbishing, there isn't a segment of technology that you cannot learn.

• In Chapter 3, we asked you to invest some time at the library, poring over back issues of your hometown newspaper to find out how well your local economy fared during the recession of the early 1980s. That may not be necessary if you worked for a stamping plant in Dayton, Ohio; you already know how hard it's been to find a job that pays better than the neighborhood McDonald's. And if you live in Nashua, New Hampshire, or Austin, Texas, you have been reading newspaper stories about the local economic boom every week for the last five years. But if you have moved since, say, 1982 or changed your career, if you are new to the job market, if your industry is just being automated, or if your memory simply is not as good as it once was, you really do need to make at least one trip to the library. Pay special attention to the business section of your local paper. In many states, you will find regional business magazines as well; they have space enough to analyze the local economy more thoroughly than most newspapers can and are well worth your attention. Stories of layoffs, foreign competition, and rising unemployment in 1981 or '82 are a clear warning of more trouble to come. Glance at the old "Help Wanted" ads, too. They will show you what jobs may be available to keep you afloat if yours abruptly disappears. You probably won't like what you find.

That economic history lesson is just the first step in evaluating your current location. Look at the local economy as it stands today. Has your hometown managed to attract new employers since the early 1980s? Are they well diversified, so that if one industry suffers during the 1990s others will be able to fend off high unemployment? Is there a good proportion of high-tech companies, or do vulnerable, labor-intensive industries still predominate? How many local employers have prospered in the new export economy? How will they fare if exports collapse? As we saw in Chapter 6, the regions that are growing fastest in today's economy will survive the next decade with the fewest problems, while those that remain depressed even in good times are headed for serious trouble.

For one view of the future, look at your city and state as a corporate planner would when choosing a site for a new plant. How high are state and local business taxes? How strong are local unions? How good is your local school system? Would it invite a company's employees to bring their children to your town? Does your area have a large population of well-educated, technically skilled workers? In an all-out recession, even the most inviting regions will find their growth curtailed, but an attractive business climate will make it easier for existing firms to retain the jobs they now offer.

Living in the wrong place is one more thing that will make life difficult in the coming decade, but a mediocre local economy does not necessarily mean that you must leave your home to survive the 1990s. It does mean that the marginal jobs—and particularly those dependent on local retail businesses—will be more vulnerable during a recession than similar positions where the business climate is healthy. Your next step is to figure out whether your job is one of these.

• We have emphasized two kinds of job in this book: the high-tech, high-skill careers that are sure winners even if the economy turns sour; and the low-tech, labor-oriented jobs that are quickly fading into business history. (You can find a comprehensive list of jobs—the good, the bad, and the obsolete—in Appendix B.) From this, one obvious rule emerges: If your job can be automated, it will be, if not today, then soon. Two-thirds of manufacturing jobs either have been lost already or soon will be, and many routine service jobs will join them. If yours is vulnerable but has not yet been cut, a sharp recession could actually provide a reprieve. Companies fighting for survival are likely to struggle on with human workers rather than invest in costly new equipment. But that is little cause for celebration; as soon as capital becomes a bit easier to spend, these firms will rush to automate and thereby maximize their profits during the upturn.

There are many other jobs where your future may not be so clear. What if you are a teacher, an ad writer, or a government employee? In those cases, and many like them, your analysis becomes much more complicated.

The Baby Boom generation is having fewer children than its parents did, so there will be fewer jobs for high school teachers in the 1990s. Maybe. If, as we expect, education becomes a national priority, the demand for teachers will rise in the core subjects of English, mathematics, foreign languages, and especially the sciences. There may be a second wave of demand if educators are required to meet even minimal standards of competence; forcing teachers in most school systems to take the final exams their students must pass would leave many new openings to be filled. For would-be college teachers, there will be no such opportunities. In a genuinely bad economy, poverty will keep young people at home, working at menial jobs to help support their families.

Advertising writers, editorial personnel, and those in similar creative positions should be relatively safe in a recession. But what if you work for a regional ad agency that specializes in promoting local retailers? That's great if you live in Florida, where business will boom even in a national recession; it's not so great if you live in Detroit, where it surely will not.

And government employees? Bureaucrats never lose their jobs, right? Unless another conservative Administration decides to close down the program they work for or to sell off the facility to private operators. Or a liberal Administration takes aim at the military budget and at the thousands of civilian employees working for Defense Department programs. Then it's anyone's guess what will happen.

All these trends and many others will affect more people than teachers, ad writers, and bureaucrats. Take a good look at your own job. Even if the past eight chapters have already given you a good idea of how vulnerable you are, start from the beginning and take stock systematically. Is your industry on our list of recessionproof fields? Has it already been so thoroughly automated that adding new machines will cost relatively few jobs? Were you hired when the export boom hit in 1987? Will you still be needed when it has collapsed? And—be ruthlessly honest about this question—how good are you at your job? Do you have special skills that will keep you at work when others in your job category are gone? If you are one of a dozen secretaries in your department, you're on shaky ground. Unless you are the only one who really understands the computerized inventory system. If you are not, could you transfer into a job that seems more secure?

Think about your company as well. Is it a market leader or ready to go under at the first sign of trouble? Has it automated its operations yet, or is there a chance that human workers will lose their jobs to robots? Is it at least as well automated as the competition, or will it lose business when they cut their prices to levels it cannot match? How heavily does it depend on exports? How closely is it tied to local business conditions? Will it survive if the government raises interest rates and provokes another round of inflation?

If you don't like the answers, and many people will not, there is another decision to make: Would it help to move to another firm in your industry? Or would you be better off finding some way to apply your skills to some more promising field? Unless you are willing to change careers completely, you will have to look as closely at your company's competitors—your most likely new employers—as at your own firm.

If you are married, there is a better-than-even chance these days that you are half of a working couple. What about your spouse's job and employer? Unless one of you works strictly by choice, you will have to go through the whole analysis twice. Could you survive on just one of your salaries? And what happens if you both lose your jobs? Could you find work elsewhere? Could one of you support your family in, say, Orlando, Florida, or Austin, Texas, while the other retrained for the local computer industry? If you cannot make do on a single income and even one of you is a candidate for unemployment in the next recession, you will have to retrain or move before the downturn arrives.

Remember, a recession will only hurry the loss of jobs that would be vulnerable even in a good economy. If your job is on the list, it's time to find some other line of work, even if you are convinced the pessimists are wrong.

• Now to money. Sharpen a few pencils, and try to get a handle on your personal economy. If you have never worked out a realistic budget, this is the time to try. How much do you spend every month? How much of that goes for essentials? How much could you cut back if your income suddenly vanished? If you are in debt, can you find enough slack in your budget to pay off what you owe? Can you save anything toward hard times?

The real question here is, how long could you hold out if you lost your job tomorrow? How much unemployment insurance would you receive, and how long would it last? How much could your spouse add to your weekly income? Do you have enough medical insurance to survive if you or someone in your family suddenly became ill? Do you have high mortgage payments? A high rent? Credit-card debt? Car payments? Are you still raising children, or is your family grown and out of the house?

Take a close look at your assets as well. How much do you have in your bank accounts? How much in stocks and bonds, corporate or Treasury? How much can you borrow against your life-insurance policy? Do you own anything you could sell to make money? Would it still be salable in a shrinking economy? Balance that off against outstanding bills and other immediate debts, and you will begin to see what you'll have left to live on if your job disappears with our national prosperity. Remember that any goods or property you hope to sell for emergency money may take a long time to move when others are also forced to sell theirs.

Given any choice in the matter, there is only one circumstance under which it makes sense to sell your house: if you have decided to move in search of a better job in a more hospitable economic climate. But if your local economy collapses and you are forced to move, will you still be able to sell your home? How much will it bring? How fast will it sell? Don't just guess. Hard facts seldom look as comforting as casual estimates. All through the oil states there are plush, empty houses whose owners stopped at the bank one day to drop off the keys as they set out to find a new life. In leaving their mortgage behind, they lost tens of thousands of dollars in equity as well, all because they had not planned for an economic decline no worse than the one that could hit much of the United States in the next decade.

Again, your local library has the information you need. Take a look at the real estate ads from the early 1980s. Did local homes hold their value during the recession? Did they drop sharply? A real estate agent will probably remember how long it took to sell a home like yours back then. There is no guarantee that your area's real estate market will act in the 1990s as it did a decade earlier, but the recent past is the best guide you have. Correlate what you find with the changes in your local business climate in the last few years. It should give you a good idea of what to expect.

• Your spouse and children are in this with you, and not just because they add to your expenses or because your wife or husband can probably help take up the economic slack if you are suddenly out of work. Treat them as full partners in the task of running your family life. In Chapter 5, we discussed their effect on your decision to start a new business. Their cooperation will be just as crucial if you have to move or find a new way to earn a living. An angry spouse and sulking youngsters are not the best companions to have when you're working full time and trying to learn a new career in your off hours. How easy will it be to uproot your spouse and school-age children? How well will the kids adapt to leaving their friends behind and finding a place in a new school system? For that matter, how good is the school system in your hometown-to-be? If it does not offer a good range of science and language courses, taught by teachers far better than the sorry national average, your move could sabotage their future. In that case, you can either pick another destination or resign yourself to paying for private schooling—if you can.

Now that you have completed this rigorous self-appraisal, what should you do about your findings? Unfortunately, we cannot tell you. Individual circumstances are so varied that there is no hope of offering a plan that will lead everyone—or even a significant minority —to a better future. Here again, you will have to do the hard work of decision-making. However, there are some guidelines that may help.

• There was a time when living on credit made sense. During the days of double-digit inflation, you could borrow large, healthy dollars today, enjoy their substantial buying power, and repay the loan in small, anemic dollars tomorrow. In today's low-inflation economy or tomorrow's recession, debts must be paid in dollars you will sorely need. So pay off your debts now, even if it means scrimping on necessities. Unless your employer is so well established in one of the growing high-tech industries that not even economic collapse can seriously threaten its profits, recession will most likely cut into your income significantly. Even if you escape unemployment, a new round of wage cuts and givebacks is all but inevitable. Having to cope with massive credit-card debt on top of mortgage or rent and car payments could tip your personal economy into collapse if the national economy suffers even a minor setback. The money you now spend paying off debts should go toward supporting your family while you train for a new career.

One exercise that can help here is to make two lists of possible expenses. One list should include all your necessities—food, basic clothing, shelter, and so on; the other list records the things you would like to have. Some items may appear on both lists, but in different forms. For example, you might like to buy a new Mercedes, while your real need is to have some way to get to work; a reliable used car will get the job done. Reduce as many of those "would-like" items to their cheapest form; then, if they qualify as necessities, transfer them to the "must-have" list. If not, they remain on the list of pleasant luxuries. When you are done, throw the list of luxuries into the trash. If you are serious about getting your finances in shape to withstand a recession, you can't afford luxuries.

• If you are nearing retirement, you can probably ignore almost everything we have said about changing careers. It will be at least 1990 before a recession strikes; with luck, it could be much later. By the time it arrives, you should be living safely on a fixed income. Even in the severest downturn, there is little threat that bad investments by your retirement-fund managers or cost-cutting measures in the Social Security program will significantly reduce your income. By now, you should already be cutting your basic living expenses to fit your postemployment economy. Continue on schedule, and all should be well. If you really need extra income, most service industries need all the help they can get. The pay scale may be relatively low and the work boring, but the flexible hours and easy availability of jobs should more than make up for any drawbacks.

• If you are just beginning your career, you are in the ideal situation: Unless you married very young and already have a family to support, your expenses should be even lower than your entry-level salary. You are not yet so tracked into your first career that it will be difficult to forfeit the time and energy invested in it, and you are unlikely to be tied down by a house that must be sold before you can move where promising jobs are plentiful. Use your current job to support your search for more future-oriented employment. Then relocate to one of the hot, high-tech job markets discussed in Chapter 6, and seek your fortune. Or move first, and train on location. As a young employee, you will probably find most companies more willing to help in your training than they would be for an older worker with only a few more active years in which to repay their investment.

• It is in the middle of your working years that seeking a new career is at its most daunting. In your thirties, you almost surely have a family to support. By the time you reach age forty, you will be making mortgage payments, trying to save money for your children's college educations, and beginning to wonder about saving for retirement. And by your fifties, a little panic is beginning to set in: If you married late, you may still have college-age children to see through school; it is time to pay off the mortgage; your retirement fund probably has not been growing as quickly as you would like; and the thought of losing your job is enough to bring on nightmares. Yet if you are not in one of the recessionproof industries, that fate is all too possible, as thousands of assembly-line workers discovered in the last recession. Changing careers may mean abandoning a high salary in your established field and temporarily accepting a far smaller paycheck in an industry with greater growth potential. Yet somehow, at any age, working around all other commitments, you must find some way to shift into a more stable career.

Unfortunately, it is in this stage of your career that we have the fewest shortcuts to offer. To make a sound decision, you must plod through each stage of the analysis outlined above, then work through the process of finding a new career described in Chapter 10. With your living expenses at their peak and your retirement years on the horizon, there is no easy way to shift careers.

However, a few random thoughts may guide your way:

If your spouse does not work and can, it is time to consider adding a second salary to the family income. Even if the job is only temporary, the extra cash can help carry you through the difficult period of retraining, when your own income may suffer and course costs may be high. If you face long training and must cope with daytime classes, there may be no other way to survive this period.

It may occur to you to redirect some long-term investments to provide extra income today. This is strictly a temporary measure, to be made only after careful thought and with the advice of a competent financial adviser—not your stockbroker! Getting caught in another stock crash will not help your short-term position and could be disastrous in the long run. (But of course, you have already learned that.) We are not at all sure the short-term income is worth the risk.

It may also occur to you that a small home-equity loan could pay for a lot of retraining. It's true. But before taking on this kind of debt, reread what we said about debt in general a few paragraphs back. If you are still convinced that a home-equity loan is the best way to finance your education, start by buying a tent. If you lose your current income before you are ready for a new career, you could wind up living in it.

If you have children nearing college age, you'd better find some way to prepare them either to pay their own way through school or to do without. Scholarships, government-backed loans, summer jobs, and college work programs will support their education when you may be unable to do so. And if the next recession turns into an all-out depression, many young people now headed toward college will find themselves staying home to help support the family.

In the early 1990s it may be much easier to pay for schooling, either your own retraining or your children's college. By then, we expect Congress to enact legislation allowing us to take money from an IRA or Keogh-plan retirement fund and use it for tuition and other education costs. It should also be possible to set up special IRA-style education funds. This money will be tax-exempt. According to recent polls, nearly two-thirds of American voters favor such a plan. This is too large a percentage for Washington to ignore.

Do not forget the possibility of starting your own business. A few courses in small-business practices could lead to a far larger, more stable income than all the career training you may consider. Reread Chapter 5 at least once before rejecting this idea.

Finally, if you cannot type, learn. Whether you keep your current job or move to a whole new career, there is almost certainly a keyboard in your future. By the year 2000, an estimated 75 percent of all jobs will include some form of information processing as a major part of the day's work. That means working with a computer terminal. You can't do it efficiently if you can't type. This, at least, is one skill you can learn at home, cheaply, fitting short practice sessions around any other duties.

10

JOB HUNTING IN THE 1990s

IF AT THIS POINT you have become convinced that there is nothing to worry about, that nothing will derail your career, even during the worst business conditions that incompetent national leaders can hurl at it, you have completed all of the hard work. Take one last glance at your life to see whether there are any minor changes that would make you even more secure, and go to work tomorrow knowing that you are where you belong. But if there is any doubt at all that your current set of job skills will see you through, the hard work has just begun.

It is time to figure out what other line of work would give you the brightest future. If it has taken very long to reach this stage, you might reread Chapters 4 and 5 to remind yourself of the brightest opportunities available now and in the 1990s. Do not neglect the possibility of starting your own business, even if it now seems an unlikely course. Five years from now, the planning you do today might coalesce into a new career far more rewarding than working for others will ever be.

If you live in a major city or a college town, you can probably find professional career counselors whose job it is to help people like you redirect their lives toward more productive, rewarding, and secure employment. For a relatively small fee, and often at no fee, they can help you organize a huge and often intimidating search into manageable pieces. Many tradition-minded counselors do have one limitation, however: Like the rest of us, they have yet to adjust to the rapidly changing employment conditions brought on by technology and the growing interdependence of the world economy. Few of them will be able to filter out all the occupations that these forces will soon make obsolete. Fewer still will be prepared to help you decide which potential jobs will survive a bad recession. A good counselor's help will probably be worth whatever it costs, but you will have to interpret his or her advice in light of the economic conditions of the 1990s.

If you have not been taking notes about your job, employer, and economic condition, please begin *now*. Finding a new career—figuring out, in effect, what to do with the rest of your life—could turn out to be one of the most difficult things you ever do. You will have to dig deep into memory for useful experiences and for the pleasures and irritations of past jobs. Even the most important insights can vanish as quickly as snow in Miami; if you don't write them down instantly, you can wind up frustratedly trying to remember just what it was you found so exciting. (Keep a pen and pad next to your bed at night; few thoughts are more enlightening or harder to recall than the ones that interrupt your sleep.) And there is nothing like a pen and paper for focusing your attention on the job at hand.

Start your job hunt with a close look at yourself. Keep things abstract at first. There are an estimated 40,000 different kinds of job to be found in the United States. There is no reason to let anything limit your choices at this stage.

We all bring three things to any job: aptitudes, values, and experience. We will save experience for last, because experience can almost always be gained as you go along and because you may have been tracked into experiences that either failed to satisfy you or failed to prepare you for a recessionproof career. Aptitudes and values are more basic and less easily changed. More than any other influence, they govern how well we can do a job, and how much pleasure we will get from it. If you hate working with numbers, becoming a computer programmer is not for you; even if you enjoy playing golf, you will never be a pro without top-notch motor coordination; and you will have a lot more luck in selling used cars if you view it as a fascinating game of strategy and influence than if it seems a kind of exploitive manipulation.

Begin by looking at your inherent aptitudes. Many are set by biology. Others are governed, at least in part, by training so deeply ingrained that it is almost impossible to separate from your genetic heritage. The Department of Labor defines eleven aptitudes that contribute to job performance:

· · ·

• Intelligence. General learning ability. The ability to "catch on" or understand instructions and underlying principles; the ability to reason and make judgments. Psychological theorists have begun to define a wide variety of separate, specialized intelligences, from the talent for learning foreign languages to ability to comprehend higher mathematics. For this purpose, "intelligence" is roughly equivalent to the ability to do well in school.

• Verbal. The ability to understand the meaning of words and to use them effectively. The ability to comprehend language; to understand relationships between words and to understand the meaning of whole sentences and paragraphs. Those college-aptitude tests in your senior year of high school put you through your paces in this field. How well did you do?

• Numerical. The ability to perform mathematical operations quickly and accurately. Part of this is training; part of it is not, as most of us are painfully aware. Again, the precollege tests should have given you a good idea of where you stand.

• Spatial perception. The ability to think visually ("see" pictures in your mind) of geometric objects and forms. The ability to "see" the inside and outside of objects in your mind; conceptually to be able to turn them around; and to understand the way objects fit together without actually seeing the objects. It's used in all sorts of mechanical disciplines. Men tend to rate higher in this category than women, but the difference between individuals is a lot greater than the difference between the sexes.

• Form perception. The ability to perceive pertinent detail in objects, pictures, or graphic materials. The ability to make visual comparisons and discriminations and see slight differences in shapes, shadings of figures, and widths and lengths of lines. It is not just artists and illustrators who use this aptitude; quality-control workers who spend their time watching for defects in tiny parts use it constantly.

• Clerical perception. The ability to perceive pertinent detail in verbal, tabular, or written materials. The ability to observe differences in written copy, to proofread words accurately, and to find errors in arithmetic computation. You will never be a good accountant, executive, or lawyer without it.

• Motor coordination. The ability to coordinate your eyes and hands (or fingers) rapidly and accurately in making precise movements with speed. How well do you type?

• Finger dexterity. The ability to move your fingers to manipulate small objects rapidly and accurately. Again, how well do you type?

• Manual dexterity. The ability to move your hands easily and skillfully, to work with your hands in precise and accurate movements. Any kind of assembly work depends on it.

• Eye/hand/foot coordination. The ability to move your hands and feet together in accordance with visual prompting or stimulation in accurate and precise movements. Babe Ruth had it in abundance.

• Color discrimination. The ability to perceive or recognize similarities or differences in colors, or in shades or other values of the same color; to identify a particular color, or to recognize harmonious or contrasting color combinations, or to match colors accurately. You will need it for arts and crafts of all kinds.

There is no particular moral virtue in having any of these abilities, and you may find no great pleasure in exercising any one of them. But more than any other factor, they limit the range of activities you can perform well. They can also be oddly difficult to evaluate for yourself. Just as most of us are convinced that we drive well, no matter that others see us as a menace on the highways, we may have no idea how well our form perception or manual dexterity compares with the ability of others. If you are not certain how you stack up in these areas, it is worth finding out for sure. Compare notes with family and friends, or go back to the library, where a little searching will probably turn up a variety of psychology and self-help books that will give you hard information. Knowing for sure what you are capable of is the first step in finding a new career.

Now values. You are going to be working for a paycheck. That's a given. If you did not need the money, you could spend your life playing golf, or fishing, or doing whatever it is that gives you pleasure in your spare time. But money is more than the buying power it provides: Money is status; money is the satisfaction of knowing that you can provide for your family; in our society, money is the reassurance that others value what you do. It may well be that one of these secondary meanings of money is more important to you than the ability to pay for material goods.

And as we saw in discussing entrepreneurship, there are a lot of other rewards your work can give. Just what is it that makes you feel going to work in the morning is worth the effort it takes to drag yourself out of bed? If your answer is "Nothing!" it's time you found work that does provide the rewards you need. Given your choice of two jobs at the same salary, which of the following values would lead you to pick one instead of the other?

• Achievement. Does it please you to know that your efforts are going toward some long-range, lasting project that is important on its own merits? If you know how the man who built the pyramids felt, you should be looking for a job that promises lasting achievement.

• Challenge. Some of us like the comfort of knowing that we've mastered our jobs. Others find easy work boring and come into our own only when taking on the problems other people find too tough to tackle. If you'd prefer climbing mountains to climbing into a hammock with a good book, challenge is high on your list of values.

• Creativity. Are you the sort who drops helpful notes into suggestion boxes? Do you get a sudden thrill of happiness when a new way to solve an old problem pops into your head? Do you have some artistic talent you have always wanted to develop? It may be time for a creative new career.

• Dominance. Do you like to manage others? To sway them to your point of view? Does it warm your ego when others come to you for guidance? Pure power may be one of your goals.

• Independence. Are you the self-reliant sort? Does it gall you to depend on others? Are you more comfortable setting your own schedule than punching a time clock? Being a self-starter can lead to success in many different fields.

• Moral Values. Do you believe that work builds character? Do you feel guilty when goofing off? Does contributing to a cause give you satisfaction? Your moral code will govern how you feel about your job.

• Personal Relationships. Is work a kind of social activity for you? Do you prefer jobs where you can be part of a team? Does staying at home alone make you feel isolated or depressed? Careers with a high level of interaction should be high on your list.

• Recognition. Does people's respect mean as much to you as money? Are you attracted by glamour and prestige? Do you find yourself backed into fads by social pressure? Think about working for a major corporation or institution whose name people will recognize even if they have not yet learned yours.

• Self-Expression. Are you an original thinker? Do you like to try out your own ideas rather than following set procedures? Was reading your first poem to the class the high point of the year in second grade? People don't all need the chance to express themselves as much as you do; find a job that gives you that opportunity.

• Social Contribution. Are you happiest when helping people in need? Do you spend your spare time working for charity organizations? Do you believe that individuals can make the world a better place to live? Find a job where you can help others, and you'll help yourself.

• Variety. Does it take constant change to keep you from feeling bored? Are you at your best when meeting new people and seeing new places? Are you most productive when you can do several different kinds of work each day? Variety is the spice of your working life.

This list of values that can be important in choosing a new career is far from complete, but it should help you to a better understanding of your needs.

If none of these items draws a strong response from you, it may help to look at your own experience. What was the best job you ever had? What made it so good? How about the worst job you ever had? What made it so awful? A few minutes spent reviewing the good and bad features of all the jobs you've held should make it clearer just what to look for and what to avoid in future.

Do not make too many judgments when looking at what matters to you in a job. Feeling that you really should contribute to society is not the same as finding pleasure in doing so. The more effort you put into finding what matters, and the more honestly you approach the task, the better are your chances of being happy in the job that carries you through the '90s.

Where do you fit into the job market? That question brings us at last to your education and experience. Poring over your old jobs is just the first step in this part of your stock-taking. The focus here is not on what you have done, but on what you can do. You must search your past for all the marketable, perhaps long-neglected, skills you have learned, both on the job and off. Many of them can be transferred to other jobs, even other industries, some of which may be more viable in the 1990s than your current field.

Start at the beginning. What did you learn in school? Don't limit yourself to thinking about your college major. Even if you dropped out of high school, you may well have picked up something that will help today. A half-forgotten typing class could make it a lot easier to master a computerized accounting system than it would be for someone who can't find his way around a keyboard. What about foreign languages? It is not just importers and exporters who need to communicate with non–English speakers. In the Southwest, many potential employees speak only Spanish. Being able to communicate in their native language could save you a lot of management problems. Your high school shop class could grow into a thriving business in machining or furniture-making. If you were on the football team, remember the drive and willingness to take your lumps that other players beat into you on the field. You're going to need them again.

How about on-the-job training? OJT is not just your employer's courses in company procedure. It's your firsthand (or even second-hand) experience in solving business problems. If you are a manager, you've seen what the finance department does, and sales and marketing, and how they accomplish their tasks. If you have not handled management duties yourself, at least you have had the chance to see how they work from the receiving end. If you have ever worked on an assembly line, you know a major part of production firsthand, and you could probably tell personnel specialists a lot about how to run a shop without provoking labor problems. Go over all your experience, all your observations, and figure out just what you've learned without noticing that you were learning. It could come in handy.

Don't forget any skills learned from hobbies or volunteer work. It's not that large a jump from fixing your own car to being paid for working on other people's. And the only thing that separates chairing a service-group committee from managing similar working groups on the job is getting someone to let you try.

At this point, you should have a fairly clear idea of what you bring to a new job and what you hope to get from it. Your next task is to match those abilities and needs with specific employment opportunities. At long last, you are nearing the end of *the first step* in finding your way to a secure future.

After the rigors of self-assessment, identifying careers that you might find suitable should be relatively easy. One reason is that so many people have passed this way before. In weighing your aptitudes,

values, and experience, you are working with a unique set of characteristics; in all the world, there is only one you. But there is an entire
profession full of career counselors, and they have devised a variety
of tools that can guide the way from your own special combination
of assets to a career that you and many other people might find
satisfying. Two of the best are the Holland career-planning model,
devised by psychologist John L. Holland of Johns Hopkins University,
and the *Jobs of the Future Career Guidance Assay,* created by Marvin
Cetron and counselor James C. Gonyea of the University of New
Hampshire. For now, let's see what Dr. Holland has to offer.

Holland divided people into six general categories, based on their
personality traits and the interests that tend to go with them. Then he
grouped occupations according to which type of personality would
find them rewarding. In theory, once you have figured out your aptitudes and interests, you should be able to recognize yourself in one
of Holland's personality groups and then pick a career from the list
of matching jobs. Simplistic as it sounds, the process works pretty
well.

Here are the six categories, with typical jobs that suit them:

Realistic. These people are practical, stable folk, strongly rooted in
the real world. No neurotic self-doubt or manipulation games here,
just frank, self-reliant types. In Holland's scheme, realists are technically and athletically inclined, happiest when working with their
hands and with tools, often outdoors. Not for them such careers as
teaching or psychotherapy, or anything else that demands working
with people. If they have weaknesses, they are probably a little re-
pelled by self-expression and by new ideas. Farmers and forest rang-
ers fit into this group. So do most engineers, draftsmen, and
machinists.

Conventional. Picture a stereotypical banker, and you are looking at
one of Holland's conventional people: controlled, conscientious, orderly. You will find them working with words and numbers, carrying
out detailed instructions. Give them a system every time. Ambiguous,
open-ended, unstructured situations drive them up them wall. Accountants, computer programmers, medical-records technologists,
and good secretaries all fit into this category.

• • •

Investigative. Biologists and chemists, doctors and detectives, mathematicians and economists all have the investigator's traits: analytical minds, powerful curiosity, and a taste for precision. They prefer to work on their own, ferreting out the answers to complex, abstract problems. Science is their home terrain, but you'll find them anywhere that independent observation, learning, and problem-solving are required.

Social. What do good teachers, psychologists, social workers, and speech pathologists all have in common? They tend to be sociable, tactful, understanding people, eager to help others. Machinery and hard physical labor are not for them, but they come into their own when working with others who need information, training, or other forms of help. And Holland classifies them all as social people.

Enterprising. Remember that taste for dominance we asked about earlier? These people have it in spades. They are persuasive, ambitious, and energetic. Like the social types, they enjoy dealing with people; but their goal is not to help, it's to manipulate, to lead. They are not like the conventional people they usually wind up managing; precision and systems leave them feeling trapped. So do long hours of intellectual work. Career salesmen, lawyers, politicians, and generals all belong in this category.

Artistic. Like investigative people, the artists deal in ideas. But where scientists analyze, artistic people create. Imagination is their domain; structure, rigid rules, and physical labor their bane. People in this category tend to be idealistic and intuitive, with a strong drive toward self-expression. Writers, artists, musicians, and philosophers all fit this description.

If you are like most people, you will find that you have traits in common with the people in two or three of Holland's categories. That can be an advantage, because it opens more possible careers to you than any single set of interests and skills would. It also makes it possible to combine differing talents in productive ways. Scientists—investigative types—from Isaac Asimov to Carl Sagan have discovered their artistic side and built enormously successful careers as writers. Literally hundreds of firmly realistic engineers have used enterprising talents to build their own companies. You may also find some fertile ways to use traits that Holland's model places in separate categories.

If you have already taken the time to probe your own inner workings, you probably have a far better idea now of what matters to you in a career than you did when you began this chapter. (If not, it may be best to seek out professional career guidance to help you around whatever is blocking your progress.) All that remains is to look systematically at all the hundreds of occupations—out of tens of thousands!—which give you the best chance of weathering an economic storm. One of them, and more likely several, should fit your needs exactly. Take notes at every step of the way. Finding a recessionproof career is just like any other job: Be systematic and diligent about it, and success will come a lot more easily.

You might begin your search for a specific job by subscribing to some out-of-town newspapers, especially if you live in one of the country's depressed labor markets. A look at the help-wanteds from Austin, Texas; Orlando, Florida; Nashua, New Hampshire; and a few other fast-growing cities could help to guide your search in productive directions. And when you sit down to find an occupation that meets your criteria, it can help to know that somewhere in the country, even if it is a thousand miles away, someone actually wants people with the skills you either have to offer or hope to learn.

There are two ways to figure out which of the thousands of jobs available in the United States best fit your needs and abilities. One is long and difficult, the other relatively quick and easy. The long, hard way is to do it all yourself: Go to your local library, and sift through two key reference books published by the U.S. Department of Labor. The *Dictionary of Occupational Titles* is a huge compendium of job descriptions. Once familiar with the nine-digit code used to classify each occupation—making sense of it will take some practice—you can look up jobs that require a given set of aptitudes or skills, find out what physical demands they will make on you, check out their working conditions and educational requirements, and in general figure out how closely they meet your needs. (This is one area in which an experienced counselor can help shorten your search.) The *Occupational Outlook Handbook* narrows the list to several hundred of the most common jobs. In addition to describing the nature of each occupation, it attempts to forecast the number of jobs likely to be available in each field and the salary you can hope to earn. (Similar forecasts can be found in Appendix B. We have spent considerable effort in updating the Labor Department predictions, which are several years out of date.) The *Handbook* is best used to filter out jobs that are obviously being made obsolete by technological or economic changes. Bear in mind that technology has not stood still since it was written; many of the jobs that seemed promising then have now joined the endangered-occupations list. Wading through these two volumes is a good deal of work, but it will eventually get you where you want to go.

Then there is the easy way. We mentioned it earlier in this chapter: The *Jobs of the Future Career Guidance Assay*. It was created as a supplement to Marvin Cetron's book *Jobs of the Future* (McGraw-Hill, 1984), a forecast of the 500 best employment opportunities of the 1990s. The assay is designed to ease both halves of the job hunt: figuring out what you want from a new occupation and identifying specific jobs that meet your criteria. In part, it works on much the same principles as the Holland profile, systematically analyzing your personality traits and interests. Its advantage over previous counseling tools is in the second step. The test is keyed to the fast-growing, technically oriented jobs that will prosper even as the careers that comfortably supported the last generation continue to disappear. You can be sure it will not aim you toward a dead end; no matter how well your aptitudes fit you for mechanical tasks, it will not suggest that you find a job on a Detroit assembly line!

The *Jobs of the Future Career Guidance Assay* is reproduced as Appendix C at the end of this book. Suitable employment possibilities are listed in Appendix B as having a fast growth rate during the next decade. Look at the job forecasts in Appendix B, then take the test and look at the jobs again. Doing this on your own should give you a head start in your search for a more promising career. For a professional analysis of your best options, you are invited to write down your answers to the assay questions and forward them to Jobs of the Future, Inc., at the address listed in Appendix C. (To make things easier, you can write and request a formal test book and answer sheet.) We know of no more efficient way of reorganizing your working life to cope with the turbulent years to come.

• • •

At this point, one way or the other, you should have identified several possible careers, any one of which would give you the security —not to mention satisfaction—that may be missing from your present employment. Of course, that is only the first step in building a more secure, rewarding future.

By far your most important tool in finding a new career is the right education. Chances are that you don't have it. Though only one American in four goes to college, nearly all high school students are pushed through college-preparatory programs that leave them unready to compete in the real world. In future, a much better grasp of the traditional "three Rs" will be taken for granted, while most other subjects that schools now teach, or claim to, will be even less relevant than they are today.

Basic computer skills will soon be necessary, even for low-level employment. We cannot stress this point strongly enough: If you are not comfortable with computers, if you are not "computer literate," it will be much harder to find a new career, or to make progress in the one you have. The difference between being a typist and being a word-processing specialist is several thousand dollars per year and often several months of job hunting. That difference is spreading rapidly from one end of the job spectrum to the other. Already, many of the nation's welders have been replaced by robots; the one survivor in their department was the welder who, by the time the machines arrived, had learned to program them. Middle-level executives are no safer. Those who pride themselves on being above such menial matters as typing, even on a computer, may have as long as five years to recognize their mistake; after that, their job will go to someone who cares more about getting the job done efficiently than about keeping his fingers off the keyboard.

All this is not to say that simply learning to use a computer will guarantee you a bright future. Computers are tools like any other; they will not do you any good at work if you don't know your job in the first place. But if you cannot use a computer, you will soon find yourself in the position of a carpenter who can wield only a handsaw competing against users of power tools. It's a position you do not want to be in.

You can find basic computer training at virtually any vocational school, high school, or college. Most offer night courses for adults who work during the day. Many computer shops offer similar classes, though at greater cost. And for those who can make a greater commitment, nothing beats buying your own computer, picking up some introductory books, and joining your local computer club, where dedicated hobbyists will be able to teach you virtually anything you have interest enough to learn. However you accomplish it, learn what a computer is for and how it can be applied to your chosen career. The knowledge will repay your effort many times over.

Most jobs will require specialized training as well. Some of what you need may be available where you work today. Many major companies offer in-house training designed to improve job performance and to aid in changing positions within the firm. IBM, for example, now spends some $900 million per year on employee education. Many in-house courses are dedicated to specialized skills that may not contribute to your career change. But many companies offer generalized education, from remedial English to advanced math. If you work for one of the Fortune 500, you can be sure that opportunities are as close as the company's human-resources department. Discovering your employer's educational program can greatly ease the task of training for a new career.

Local high schools, vocational schools, and colleges nearly all offer continuing-education programs in a wide variety of fields, many of them suited to the career changer's needs. In the last decade, colleges especially have adapted their programs to working adults. While these programs vary widely in their educational standards—the continuing-ed courses at many colleges are far less rigorous than the institution's daytime classes—many are of high quality, and all offer at least a place to start the process of training for a new career.

Finally, do not overlook that menacing appliance now found in many households: the home computer. Thanks largely to the growing demand from the nation's high schools, software makers have published tutorial programs on topics ranging from Civil War history to calculus. Many more such automated learning tools will appear each day for the foreseeable future. Though few of the programs now available offer specific vocational training, many can help to shore up weaknesses in such basic skills as typing, grammar, and mathematics. For that purpose, computerized learning programs may be the quickest, easiest way to begin training for a new career.

Just how much specialized vocational training you need will naturally depend on the career you choose. Turning a hobby of tinkering with cars into a new profession as an auto mechanic could be as easy as announcing that you are open for business. Becoming an emergency medical technician requires two years of hard study, only part of which will be available at night. How well you can cope with these demands may help decide whether a given career is the right choice for you.

For most of us, retraining will be a matter of grinding through night courses while holding down a full-time job. If that is not possible, either because night classes are not available in your chosen field or because your current job cannot be contained in its theoretical 9-to-5 schedule, there are several alternatives, none of them easy. If your spouse works, you can quit your job and make do on one salary until you are qualified to find work in your new field; if not, perhaps he or she can take a job. If you are certain that your current job will not last, you can plan ahead and go to school as soon as the ax falls, supporting your family on the combination of unemployment compensation and your spouse's income. In some fields, it is possible to get a job before your training is complete and learn the rest while being paid and enjoying such fringe benefits as health insurance and vacations. One way or another, the price must be paid. If you cannot make the time to train for your chosen career, it may be necessary to find some other line of work for which the educational demands are easier to meet.

For vocational training in many fields, including computer technology and other high-tech skills, it may help to move to one of the nation's fastest-growing job markets as soon as you choose your new career. Florida offers what is probably the best program of vocational education in the country. In fact, the high quality of vocational training in Florida is one of the major attractions that have led IBM, DEC, and many other companies to locate their artificial-intelligence research units in the long corridor from Orlando to Tampa–St. Petersburg. Today, Florida's voc-ed program is as strong as ever, and its graduates have a host of would-be employers waiting for them at the schoolhouse door.

In the long run, it may be that the most important thing you learn in training for a new career is the skill of learning itself. Within the next decade, roughly 4 percent of workers are expected to be in some kind of training program each year. Many of us will find ourselves going through the whole process of job changing every ten years, with all the specialized reeducation that implies. The learning skills you acquire in this first, forced step into the turbulent future will be used constantly for the rest of your working life.

That leaves the last step: finding a new job once you have trained for it. There is nothing we can add here to the advice you will find in Don Bolles's fine book *What Color Is Your Parachute?* (Ten Speed Press, updated yearly). When the time comes to go job hunting, pick up a copy of Bolles's how-to, and follow his suggestions. You will probably find that stepping into a whole new career in a fast-growing industry is a good deal less painful than it would have been to find a new job in your old line of work.

Well, after all your work, *something* should be easy. We never said that choosing a new career would be, even with the *Jobs of the Future* test to help. And certainly training for it will not be, not while holding down your current job. But these are exercises that will serve you well, no matter what happens to the economy. In the worst case, survival will be a lot easier if you can find your way into a depression-proof job in a fast-growing area. And in the postrecession years of the late 1990s, or the boom years that the entire decade could be (given sensible economic policies in Washington), your chances of prosperity and happiness will be a lot brighter if you plan your career well today.

11
A TIME OF OPPORTUNITY

THROUGHOUT THIS BOOK, we have hedged our bets about whether the United States and its trading partners are headed for a recession or depression. The simple fact is that we don't know. Neither does anyone else, much as some professional pundits want you to think otherwise. We would like to believe that world trade will flourish as it has since the early 1980s, led in the future by a more vigorous American economy; this is surely possible. In fact, we suspect that it will continue much as it has, muddling through as best it can while burdened by the excesses of a United States whose leaders find it politically impossible to follow responsible fiscal or economic policies. Yet even this limited hope rests on our belief that these same politicians will significantly reduce the national budget deficit. To date, there has been little to justify optimism on that score; economic disaster thus remains frighteningly possible.

But for the purposes of this book, it does not matter whether the early 1990s bring the worst of times or the best. As we have already seen, the economies of the United States and its trading partners are now undergoing a metamorphosis in which electronic technology will supplement human skill, and in many cases replace it, much as machines replaced human muscle in the 19th and early 20th centuries. If the economy flourishes early in the coming decade, companies will rush to adopt the new varieties of automation in order to match their competition. If it collapses, the least automated, most vulnerable companies will go under almost immediately, and the shortage of investment capital will delay the economic transformation until the late 1990s. Either way, many traditionally desirable jobs will be lost, and a host of new, well-paid, technically sophisticated jobs will soon go begging for trained people to fill them, even as armies of the unemployed search for the vanished work they were trained to perform. If not tomorrow, then within ten years, many of us will be forced to train for new careers, even while struggling to earn a living. Our economic survival will depend on it.

For the moment, let us assume the worst: In 1990, perhaps as late as 1992, the American economy will collapse, taking the nation's trading partners down with it. Mass unemployment will result.

What then?

After six or seven years, the crash of the 1990s will be over; business will recover, slowly at first, but ever faster; then international trade will find new life; and a new, more permanent boom will begin. For those lucky enough to survive the chaos relatively unharmed or strong enough to build new lives from adversity, the years that follow will bring prosperity now available only to a few. We could subtitle this chapter "What all the 1990s should have been, and might still be," for this optimistic picture of the future ten years hence is no more than we could expect almost immediately if our leaders in Washington took our economy as seriously as they do their next election campaigns.

The boom will lift both manufacturing and the service industries. As it progresses, virtually all segments of the U.S. economy will come to demand as many trained technicians as a modernized educational system can turn out. Because these are skilled employees, they will be well paid. Eventually, the local McDonald's will install automated burger makers, because human workers no longer need accept whatever boring job will bring them the minimum wage.

Even if we avoid a recession or depression in the 1990s, the transition to a new, more prosperous economy will be far from painless. In all the industrialized nations, it will be bought at the cost of jobs that now support millions of workers and their families. Nowhere will that pain arrive sooner or be more severe than in the United States, where we habitually talk about the future but seldom prepare for it.

The growing interdependence of the world economy has created a demand for ever-greater productivity throughout industry. Japan's total dependence on imported energy and raw materials has forced its industries to build better products with less human effort and to improve their performance each year. South Korea, Taiwan, and the other Pacific nations have fought even harder for their share of the world's prosperity. These countries have set a standard of output and quality that American workers have yet to equal. Yet if we are to repay the enormous international borrowing of the 1980s, we must not merely equal that standard but improve on it. This is the great force bringing change to the U.S. economy.

Its tools are automation and the bimodal economy, in which both large and small companies flourish, while mid-sized firms go under. Automation makes up for all the shortcomings of human workers: Robots and flexible manufacturing systems are relatively cheap, fast, consistent, easily trained for new tasks, and unlikely to strike for higher wages and benefits. Products built by machines cost less and suffer fewer defects than those made by human hands. Moreover, machines are rapidly becoming easier to find than trained or trainable workers; the declining birthrate and low educational standards have seen to that.

The bimodal economy has other benefits in an increasingly competitive world: Large companies enjoy the classical economies of scale. Raw materials are cheaper for them, management costs are lower, and they find it easier to amass the capital to invest in modern equipment and to survive a profit-bruising battle with competitors. Small businesses find it easier to deliver personal service, not only in such traditional service industries as housecleaning and travel planning, but in manufacturing and marketing as well. As automation comes to dominate our economic and professional lives, demand for that personal touch will grow steadily. As future entrepreneurs recognize this potential market, products and services tailored to individual customers will become an ever larger and more profitable part of the economy. But mid-sized companies, saddled with relatively high expenses and able neither to automate as quickly as their larger competitors nor to provide the personal service of smaller firms, will continue to disappear from the economic scene. Either they will go out of business, or they will be absorbed by the giants of their industries.

In the short run, these changes mean widespread unemployment of the kind we have already seen in the industrialized North-Central States. Automation replaces human workers, leaving them searching for employment and prepared only for jobs that no longer exist. Computers also make it possible for one manager to oversee as many as twenty workers, rather than the six found in traditional corporate structures. Thus, companies are eliminating whole levels of middle management, and white-collar employees have become just as vulnerable to sudden loss of their careers as assembly-line personnel. Because the computer revolution is only just beginning to change management methods, the executive purge will gain momentum in the next decade.

Yet in only a few years, these same forces will bring new opportunities for prosperity. As the computer and health-care industries continue to grow explosively, they will demand a vast new supply of technically trained workers. Telecommunications, biotechnology, legal services, and old-fashioned teaching will face similar shortages of skilled personnel. With government assistance, business will meet this need by training and retraining hundreds of thousands of people who today have little hope of finding a highly paid career. These new members of the middle class will provide a new market for goods and services, adding to consumer demand. This will stimulate business and further increase the need for trained, well-paid workers. And so on, in a very beneficial cycle.

As the high salaries of tomorrow's professionals spread new wealth throughout the economy, automation will cut the cost of goods. By the year 2000 (somewhat later if an economic collapse delays this transformation), human workers (aided by automation) will be five times as productive as they are today, and the goods they make will cost half as much. A car like today's Toyota Camry, which with a few accessories sells for about $14,000, will cost only $7,000—and be made by an American manufacturer. (More precisely, as a percentage of tomorrow's average salary, it will cost the equivalent of $7,000 today.) Thus, in real terms, most of us will soon be twice as rich as we are today; the American standard of living will soar.

Rising affluence and the spread of technology will improve our lives in other ways. Computer-controlled, manufactured homes will bring new comfort and convenience within reach of the average worker. One-fourth of us will work in those homes, linked to our jobs only by our telecommunications equipment and our paychecks. More than 500,000 of us each year will start our own businesses, seeking a chance at genuine wealth. As the need to spend a set working period at a factory or office fades away, flexible working hours—

only thirty-two per week—and job sharing will become popular ways both to ease the task of earning a living and to provide incomes to more workers. In off hours, the huge new middle class will enjoy international travel, adventure tours and luxury cruises, and a host of other diversions now reserved for the wealthy.

We will have more years in which to enjoy those pleasures, and not only because of breakthroughs in medical care. In preparing to become the professionals demanded by tomorrow's economy, we will have to improve our education, and well-educated people are traditionally more conscious of their health than others. Thus, more of us will pay attention to the four basics of "wellness": regular exercise, proper diet, avoidance of tobacco and other "recreational" drugs, and finding relief from stress. Our life spans will stretch much longer than today's actuaries project.

That education will continue throughout our lives. It must. Even today, half of an engineer's professional knowledge is obsolete in five years. That will be equally true in many of the new technical specialties that will appear in the next decade. In order to retain almost any job that pays well, we will have to retrain constantly. Of course, if we are taking classes anyway, we can also train for some other profession. Job mobility in the future will make today's peripatetic workers seem as locked to their employers as their parents were thirty years ago.

This new economic order has one great flaw: There is no place in it for the poorly educated or for those with obsolete skills. Even today, there is little room for the educationally disadvantaged. Only 18 percent of jobs are open to high school dropouts; that is quickly declining to 14 percent—a way station on the route to even lower levels. Today 22 percent of jobs require a college education or an advanced degree; in the next decade, that will climb to nearly one-third. These changes are being felt in the workers' wallets. In 1986, men with a high school education earned 28 percent less (adjusted for inflation) than in 1973.

There is every reason to believe this trend will continue. Only seven years from now, fully 80 percent of jobs will demand some kind of education beyond the high school level. The nature of that training will change more than the simple statistic reveals; two jobs out of three will require specialized vocational classes, either instead of or in addition to a traditional liberal-arts college program. And that job-specific education will teach skills far different from those which support today's remaining factory workers and farmers. Technical training is the only visa that will gain admission to the prosperity of the late 1990s and early 21st century.

What will happen to people who lack this necessary entrée? Some will take dead-end service jobs, only to discover that they too succumb to automation. Others will find their way into training programs run by companies desperate to find any workers they can get. The rest may well join an underclass of the permanently unemployable, doomed to live on "workfare," trading menial labor for public support until they can correct the flaws in their basic education and train for a technical career. Even after the public and private educational systems gear up for the new demands soon to be placed on them, this will require years of effort. Many will find that a defective education is an obstacle never to be overcome.

Though some of the new disadvantaged will be the school dropouts and chronic indigents who cannot make it even in today's economy, many will be men and women who have worked conscientiously and supported themselves all their adult lives. Their only sin will be their failure to adapt to an increasingly technological world before their old way of life collapsed around them. More than half of the factory workers who lost their jobs during the early 1980s have already found that there is no place for their skills in today's economy.

If your training is general-purpose and nontechnical, there is little hope of retaining your current way of life. There will be assembly-line workers and middle managers in the 21st century, just as there are drywall plasterers, blacksmiths, and even buggy-whip makers today. But for most such people, the fact that a few of their colleagues retained their jobs will be little consolation.

There are two ways to meet the coming cataclysm. One way is to do nothing and trust that you will find some way to make a living when your old job is gone. In the short run, that is by far the easier approach. But the price is high: Eventually, you will find yourself scrambling to learn a new career while living on welfare or borrowing from friends and relatives in order to survive. The other way is to begin now, choose a new career, train for it while working full time at the job you now have, and perhaps then move to an area where high-tech jobs are more plentiful than they are where you live today.

It means paying for classes, most likely with money needed for more immediate purposes, studying nights and weekends, losing sleep, sacrificing holidays and vacations, and reverting to the student habits reluctantly learned in childhood. For the moment, all this will be far more difficult than plodding on as though we still lived in the world of the 1950s. But in the long run, it means that you will be able to slip into your new career without the pain of long-term unemployment.

The 1990s will usher in a time of growing freedom and prosperity —for those who plan and work for it today. We will be able to choose our jobs, our working conditions, our careers, and our amusements from a vast array of possible lifestyles now either unavailable or far out of reach for most American workers. And then, we will be able to change our minds and make new choices at any moment. It is up to us to make the most of our new opportunities. The time to begin is now.

APPENDIX A:
SKIRTING THE ABYSS

THOUGH NEW TECHNOLOGY must replace many of today's jobs, it is entirely possible to avoid the economic crash that now seems destined to disrupt the employment market further. We need only balance the Federal budget without confiscatory taxation, pay off our foreign debt, and, for long-term security, reform our educational system to give high school graduates the skills they need to compete in the modern world.

As Chapter 1 made clear, any plan that seeks to balance the Federal budget without causing at least a severe recession must cut Federal spending to a size that we can support and avoid a heavy tax burden that would discourage savings and investment. In theory, nothing could be easier; the thousands of pages of that intimidating document offer up gobbets of fat for the carver's knife in almost every program. But that theory ignores political reality.

One significant drain on our national income simply cannot be cut. It consists of interest payments on the national debt—roughly $129 billion per year by the end of 1985 and estimated at $150 billion in fiscal year 1988. The only way to reduce them is to repay our foreign loans faster than the interest mounts up. The alternative is to default on repayment of foreign loans—and learn to live without borrowing the offshore dollars to which the government has become addicted.

Two more areas of government spending have been nearly as difficult to cut: the defense budget and entitlement programs. The defense budget, ferociously defended by conservative politicians, is expected to account for $291 billion in fiscal 1988, or nearly one-third of government spending. Entitlement programs, such as Social Security and Medicare, are just as vigorously defended by liberals; they will eat up just less than 47 percent of the FY 1988 budget, some $506 billion.

That leaves discretionary nondefense spending for such commitments as foreign aid, Federally funded medical research, and the NASA space program. These are the easy cuts, with few defenders and those easy to ignore. Thus, these programs have already been hit hard by previous attempts to trim the budget. Net real investment to build and maintain our roads, bridges, and other public works has shrunk by 75 percent over the last twenty years. Research fell by 25 percent from 1979 to 1986. Aid to schools was cut by 14 percent. And when it comes to balancing the Federal budget, these cuts are virtually meaningless. The total bill for all forms of discretionary nondefense spending will come to only $189 billion in 1988. Cut *all* such programs, and the Federal budget will still be in the red.

So, though there is a little more to be squeezed from discretionary spending, the burden of budget cuts must fall on defense and entitlements. Murray Weidenbaum, formerly chairman of President Reagan's Council of Economic Advisers and now director of the Center for the Study of American Business at Washington University, recently suggested in his book *Rendezvous with Reality* ten programs ripe for the cutting. They make a good place to begin the search. Most of them make it all too clear how difficult it will be to gain political support for truly effective budget cuts. Here is Dr. Weidenbaum's list, supplemented with a few thoughts of our own:

• The Veterans Administration hospitals were built to care for servicemen who had been injured in the service of their country. Instead, they have turned into a source of free medical care for every ex-draftee who breaks his leg while skiing. So eliminate VA-hospital stays for those whose medical problems have nothing to do with their military service. Then stop building VA hospitals in cities where there are already enough private and public hospitals to serve the region.
• Either retire NASA's space shuttles permanently, or take them off the civilian budget and hand them over either to the military or to private industry. True, operating them does not cost much more than $5 billion per year, but few space scientists believe their contribution to research merits even that relatively small expense.
• Eliminate farm price supports. Do it gradually, over a few years, to soften the blow. But do it. Federal government subsidies to agriculture totaled about $25 billion last year, nearly one-third of net farm income. Much of that money went to huge corporate farms that would have survived quite well without the aid.
• Stop building needless dams and other huge pork-barrel projects. For many years now, most projects built by the Bureau of Reclamation and the Corps of Engineers have been little more than disguised subsidies to local businessmen.
• Cut aid to the few countries that soak up most of our foreign-aid dollars. That includes Israel, its Arab neighbors, and most of South America, where all too many of these donations end up in the pockets of the politicians whose citizens are supposed to receive them.
• Put a cap on Cost-of-Living Adjustments for Social Security benefits. Contrary to popular belief, COLAs do not come from the contributions that recipients paid into the system during their working years; they are stolen from the pockets of the generations still working. It is simply unfair to take from the Baby Boom generation—and soon, from *their* children—money that will never be repaid.
• Raise the military retirement age to 50. And let's make servicemen stay in

for 25 years as well. As it stands, those with 20 years of active duty can retire at 40 and receive half to three-fourths of their maximum salary for life—adjusted each year to compensate for inflation—no matter how much additional income they earn. Only one recipient in four is now over age 65. Most go on to a second pension-paying career. They are eligible for Social Security as well. There is no reason personnel in a peacetime military should be accorded such costly privileges. (In wartime, we could give them two years of credit for each year of hazardous duty.) It would be unfair to change the rules for today's military personnel, but the potential career soldier who enlists tomorrow morning should have something that resembles a full-length career in store.

• Change the way Federal salaries are computed. Regulations dictate that government employees should be paid as much as those doing similar jobs in the private sector. Fair enough. But add in the generous fringe benefits that Federal employees also receive. Those benefits were adopted as a way to attract people who otherwise would have gone into industry at a time when government salaries were relatively low. But those salaries have essentially caught up with private pay scales. There is no reason to continue such generous benefits as well. It is not just salaries that should be indexed against the private sector, but total compensation packages.

In addition, we should consider eliminating the Civil Service retirement program and enroll government employees under Social Security. Doing so would provide them with the same benefits the rest of us receive and add needed funds to the Social Security pool. It's hard to say exactly how much money this would save, but there is no doubt it would be a substantial sum.

• Repeal the Federal controls on private construction wages that were enacted in the depression-era Davis-Bacon Act. At this point, their sole effect is to raise the cost of government building projects.

• And charge normal, market-level interest rates for Federal loans. Higher prices always reduce demand, and we have other, more pressing uses for that money.

As Weidenbaum points out, "These ten proposals would arouse the opposition of organizations representing veterans, farmers, senior citizens, unions, aerospace companies, construction interests, and both Arabs and Zionists. And we have not yet tackled the large budgets for defense and welfare."

The defense budget may be the easier to cut. We are not going to advocate anything that resembles unilateral disarmament. Anyone who thinks America's best defense—or the world's—is to be so inoffensive that no self-respecting nation would stoop to attacking our interests should rethink his position, preferably after carrying a fat wallet around New York City's Central Park for a few hours on a warm summer night. But Pentagon spending is replete with appropriations that either do nothing to improve our defense posture or should be paid for by others. Five items come to mind immediately:

• The Strategic Defense Initiative, or "Star Wars." The problem with Star Wars is not that it won't work. Hear and believe: It is perfectly possible to design and build an effective space-based antimissile defense system, no matter how much some antidefense activists would like to hide the fact. Whether it could completely shield American civilians against Soviet missiles or merely ensure that our own ICBMs survived to retaliate is still open to question, but it really does not matter. Either would make nuclear war impractical, even in the eyes of the most hawkish military planner.

The real problem is cost. As nearly as Forecasting International can figure it, a fully deployed space defense system would cost roughly three times America's Gross National Product. Our entire defense budget comes to roughly 7 percent of our GNP. It is hard to say that the hope of eliminating the threat of nuclear war is not worth the price. But when the time comes to deploy the products of today's research and the voters recognize that the bill adds up to long-term poverty for the country that builds its long-sought shield, the program will die instantly. Killing it now could save tens of billions of dollars. Exactly how much is unclear, because the budget for Star Wars is classified.

• The 600-ship Navy. The Navy has two kinds of ships: submarines and targets. To date, we have specialized in building targets. It costs us some $750 million to pull a World War II battleship out of mothballs, a mistake we have made four times during the current military buildup, and that seems cheap next to the cost of the huge carrier flotillas that now form the centerpiece of American naval strategy—and an unmissable bull's-eye for nuclear missiles. In an all-out war, their life expectancy is less than three days—far too brief for them to make any major contribution to a defense effort. And in a conventional war, they are too ponderous to serve any useful role. Midway and the other gigantic sea battles of the Pacific theater are only fading memories; they will never be fought again. Massive troop movement is now better served by air transport, and in any case is not the role for which today's Navy was designed. Shelling of enemy strongholds can be replaced by missiles and long-range bombers. And blockading enemy harbors, the one remaining use for a large navy in a conventional war, is more effectively done by submarines, mining, or even small, high-speed surface craft, as used by Iran in the Persian Gulf.

All this is not to say that surface ships have suddenly become useless. There is still a place for small, fast—and relatively cheap—surface-effect ships and hydrofoils that can get from place to place faster than an enemy can conveniently draw a bead on them. The Navy must learn the tactic the Army calls "dash and hide": Hit the enemy as hard as possible, and then disappear. If the Navy is not willing to trust small surface vessels for the task, submarines with a working depth of only 10 or 20 feet would be even more effective and little more expensive. So let's stop building targets and, as soon as possible, retire the ones we have.

• The Rapid Deployment Force. The Army supports the two divisions of the so-called "Rapid Deployment Force" at enormous cost. This is among the most wasteful items in the military budget, for at least three reasons. Their state of readiness, though far better than during the budget-starved Carter years, remains deplorable; officers within the RDF itself privately concede that they could hardly invade Hoboken, NJ, with an effective fighting force in less than a month. Further, we are unlikely to need the RDF so long as the President must report to Congress when committing American troops to a combat zone. Though the Rapid Deployment Force was mildly useful in our well-planned, poorly executed assault on Grenada, the days of sudden scrambles to the battlefield by substantial invasion forces are past. And finally, there are the U.S. Marines. The traditional role of the Marines is to carry out amphibious landings on hostile shores, and shoulder-mounted missiles such as the Stinger have made that role obsolete. One enemy soldier can now sink a landing craft every few minutes until his ammunition runs out, killing all 250 Marines on board and destroying two tanks. So reorganize the Marines to do effectively what the Rapid Deployment Force can hardly do at all. It will save us several hundred million dollars a year; the exact amount is classified.

• Overseas military commitments. The United States has mutual-defense treaties with about forty countries across the globe. Near the end of the Vietnam War, we had more than one million troops overseas. The figure still stands at about 540,000. These commitments represent an unjustifiable subsidy to the very trading partners whose corporations, unburdened by taxes that would otherwise be needed to defend their own countries, are trouncing ours in international trade. It is time our allies paid for their own defense. If they do not want to support their own military, or like Japan are forbidden to field a large army by their constitution, they can start paying a fair price for the use of ours.

Consider only our commitments in Europe and Asia. Next to them, our spending for such adventures as our intervention in Lebanon under President Carter and President Reagan's Persian Gulf flotilla seem almost free.

The world has changed dramatically since the United States agreed to defend our then-new allies, Germany and Japan. Even before the Second World War, the United States made about one-third of the world's manufactured goods. Nazi Germany accounted for about one-sixth, and Japanese industry produced only 3 percent or so of the world's goods. By 1945, America manufactured fully half of the world's industrial output, and the factories of Germany and Japan had been reduced to rubble. (By contrast, at the peak of its power, Britain accounted for only one-fourth of the world's manufactured goods.) Today, the European Common Market is the second-largest economic bloc in the world. Japan ranks third, though on a per capita basis it comes in first.

And still we spend vastly more to defend Europe and Asia than those regions spend on themselves. In 1986, our budget for the defense of Europe was $134 billion—and that does not include nuclear weapons; Europe itself spent only $83 billion on defense. That same year, we sank $42 billion into our Asian military forces. Japan spends only 1 percent of its Gross National

Product on defense; in FY 1988 that will come to $22 billion. And maintaining our 43,000 soldiers in South Korea costs $4.8 billion per year, more than three-fifths of our trade deficit with that country. Neither country can afford to have the United States pull its troops out of Asia. Both should be easily persuaded to pay a substantial part of the cost of keeping them there.

In Europe, at least, our 350,000 soldiers are hardly needed. West Germany alone has some 500,000 men under arms, and former West German Chancellor Helmut Schmidt concedes that 800,000 more can be called up in less than a week.

So: Bring the soldiers home. Or make the countries we defend pay for the benefits they receive. Returning just 100,000 of our soldiers in Europe—fewer than one-third of the men stationed there—would save the United States at least $30 billion per year.

• Military pensions. Murray Weidenbaum is right. Though classified as an entitlement program and not appropriated as part of the Pentagon budget, in the long run these will be the costliest defense-related expense of all. Unlike Social Security, military pensions do not come from a trust fund paid into during the working years. They are one more drain down which we pour tax dollars. Raising the military retirement age to 50 is just a start. We should also trim cost-of-living adjustments to no more than 80 percent of any change in the Consumer Price Index—it simply does not cost as much to live in retirement as it does to follow a career, even in the military—and count military pensions against Social Security eligibility.

That brings us to the general-purpose entitlement programs: Social Security, Medicare, Medicaid, and the dozens of lesser expenses. Entitlement programs are by far the largest and fastest-growing segment of our national budget. Large as defense spending appears, at 6.6 percent of the Gross National Product it has grown in the 1980s only half as much as it declined during the preceding decade; it remains lower than in any year from 1950 to 1973. Contrast that with entitlement programs, which have grown from 5.4 percent of the GNP in 1965 to 11.5 percent last year. As former Secretary of Commerce Peter G. Peterson has pointed out, just the growth in entitlements in the last twenty-one years, not even the total cost, is an amount greater than we spend on public infrastructure, such as roads and dams, all investment in business plants and equipment, and all civilian research and development work *combined.*

These are the most difficult programs to cut, because they have by far the widest political backing. The National Committee to Preserve Social Security and Medicare alone boasts some 4.8 million highly vocal members. The American Association of Retired Persons is even larger, and there are dozens of similar organizations dedicated to defending the entitlements of their members. But if our leaders in Washington have the courage to eliminate those portions of the social "security net" that have nothing to do with aiding the impoverished, that alone could balance the Federal budget.

It can be accomplished without in any way harming the truly needy. In

1986, Federal, state, and local governments paid out about $525 billion—one-eighth of the Gross National Product—in benefits; some $455 billion of that was drained from Federal tax revenues, $360 billion in cash and the rest in the form of food stamps, health care, and other nonmonetary benefits. The total includes Civil Service and military pensions, farm subsidies, Veterans Administration health benefits, the gigantic Social Security and Medicare programs, and the tiny $18 billion—slightly less, actually—paid for unemployment compensation.

Only $100 billion of that went to the poor, at best guess. But it is only a guess. Only 15 percent of Federal benefits, about $68 billion, is reserved for people living in poverty. The rest goes to all who can qualify, and actually needing the money is not one of the criteria. An estimated 250,000 millionaires receive Social Security and Medicare.

Those two programs alone account for $271 billion in Federal entitlements, about half of the benefits paid out by all levels of government. Those with the highest lifetime incomes, and presumably with the most comfortable retirement plans, receive the largest Social Security payments; those who actually need the money get least. But those who need the money are a small minority. With the exception of a few orphaned dependents receiving payments that otherwise would have gone to their parents, Social Security funds go to the elderly, and of all age groups the elderly have the lowest poverty rate. And virtually no one who qualifies for Social Security at all receives as little as he paid into the system over his working life. The average lifetime benefit received from the program is five to ten times what the recipient paid in.

Writer Bernard Gavzer, reporting in *Parade* magazine last year, put some hard numbers on it. Gavzer entered the Social Security program in 1941 and had paid $20,490.63 into the system by October 1987. If he retires at age 67, he will receive at least $9,480 per year. That is, in roughly two years and two months of retirement, he will receive every penny that he paid in. Given a life expectancy of 79, he will collect an additional $142,200, not counting annual cost-of-living raises. So much for the argument that all those who qualify for Social Security under the present rules should receive it regardless of need, because they are only getting back what they paid in.

The first step toward plugging the Social Security drain is to apply a means test to recipients. People living in comfort should not receive Federal benefits that amount to welfare for the well off. Limiting Social Security payments to retirees with a median income or less would save an estimated three-fourths of the money this program now spends.

Next, change the way we figure cost-of-living adjustments. As it stands, Social Security payments are supposed to be raised by an amount equal to the rise in the Consumer Price Index whenever inflation lifts the CPI by 6 percent. In fact, when inflation reached only 4 percent in 1986, election-minded Congressmen voted a 4.1 percent raise in Social Security benefits for fiscal year 1988, a bonus that will cost taxpayers $8.6 billion. But retirement frees ex-workers from a host of expenses that beset them while still on the job: commuting to work each day, business suits or work clothes, and the like. So instead of COLAs equal to the change in the CPI, raise benefits by only 80 percent of the inflation rate. Retirees will still live quite comfortably, thank you, and the Federal deficit will shrink dramatically.

Former Commerce Secretary Peterson would go even further. He prescribes cutting the cost-of-living adjustment on Social Security and other benefit programs not aimed at the poor—that is, programs that do not apply a means test for eligibility—to only 60 percent of the inflation rate. By the year 2000, he estimates, we would be saving $150 billion per year in Federal payments.

Finally, and this is where the real saving will come in the long run, raise the retirement age gradually from 65 to 70. There is nothing sacred about retiring at 65. Bismarck chose that as the pensionable age for German government workers specifically because fewer than one in 20 ever reached his 65th birthday. With the national life expectancy for men at 79 years and climbing, we can no longer afford to meet the standard of the 1880s. Beginning next year, we should add two months to the retirement age each year. Workers would be eligible for Social Security benefits at age 65-and-two-months in 1989, 65-and-four-months in 1990, and so on. For each two months added to the retirement threshold, we would save $3 billion per year.

Saving on Medicare is a more difficult proposition. We spent a total of nearly 11 percent of our Gross National Product on health care last year. Federal health benefits alone reached $120 billion in 1987. The cost of the entire Medicare program was only $14 billion in 1975; in 1986, it was more than five times that, and by 1990, the total is expected to reach $100 billion. All this despite cost-cutting measures that many critics have charged already deprive some patients of necessary medical treatment.

Though public-health analysts can cite endless cases of waste in our medical delivery system, most of the growth in this expense category is due to two inescapable trends: Medical research continually devises new, increasingly technological therapies that are both more effective and more costly than the treatments they replace. And better health care allows ever more people to live into their seventies and eighties, when medical expenses rise sharply. There seems no way to reduce these ever-growing costs. Yet by the year 2000, health-care spending is forecast to reach 15 percent of our GNP, a drain on our economy that may well be unsupportable. The ugly fact is that we may be forced to limit our support for medical costs, even if it means that people die who might otherwise be saved. Many other countries have already taken that sad path.

Budget cuts, difficult as they will be to achieve, are not enough to insure our future standard of living. We must also take positive steps to promote a better future. There are only two. We must promote savings and investment, so that American business can afford the modern equipment it needs to compete with its highly automated competitors in Japan, Germany, Korea, and other more modern nations. And we must bring American educational standards up to those of the nations against which we compete.

Our national net savings rate—that is, the amount saved by private citizens less the Federal deficit—is among the lowest in the industrialized world. Today, it lies somewhere between 2 percent and 3 percent of the Gross National Product; in 1982, 1983, and 1986, it fell below 2 percent. By contrast, our savings rate in the 1970s averaged 8.1 percent, while the average among industrialized nations is between 10 percent and 20 percent. In Japan it consistently tops 20 percent. In 1986, our net savings totaled only $125 billion. In Japan, with half our population, the figure was $380 billion. This, combined with the enormous load of government borrowing to finance the budget deficit, explains why American companies have been unable to do without the capital provided by foreign investors—and why those investors have been able to supply it.

Our net investment—the force that shapes our economic future—mirrors those savings figures. Our net investment for houses, factories, laboratories, and public works in the 1980s averaged 5.3 percent of our GNP; in 1986 it amounted to $300 billion. Japan invested $270 billion, or 16.1 percent of its GNP, in 1986 and still had $80 billion to lend overseas—$50 billion of it lent to us. At that, the Japanese investment rate is actually falling. In the 1960s, it averaged 22.6 percent per year.

The Tax Reform Act of 1986 "leveled the economic playing field" in the United States, eliminating not only loopholes through which corporations and the wealthy were said to evade their fair share of taxation, but also such incentives as research-and-development exemptions, capital-investment tax credits, and lower tax rates on capital gains. Fair as this sounds, popular as it remains, we must restore those provisions which used to promote savings and investment, and perhaps add some new ones. If lower tax rates on capital gains promote investment, and they do, then we must lower them. If tax credits encourage corporations to modernize their industrial plants, then credits we must offer them. Such provisions are not just another form of welfare for the rich. They are ways to speed our return to economic health. We need the help they can provide far more than we need the taxes they will cost us. An expanding economy will more than make up the loss.

Shoring up our educational system will also cost us, and it will be most of a generation before we gain the benefits of our commitment. But the cost of our current educational practices is horribly clear. Fewer than half the geography students in one Florida survey could find America on a world map. Fewer than one high school student in ten takes more than two years of a foreign language. Colleges across the country have been forced to start classes in remedial English because incoming freshmen can neither read nor write. In one large Texas city, highly motivated mathematics teachers, themselves victims of the long decline in our educational standards, volunteered to teach extra classes for high school students having trouble in their normal studies. As conscientious educators, they decided first to test their own knowledge to make sure they were up to the task. Only 48 percent could pass a standard high school–level math test. As a result, this is the first generation in which children have had lower IQ and SAT scores than their parents. Measuring even by today's low standards of achievement, by the year 2000 we will have produced nearly 20 million young people wholly unable to compete in an increasingly technological world.

Such deficiencies are quickly felt in economically devastating ways. To pick just one example of many, Japan, with half our population, graduates more than twice as many engineers as the United States.

We can ignore here calls to test the competence of teachers. That debate is being carried out in depth in newspapers, on the evening news, and in every PTA meeting in the country. But it is worth noting that the old rule holds true: You get what you pay for. If we want capable teachers, we must offer pay scales comparable to those that competent mathematicians and linguists and biologists can find in industry, then hold out for the best applicants.

One other point: Children cannot be expected to learn as much in six months as they would in eight. Even the poorest student in the rigorous Japanese educational system has a better chance of becoming an educated, capable adult than any but the brightest, most diligent American child. We cannot hope to compete in a worldwide economy unless we bring our students much closer to their standards. We can begin by going to a seven-hour classroom day, 210 days per year, with at least one hour of homework. Even this half-measure will not be cheap, but the alternative is to become a Third World nation.

Just what can we expect from all this effort? As noted in Chapter 1, it depends in part on the reception we receive from our trading partners. If they are unwilling to sacrifice a bit of their export profits and stimulate their economies slightly to promote demand—if, in short, they refuse to give us the room to repair our damaged economy—it will be very difficult to avoid a sharp decline in our standard of living. If they, and our own leaders, choose a trade war rather than mutual cooperation, we may well be in for an indefinite period of poverty much like the one that gripped the world nearly sixty years ago. Our only consolation will be that the people who made it inevitable are suffering as badly as we are.

If we can act together to prevent an otherwise certain calamity, things look much brighter. Balancing the Federal budget, promoting foreign trade, and revising the tax system yet again will quickly raise not only our GNP but, as savings are invested to modernize our industries, our per-worker productivity. That means a better standard of living for all.

It's a matter of personal income. The more we produce, the faster we can afford to pay our debts, and the more we will have left to spend. That is as true for a nation as it is for an individual. Add new investment to our economy, and we will all wind up with more to spend.

That kind of progress will be a marked change from the America of recent experience. For the last eight years, our GNP has grown, on average, at a real rate of about 2.1 percent per year. Yet our national standard of living has remained just about the same. The reason is that, in large part, what we have added to raise our GNP is not more output per worker, but simply more workers. The Commerce Department likes to brag, on the Administration's behalf, that we added the equivalent of 9 million new jobs between 1981 and 1986. That statistic omits crucial details: Many of those jobs were part-time, and the vast majority were in service industries in which both pay and productivity are low. The GNP of India has grown that way for years, but still the millions starve.

In Chapter 1, we looked at the consequences of our dependence on foreign borrowing: To pay our overseas debts within the foreseeable future, we must greatly increase our exports. We cannot do that without lowering the value of the dollar, perhaps to a degree that would end foreign investment here before we are in a position to do without it. That would plunge us deep into recession. Alternatively, we could raise our interest rates to draw offshore money back—and in the process make it too expensive for American companies to borrow the money they need to finance expansion. In the end, that too leads to recession. We will face that risk until we have repaid our foreign debt.

For the last few years, our productivity has grown so slowly that it would take twelve years to wean ourselves away from foreign investment and begin to reduce our net debt, even if the Federal government manages to hold its spending to current levels. How much faster can we accomplish that if our per-worker productivity grows? Two decades ago, we could have done it in three years; three decades ago, it would have taken only two.

Look at it another way. The average worker today produces just over $35,000 per year in goods and services. At the current rate of growth, in the year 2020, when today's 25-year-olds are nearing retirement and their babies are in their most productive working years, that will have risen by less than $6,000, or 14 percent. The standard of living will have risen only 8 percent, after declining for the rest of this century. If productivity were to begin growing today at the average rate for the 1950s and '60s, about 2.4 percent per year, we would have paid off our foreign debt by 1991 or '92. Thirty years later, the average American worker would be producing more than $77,000 worth of goods, and the standard of living would have grown by about 120 percent. Our own generation would have escaped the grim years we now face.

It is a simple question, really. Do you want a better standard of living for yourself and a much better life for your grandchildren? Or will you settle for living less well than the generation now retired and pass on to your heirs the second-rate remains of a once-great nation? Melodramatic as it sounds, that is our choice. We can make it deliberately, by convincing our Senators and Congressmen and President that tampering with the defense and entitlement programs will not cost them their jobs, but continued inaction will. Or we can make it by default, allowing Washington to continue its business as usual, and watch a brighter future slip away. The choice is yours.

APPENDIX B:
WINNERS AND LOSERS IN THE
NEW JOB MARKET

CHAPTER 4 provided an in-depth analysis of the job market in the coming decade. This appendix lists some 500 of the most common jobs and gives Forecasting International's assessment of each occupation's prospects. As an aid to creative thinking, we have also included a few "jobs of the future," employment opportunities that we expect to open up in the next decade. Included are estimates of the number of job openings available in the 1990s, the fields' growth rates, and some basic information about training requirements, probable income, and working conditions.

The table is divided into three major sections. In the first, we present the winners in the job market of the 1990s—fast-growing jobs, many of them new opportunities spawned by high technology. The second section details the losers, occupations that are growing slowly or not at all; some are disappearing quickly. The third section is a general catalog subdivided into categories such as "Administrative Specialties" and "Sales and Services." If your job is listed in the first section, it probably offers as secure a future as is possible in the chaotic economy of the next decade. If it is listed in the second, you can expect to spend some time job-hunting in the near future; check the first part for possible new careers. If it cannot be found in either of the first sections, check the third; occupations listed there include the good, the bad, and the merely boring.

Most of the terms and abbreviations used in the table are self-explanatory, but a few may be puzzling. "Avg," of course, means that an occupation is likely to grow at an average rate during the 1990s. "Obs" means that an occupation is obsolescent and employment in the field is shrinking. "Voc" indicates that applicants can find suitable training at a vocational school. Probably the most opaque term is the catchall "non-office," which appears frequently in the "Location" column. Jobs with this description are performed indoors, virtually anywhere but in an office. Factories, hospitals, stores, and auto body shops all fit here.

WINNERS IN THE NEW JOB MARKET

JOB	NEEDED (000s)	LOCATION	ENTRY SALARY (000s)	MEDIAN INCOME (000s)	TRAINING REQUIRED
Accountant or Auditor	1,090	Office/Home	$20.4	$30	4yr Coll
Advertising Worker	100	Office	$12	$48	4yr Coll
Architect	74	Office/Home	$16.8	$48	4yr Coll
Attorney	372	Office/Home	$25.2	$72	Grad
Auto Body Repairer	118	Non-office	$9.6	$18	Voc
Auto Mechanic	638	Non-office	$10.8	$16.8	Voc
Automated Office Data Management Analyst or Supervisor	250	Office	$19.2	$30	4yr Coll
Automated Office Information Management Director	150	Office	$26.4	$60	4yr Coll
Automated Office Records, Data Information Security Manager	260	Office	$21.6	$30	4yr Coll
Automated Office Terminal/Message Center Manager (Corporate Office)	500	Office	$21.6	$44.4	4yr Coll
Automated Office Terminal/Message Center Manager (Single Office)	300	Office	$19.2	$25.2	4yr Coll
Baker	77	Non-office	$10.8	$20.4	Voc
Bank Officer or Administrator	643	Office	$19.2	$34.8	4yr Coll
Bank Teller	336	Office	$9.6	$14.4	Jr Coll
Battery Technician, Fuel Cell	25	Non-office	$10.8	$16.8	Voc
Biomedical Engineer	4	Varied	$21.6	$33.6	Grad
Blue Collar Worker Supervisor	1,300	Non-office	$19.2	$22.8	OJT
Bricklayer or Stonemason	120	Mobile	$19.2	$37.2	Apprent
Broadcast Technician	17	Non-office	$14.4	$26.4	Voc
CAD Engineering Software Specialist	360	Non-office	$22.8	$36	Jr Coll
CAD Information Retrieval & Reproduction Clerk	300	Non-office	$12	$14.4	OJT
CAD Product Design Technician	190	Non-office	$18	$33.6	Jr Coll

WINNERS IN THE NEW JOB MARKET

JOB	NEEDED (000s)	LOCATION	ENTRY SALARY (000s)	MEDIAN INCOME (000s)	TRAINING REQUIRED
CAD Product or Systems Inspector	280	Non-office	$14.4	$26.4	OJT
CAD Terminal Draftsman	300	Non-office	$16.8	$30	Jr Coll
CAD Terminal Parts	125	Non-office	$13.2	$21.6	Jr Coll
CAD Terminal Product Testing Engineer	450	Non-office	$16.8	$42	4 yr Coll
CAD Training & Educational Materials Salesperson	95	Non-office	$14.4	$24	Jr Coll
CAD Vocational Training & Educational Simulation Instructor	300	Non-office	$16.8	$26.4	OJT
CAD Vocational Training & Educational Simulation Software Specialist	150	Non-office	$16.8	$22.8	Jr Coll
CAG Layout Artist	40	Non-office	$12	$21.6	Jr Coll
CAG Operations Supervisor	20	Non-office	$18	$30	Voc
CAG Sales Representative	30	Varied	$18	$36	Voc
CAG Terminal Input Artist	40	Non-office	$20.4	$21.6	Jr Coll
CAM Holographic Inspector	135	Non-office	$14.4	$25.2	OJT
CAM Machine & Manufacturing Materials Setup Mechanic	300	Non-office	$14.4	$24	Voc
CAM Manufacturing Material/Finished Parts Traffic Controller	20	Non-office	$14.4	$16.8	Jr Coll
CAM Production Scheduler & Progress Controller	90	Non-office	$14.4	$21.6	Voc
CAM Production Superintendent	90	Non-office	$18	$30	Voc
CAM Records Supervisor, Inventory, Stocking & Shipping	14	Non-office	$14.4	$16.8	Voc

CAM Special Tooling Design Engineer	170	Non-office	$16.8	$22.8	Voc
CAM Technician	75	Non-office	$19.2	$26.4	OJT
CAM-CAD Software Coordinator	80	Non-office	$20.4	$30	Jr Coll
Cable TV Installer	300	Mobile	$13.2	$15.6	OJT
Cardiopulmonary Technologist	——	Non-office	$10.8	$30	Jr Coll
Carpenter	901	Non-office	$19.2	$33.6	OJT
City Manager	4	Office	$39.6	$558.8	4yr Coll
Civil Engineer	200	Non-office	$24	$32.4	4yr Coll
Computer Axial Tomography Technologist	25	Non-office	$14.4	$24	Jr Coll
Computer Console & Equipment Operator	812	Office/Home	$12	$21.6	Jr Coll
Computer Drafting Technician	300	Non-office	$21.6	$36	Jr Coll
Computer Graphics Technician	150	Non-office	$24	$42	Jr Coll
Computer Manufacturing Inspector	250	Non-office	$20.4	$38.4	Jr Coll
Computer Programmer	474	Non-office/ Home	$22.8	$32.4	Jr Coll
Computer Service Technician	93	Home/Mobile	$21.6	$33.6	Jr Coll
Computer Software Writer, General	1,830	Non-office/ Home	$24	$36	Jr Coll
Computer Systems Analyst	399	Office/Home	$24	$31.2	Jr Coll
Computer Terminal Information Processor	270	Office/Home	$24	$36	Jr Coll
Construction Laborer & Carpenter's Helper	851	Mobile	$15.6	$28.8	OJT
Correctional Institution Officer	169	Non-office	$14.4	$30	Jr Coll
Dental Assistant	96	Office	$9.6	$14.4	Jr Coll
Dental Laboratory Technician	53	Non-office	$20.4	$36	Voc
Diesel Mechanic	——	Non-office	$12	$27.6	Voc
Dietitian	49	Non-office	$19.2	$31.2	4yr Coll
Dishwasher	——	Non-office	$7.2	$8.4	OJT
Drywall Installer & Finisher	103	Mobile	$21.6	$33.6	Apprent
Economist	92	Office	$16.8	$30	4yr Coll
Editor, Writer or Reporter	220	Non-office/ Home	$14.4	$60	4yr Coll

WINNERS IN THE NEW JOB MARKET

JOB	NEEDED (000s)	LOCATION	ENTRY SALARY (000s)	MEDIAN INCOME (000s)	TRAINING REQUIRED
Electric Power Line & Cable Maintenance Mechanic	106	Non-office/ Mobile	$14.4	$21.6	Voc
Electrical/Electronic Engineer	513	Non-office	$26.4	$39.6	4yr Coll
Electrical/Electronic Engineering Technician	478	Varied	$14.4	$28.8	Voc
Electrician (Construction)	582	Non-office/ Mobile	$24	$37.21	Apprent
Electronic Mail Operations Specialist	300	Office	$14.4	$19.2	OJT
Emergency Medical Technician	120	Mobile	$12	$27.6	Jr Coll
Energy Auditor	150	Mobile	$14.4	$19.2	Voc
Energy Conservation Technician	1,500	Non-office	$15.6	$31.2	Voc
Engineering & Science Technician	996	Non-office	$12	$26.4	Voc
Engineering Aide	——	Non-office	$12	$21.6	Voc
Firefighter	197	Mobile	$16.8	$24	OJT
Food Service Worker (Commercial Cook)	4,436	Non-office	$ 8.4	$24	OJT
Genetic Engineer	150	Non-office	$27.6	$45.6	Grad
Genetic Engineering Technician	250	Non-office	$24	$36	4yr Coll
Geriatric Social Worker	450	Non-office/ Home	$18	$25.2	4yr Coll
Hazardous Waste Disposal Technician	1,500	Non-office	$18	$33.6	Jr Coll
Holographic Inspector	200	Non-office	$21.6	$24	Jr Coll
Home Electronic Interactive Systems Technician	180	Office	$16.8	$24	Voc
Housing Rehabilitation Technician	1,750	Non-office/ Home	$16.8	$28.8	Apprent
Illustrator/Commercial Artist	——	Non-office	$10.8	$21.6	Voc
Industrial Engineer	225	Non-office	$26.4	$36	4yr Coll
Industrial Laser Process Technician	600	Non-office	$36	$60	OJT
Industrial Robot Production Technician	800	Non-office	$18	$28.8	Jr Coll

Legal Secretary	——	Office	$9.6	$21.6	Voc
Materials Utilization Technician	400	Non-office	$18	28.8	4yr Coll
Mechanical Engineer	250	Non-office	$24	$33.6	4yr Coll
Medical Laboratory Technician	205	Non-office	$14.4	$25.2	Jr Coll
Meteorologist	——	Non-office	$19.2	$37.2	4yr Coll
Microcomputer Diagnostician	200	Varied	$24	$42	Jr Coll
Midwife	15	Home	$12	$24	Apprent
Nuclear Medical Technician	——	Hospital	$15.6	$21.6	Jr Coll
Office Information Center Terminal Operator	600	Office	$16.8	$27.6	Voc
Office Machine Servicer	——	Non-office/ Mobile	$ 9.6	$18	Voc
Painter & Paperhanger	317	Mobile	$18	$34.8	OJT
Painter, Construction & Maintenance	469	Non-office/ Mobile	$19.2	$28.8	OJT
Personnel Administrator	405	Varied	$33.6	$60	4yr Coll
Pest Control Worker	40	Mobile	$ 8.4	$14.4	Jr Coll
Physician Assistant	51	Office	$21.6	$26.4	Jr Coll
Plasterer	30	Mobile	$22.8	$33.6	Voc
Positron Emission Technologist	25	Non-office	$14.4	$24	4yr Coll
Psychologist, Counseling	——	Non-office	$14.4	$26.4	Grad
Radio & TV Mechanic	120	Non-office/ Home	$13.2	$22.8	Voc
Real Estate Agent or Broker	356	Office	$15.6	$34.8	4yr Coll
Receptionist	490	Office	$ 9.6	$14.4	OJT
Rehabilitation Counselor	25	Office	$15.6	$21.6	4yr Coll
Robot Installation & Operations Technician	75	Non-office	$14.4	$26.4	OJT
Robot on-the-Job Programmer	125	Non-office	$14.4	$24	Jr Coll
Robot-Pogrammed Tool Handler	75	Non-office	$14.4	$21.6	OJT
Robot Repairman	100	Non-office	$16.8	$26.4	Voc
Robotic Engineer	200	Non-office	$27.6	$42	4yr Coll
Sales Agent, Stocks & Bonds	67	Office	$13.2	$60	4yr Coll
Sales Representative, Consumable Commodities, Wholesale	1,001	Non-office	$21.6	$39.6	4yr Coll

WINNERS IN THE NEW JOB MARKET

JOB	NEEDED (000s)	LOCATION	ENTRY SALARY (000s)	MEDIAN INCOME (000s)	TRAINING REQUIRED
Sales Representative, Manufacturing	440	Varied	$19.2	$44.4	4yr Coll
Sales Representative, Wholesale	1,001	Varied	$21.6	$39.6	4yr Coll
Secretary or Stenographer	3,320	Office/Home	$10.8	$14.4	Voc
Security Guard	548	Varied	$14.4	$21.6	OJT
Social or Recreational Worker	480	Non-office	$12	$31.2	4yr Coll
Surgical Technician	——	Non-office	$ 9.6	$19.2	Voc
Teacher, Secondary School	1,243	Non-office	$21.6	——	4yr Coll
Telemarketing Advertising & Scenario Writer	110	Office	$21.6	$42	4yr Coll
Telemarketing Audio-Visual Technician	50	Non-office	$30	$48	4yr Coll
Telemarketing Computer Programmer	60	Office	$24	$42	Jr Coll
Telemarketing Sales Program Supervisor	65	Office	$30	$120	4yr Coll
Telemarketing Sales— Shipping, Billing Clerk, Supervisor	50	Office	$ 9.6	$21.6	OJT
Telemarketing Specialist, Recording/ Customer Order Takeoff	80	Office	$18	$36	OJT
Teletext Broadcast Communications Engineer	40	Non-office	$24	$48	4yr Coll
Teletext Computer Specialist Composition, Formatting & Editing	65	Office	$19.2	$48	4yr Coll
Teletext Interactive Correspondent	30	Varied	$21.6	$30	4yr Coll
Teletext Operations Supervisor	25	Office	$24	$40.8	Voc
Teletext Senior Editor & Director	25	Office	$36	$60	4yr Coll

Teletext Specialist—CATV Liaison & Scheduling	30	Office	$20.4	$45.6	OJT
Teletext Specialist—Marketing	30	Office/Home	$21.6	$48	4yr Coll
Teletext Specialist—Software Programming	30	Office/Home	$21.6	$36	Jr Coll
Teletext Supervisor—Library Research, Copy, Distribution	20	Office	$24	$36	4yr Coll
Travel Agent	52	Office	$12	$21.6	Jr Coll
Urban or Regional Planner	31	Office	$22.8	$42	4yr Coll
Vocational & Educational Counselor	166	Non-office	$16.8	$31.2	4yr Coll

LOSERS IN THE JOB MARKET

JOB	NEEDED (000s)	LOCATION	ENTRY SALARY (000s)	MEDIAN INCOME (000s)	TRAINING REQUIRED
Actuary	11	Office	$15.6	$36	4yr Coll
Aeronautical Engineer	——	Varied	$19.2	$60	4yr Coll
Air Traffic Controller	29	Non-office	$18	$37.2	4yr Coll
Aquatic Biologist	——	Varied	$22.8	$33.6	4yr Coll
Assembler	1,014	Factory	$ 9.6	$24	Voc
Athletic Coach	——	Non-office	$18	$30	4yr Coll
Biologist	66	Varied	$14.4	$42	4yr Coll
Boatbuilder	——	Non-office	$12	$21.6	Apprent
Boiler Tender	62	Non-office	$13.2	$28.8	Apprent
Botanist	——	Varied	$14.4	$35	4yr Coll
Cabinetmaker	28	Non-office	$12	$25.2	Voc
Cartographer	——	Non-office	$16.8	$28.8	Jr Coll
Cashier	941	Non-office	$14.4	$20.4	OJT
Cement Mason	——	Non-office	$12	$26.4	Voc
Clergy Member	240	Non-office	$14.4	$30	Grad
Collection Clerk	——	Office	$8.4	$15.6	Voc
Compositor/Typesetter	54	Non-office	$21.6	$26.4	Apprent
Computer Terminal Distributive Information Processor	140	Office/Home	$24	$42	Jr Coll
Copywriter	——	Office	$ 9.6	$33.6	4yr Coll
Counter Clerk	89	Non-office	$ 9.6	$18	OJT
Darkroom Laboratory Technician	——	Non-office	$ 8.4	$18	Jr Coll
Dentist	15	Office	$26.4	$66	Grad
Disc Jockey	——	Non-office	$10.8	$33.6	Voc

LOSERS IN THE JOB MARKET

JOB	NEEDED (000s)	LOCATION	ENTRY SALARY (000s)	MEDIAN INCOME (000s)	TRAINING REQUIRED
Dog Groomer	——	Non-office	$ 8.4	$16.8	Voc
Dressmaker & Seamstress (nonfactory)	49	Home	$12	$28.8	OJT
Engineering Draftsman	335	Non-office	$12	$26.4	Voc
Farm Laborer (wage worker)	895	Farm	$ 8.4	——	OJT
Farm Worker or Supervisor	26	Farm	$15.6	$26.4	OJT
Farmer or Farm Manager	70	Farm	——	——	Voc
File Clerk	191	Office	$9.6	$16.8	OJT
Forester (except logging)	12	Varied	$15.6	$24	Jr Coll
Freight, Stock, or Materials Handler	986	Non-office	$12	$28.8	Voc
Funeral Director	19	Office	$14.4	$33.6	Voc
Glazier	35	Mobile	$ 9.6	$14.4	Apprent
Horticulturist	——	Non-office/ Farm	$12	$31.2	4yr Coll
Industrial Designer	——	Non-office	$12	$25.2	4yr Coll
Interior Designer	——	Non-office/ Mobile	$ 9.6	$26.4	Jr Coll
Jeweler	——	Non-office	$16.8	$24	Apprent
Key Punch Operator	200	Office	$18	$25.2	Voc
Lithographic Press Operator	81	Non-office	$16.8	$20.4	Apprent
Locksmith	11	Non-office	$ 7.2	$21.6	Voc
Machine Operator	736	Non-office	$13.2	$39.6	OJT
Mail Carrier	300	Mobile	$22.8	$25.2	OJT
Manufacturing Inspector	336	Non-office	$14.4	$26.4	Jr Coll
Marina Worker	——	Non-office	$ 9.6	$15.6	OJT
Marine Engineer	3	Non-office	$25.2	$43.2	4yr Coll
Marine Surveyor	——	Non-office/ Mobile	$9.6	$16.8	4yr Coll
Microbiologist	——	Non-office	$14.4	$42	4yr Coll
Millwright	92	Farm	$12	$24	Apprent
Oceanographer	——	Non-office	$14.4	$20.4	4yr Coll
Office Communications Equipment Installer	25	Mobile	$15.6	$34.8	Voc
Packer or Wrapper (Not meat or produce)	600	Non-office	$10.8	$16.8	OJT

Painter, Automotive	41	Non-office	$21.6	$33.6	OJT
Painter, Manufactured Goods	181	Non-office	$15.6	$31.2	OJT
Park Ranger	——	Non-office/ Mobile	$13.2	$26.4	4yr Coll
Parole Officer	——	Office	$10.8	$19.2	4yr Coll
Patternmaker	4	Non-office	$21.6	$34.8	Apprent
Photoengraver	38	Non-office	$12	$14.4	Voc
Photographic Process Worker	——	Non-office	$ 8.4	$14.4	Voc
Physician	239	Varied	$45.6	$88.8	Grad
Physicist or Astronomer	35	Non-office	$18	$26.4	4yr Coll
Political Scientist	15	Office/Home	$18	$26.4	4yr Coll
Postal Clerk	281	Non-office	$21.6	$25.2	OJT
Printing Press Operator	178	Non-office	$20.4	$27.6	Apprent
Public Relations Manager	131	Office	$14.4	$38.4	4yr Coll
Punch Press & Stamping Operator	183	Non-office	$24	$37.2	OJT
Radiologic (X-Ray) Technologist	109	Non-office	$16.8	$22.8	Jr Coll
Real Estate Appraiser	——	Non-office/ Mobile	$15.6	$21.6	OJT
Roofer	112	Mobile	$ 9.6	$20.4	OJT
Sailor or Deckhand	17	Mobile	$18	$26.4	Voc
Salesclerk, Retail	2,345	Non-office	$ 7.2	$16.8	OJT
School Administrator	455	Non-office	$27.6	$51.6	4yr Coll
Sewer & Stitcher	788	Non-office	$10.8	$19.2	OJT
Sheet Metal Worker	112	Non-office	$21.6	$33.6	Apprent
Shipping & Receiving Clerk	432	Non-office	$ 9.6	$21.6	OJT
Stock Handler or Bagger	332	Non-office	$ 9.6	$14.4	OJT
Structural Metal Worker	58	Non-office/ Mobile	$18	$22.8	Apprent
Surveyor	——	Mobile	$10.8	$24	4yr Coll
Tailor	48	Non-office	$ 7.2	$16.8	Voc
Telephone Operator	182	Non-office	$ 9.6	$12	OJT
Textile Machine Operator	323	Non-office	$10.8	$20.4	OJT
Tool & Die Maker	138	Non-office	$25.2	$44.4	Jr Coll
Welder & Cutter	517	Non-office	$26.4	$33.6	Apprent
Zoologist	——	Non-office	$14.4	$30	4yr Coll

Guide to Specialized Job Markets

ADMINISTRATIVE SPECIALTIES

JOB	NEEDED (000s)	LOCATION	ENTRY SALARY (000s)	MEDIAN INCOME (000s)	GROWTH RATE	TRAINING REQUIRED
Accountant	1,090	Office/Home	$20.4	$30	Fast	4yr Coll
Administrative Assistant	11	Office	$15.6	$36	Avg	OJT
Automated Office Work Station Analyst	240	Office	$21.6	$30	——	4yr Coll
Buyers (Wholesale & Retail)	186	Varied	$20.4	$37.2	Avg	Jr Coll
CAD Terminal Parts Cataloguer	125	Non-office	$13.2	$21.6	Fast	Jr Coll
CAG Operations Supervisor	20	Non-office	$18	$30	Fast	Jr Coll
Estimator & Investigator	534	Varied	$13.2	$20.4	Avg	Jr Coll
Health Service Administrator	220	Office	$22.8	$60	Ave	4yr Coll
Holographic Inspector	200	Non-office	$21.6	$24	New	Jr Coll
Manufacturing Inspector	336	Non-office	$14.4	$26.4	Slow	Voc
Personnel Administrator	405	Varied	$33.6	$60	Fast	4yr Coll
Personnel & Labor Relations Worker	93	Office	$18	34.8	Avg	4yr Coll
Public Relations Manager	131	Office	$14.4	$38.4	Slow	4yr Coll
Purchasing Agents & Buyers (Not wholesale/retail)	227	Office	$19.2	$37.2	Avg	Jr Coll
Sales Managers	705	Office	$14.4	$54	Avg	Jr Coll
Telemarketing Sales Program Supervisor	65	Office	$20	$120	New	4yr Coll

JOB	NEEDED (000s)	LOCATION	ENTRY SALARY (000s)	MEDIAN INCOME (000s)	GROWTH RATE	TRAINING REQUIRED
Teletext Senior Editor & Director	25	Office	$36	$60	New	4yr Coll

ART

JOB	NEEDED (000s)	LOCATION	ENTRY SALARY (000s)	MEDIAN INCOME (000s)	GROWTH RATE	TRAINING REQUIRED
Floral Designer	56	Non-office	$10.8	$22.8	Avg	Voc
Illustrator/ Commercial Artist	——	Non-office	$10.8	$21.6	Fast	Voc
Industrial Designer	——	Non-office	$12	$25.2	Slow	4yr Coll
Interior Designer	——	Non-office/ Mobile	$9.6	$26.4	Slow	Jr Coll
Photographer	60	Varied	$16.8	$25.2	Slow	OJT

CLERICAL OCCUPATIONS

JOB	NEEDED (000s)	LOCATION	ENTRY SALARY (000s)	MEDIAN INCOME (000s)	GROWTH RATE	TRAINING REQUIRED
CAM Records Supervisor, Inventory, Stocking & Shipping	14	Non-office	$14.4	$16.8	Fast	Voc
Credit Investigator	——	Office	$ 8.4	$14.4	Avg	Jr Coll
Hotel/Motel Clerk	67	Non-office	$ 7.2	$14.4	Avg	OJT
Medical Office Assistant	——	Non-office	$ 8.4	$16.8	Avg	Voc
Shipping, Traffic & Receiving Clerk	432	Non-office	$ 9.6	$21.6	Avg	OJT
Stock Clerk or Storekeeper	533	Non-office	$ 9.6	$21.6	Avg	OJT
Ward Clerk, Hospital	——	Non-office	$ 7.2	$14.4	Avg	Voc

COMPUTING AND ACCOUNT RECORDING

JOB	NEEDED (000s)	LOCATION	ENTRY SALARY (000s)	MEDIAN INCOME (000s)	GROWTH RATE	TRAINING REQUIRED
Automated Office Data Management Analyst or Supervisor	250	Office	$19.3	$30	New	4yr Coll
Bank Teller	336	Office	$ 9.6	$14.4	Fast	OJT
Bookkeeper	1,904	Office/Home	$12	$20.4	Avg	Voc
Bookkeeping Machine Operator	——	Office	$ 9.6	$16.8	Avg	Voc
Cashier	941	Non-office	$14.4	$20.4	Slow	OJT
Computer Console & Equipment Operator	812	Office/Home	$12	$21.8	Fast	Voc
Medical Records Technician	20	Non-office	$14.4	$27.6	Avg	Jr Coll
Statistical Clerk	82	Office/Home	$ 8.4	$14.4	Avg	Jr Coll
Teletext Supervisor— Library Research, Copy, Distribution	20	Office	$24	$36	New	4yr Coll

CONSTRUCTION OCCUPATIONS

JOB	NEEDED (000s)	LOCATION	ENTRY SALARY (000s)	MEDIAN INCOME (000s)	GROWTH RATE	TRAINING REQUIRED
Bricklayer or Stonemason	120	Mobile	$19.2	$37.2	Fast	Apprent
Carpenter	901	Non-office	$19.2	$33.6	Fast	OJT
Cement Mason	——	Non-office	$12	$26.4	Slow	Apprent
Construction Laborer and Carpenter's Helper	851	Mobile	$8.8	$15.6	Fast	OJT
Drywall Installer & Finisher	103	Mobile	$21.6	$33.6	Fast	Apprent

CONSTRUCTION OCCUPATIONS

JOB	NEEDED (000s)	LOCATION	ENTRY SALARY (000s)	MEDIAN INCOME (000s)	GROWTH RATE	TRAINING REQUIRED
Excavating, Grading & Road Machine Operator	456	Mobile	$24	$36	Avg	Voc
Housing Rehabilitation Technician	1,750	Non-office/Home	$16.8	$28.8	New	Apprent
Operating Engineer, Construction Machinery	190	Non-office	$25.2	$33.6	Avg	4yr Coll
Painter, Construction & Maintenance	469	Non-office/Mobile	$19.2	$28.8	Fast	OJT
Painter or Paperhanger	317	Mobile	$18	$34.8	Fast	OJT
Plasterer	30	Mobile	$22.8	$33.6	Fast	Voc
Plumber or Pipefitter	390	Non-office/Mobile	$18	$36	Avg	Voc
Roofer	112	Mobile	$ 9.6	$20.4	Slow	OJT

EDUCATION

JOB	NEEDED (000s)	LOCATION	ENTRY SALARY (000s)	MEDIAN INCOME (000s)	GROWTH RATE	TRAINING REQUIRED
CAD Vocational Training & Educational Simulation Instructor	300	Non-office	$16.8	$26.4	Fast	4yr Coll
Rehabilitation Counselor	25	Non-office	$15.6	$21.6	Fast	4yr Coll
School Administrator	455	Non-office	$27.6	$51.6	Slow	4yr Coll
Teacher Aide	189	Non-office	$ 8.4	$10.8	Avg	Jr Coll
Teacher, College & University	480	Non-office	$27.6	$37.2	Slow	Grad
Teacher, Elementary School	1,173	Non-office	$20.4	——	Avg	4yr Coll
Teacher, Kindergarten	243	Non-office	$20.4	——	Avg	4yr Coll

EDUCATION

JOB	NEEDED (000s)	LOCATION	ENTRY SALARY (000s)	MEDIAN INCOME (000s)	GROWTH RATE	TRAINING REQUIRED
Teacher, Preschool	——	Non-office	$12	$19.2	Slow	4yr Coll
Teacher, Secondary School	1,243	Non-office	$21.6	——	Fast	4yr Coll
Teacher, Special Needs	189	Non-office	$16.8	$19.2	Avg	4yr Coll
Vocational & Educational Counselor	166	Non-office	$16.8	$31.2	Fast	4yr Coll
Youth Counselor	——	Non-office	$ 9.6	$18	Avg	4yr Coll

ELECTRICAL EQUIPMENT ASSEMBLY, INSTALLATION, AND REPAIR

JOB	NEEDED (000s)	LOCATION	ENTRY SALARY (000s)	MEDIAN INCOME (000s)	GROWTH RATE	TRAINING REQUIRED
Air Conditioning, Heating, and Refrigeration Mechanic	55	Non-office	$15.6	$22.8	Avg	Voc
Appliance Repairer	28	Non-office/ Mobile	$12	$30	Avg	OJT
Cable TV Installer	300	Mobile	$13.2	$15.6	Fast	OJT
Computer Service Technician	93	Home/Mobile	$21.6	$33.6	Fast	Jr Coll
Electric Power Line & Cable Maintenance Mechanic	106	Non-office/ Mobile	$14.4	$21.6	Fast	OJT
Electrical/ Electronic Engineering Technician	478	Varied	$14.4	$28.8	Fast	Jr Coll
Electrician (Construction)	582	Non-office/ Mobile	$20	$37.2	Fast	Apprent
Engineering & Science Technician	996	Non-office	$14.4	$26.4	Fast	Voc

JOB	NEEDED (000s)	LOCATION	ENTRY SALARY (000s)	MEDIAN INCOME (000s)	GROWTH RATE	TRAINING REQUIRED
Home Electronic Interactive Systems Technician	200	Home/Mobile	$18	$25.2	New	OJT
Home/Office Interactive Work Systems Technician	180	Office	$16.8	$24	New	OJT
Microcomputer Diagnostician	200	Varied	$24	$42	New	Voc
Office Machine Repairer	59	Non-office	$12	$16.8	Avg	Voc
Office Machine Servicer	——	Non-office/ Mobile	$ 9.6	$18	Fast	Voc
Radio & TV Mechanic	120	Non-office Home	$13.2	$22.8	Fast	Voc
Telemarketing Audiovisual Technician	50	Non-office	$30	$48	New	Voc

ENGINEERING AND ARCHITECTURE

JOB	NEEDED (000s)	LOCATION	ENTRY SALARY (000s)	MEDIAN INCOME (000s)	GROWTH RATE	TRAINING REQUIRED
Aeronautical Engineer	——	Varied	$19.2	$60	Slow	4yr Coll
Agricultural Engineer	1	Farm	$19.2	$48	Avg	4yr Coll
Architect	74	Office/Home	$16.8	$48	Fast	4yr Coll
Biomedical Engineer	4	Varied	$21.6	$33.6	Fast	4yr Coll
Biomedical Technician	——	Non-office	$15.6	$30	Avg	Jr Coll
Bionic Electronic Technician	90	Non-office	$13.2	$22.8	Avg	Jr Coll
CAD Terminal Draftsman	300	Non-office	$16.8	$30	Fast	Jr Coll
CAD Terminal Product Testing Engineer	450	Non-office	$16.8	$42	Fast	4yr Coll
CAM Special Tooling Design Engineer	170	Non-office	$16.8	$22.8	Fast	Voc
CAM Technician	75	Non-office	$19.2	$26.4	Fast	OJT
Cartographer	23	Non-office	$16.8	$28.8	Slow	Jr Coll
Chemical Engineer	58	Non-office	$26.4	$39.6	Avg	4yr Coll

ENGINEERING AND ARCHITECTURE

JOB	NEEDED (000s)	LOCATION	ENTRY SALARY (000s)	MEDIAN INCOME (000s)	GROWTH RATE	TRAINING REQUIRED
Civil Engineer	200	Non-office	$24	$32.4	Fast	4yr Coll
Computer Drafting Technician	300	Non-office	$21.6	$36	Fast	Jr Coll
Electrical/ Electronic Engineer	513	Non-office	$26.4	$39.6	Fast	4yr Coll
Engineering Aide	——	Non-office	$12	$21.6	Fast	Voc
Genetic Engineer	150	Non-office	$27.6	$45.6	New	Grad
Genetic Engineering Technician	250	Non-office	$24	$36	New	4yr Coll
Landscape Architect	——	Non-office	$20.4	$33.6	Avg	4yr Coll
Laser Electro Optics Technician	——	Non-office	$10.8	$26.4	Avg	Jr Coll
Marine Engineer	3	Non-office	$25.2	$43.2	Slow	4yr Coll
Marine Surveyor	——	Non-office/ Mobile	$ 9.6	$16.8	Slow	4yr Coll
Mechanical Engineer	250	Non-office	$24	$33.6	Fast	4yr Coll
Nuclear Engineer	16	Non-office	$19.2	$33.6	Avg	4yr Coll
Robotic Engineer	200	Non-office	$27.6	$42	New	4yr Coll
Solar Energy Technician	——	Non-office/ Mobile	$16.8	$24	New	OJT
Surveyor	——	Mobile	$10.8	$24	Slow	4yr Coll
Teletext Broadcast Communications Engineer	40	Non-office	$24	$48	New	4yr Coll

FARMING, FORESTRY, AND RELATED OCCUPATIONS

JOB	NEEDED (000s)	LOCATION	ENTRY SALARY (000s)	MEDIAN INCOME (000s)	GROWTH RATE	TRAINING REQUIRED
Animal Keeper (except farm)	37	Non-office	$ 7.2	$12	Avg	Jr Coll
Farm Laborer (wage worker)	895	Farm	$ 8.4	——	Slow	OJT
Farm Worker or Supervisor	26	Farm	$15.6	$26.4	Slow	OJT

Job	Needed (000s)	Location	Entry Salary	Median Income	Growth Rate	Training Required
Farmer or Farm Manager	70	Farm	—	—	Slow	Voc
Forester (except logging)	12	Varied	$15.6	$24	Slow	Jr Coll
Gardener or Groundskeeper (Non-farm)	438	Non-office/Mobile	$ 7.2	$25.2	Avg	OJT
Horticulturist	—	Non-office/Farm	$12	$31.2	Slow	4yr Coll

FOOD/BEVERAGE PREPARATION AND SERVICES

JOB	NEEDED (000s)	LOCATION	ENTRY SALARY (000s)	MEDIAN INCOME (000s)	GROWTH RATE	TRAINING REQUIRED
Baker	77	Non-office	$10.8	$20.4	Fast	Voc
Bartender	188	Non-office	$12	$37.2	Avg	Voc
Caterer	—	Mobile	$ 7.2	$12	Avg	Voc
Commercial Airline Flight Attendant	56	Mobile	$13.2	$25.2	Avg	Voc
Dishwasher	—	Non-office	$ 7.2	$ 8.4	Fast	OJT
Food Counter Worker	125	Non-office	$ 8.4	$16.8	Avg	OJT
Food Service Worker (Commercial Cook)	4,436	Non-office	$ 8.4	$24	Fast	OJT
Meat Cutter or Butcher (Not plant)	230	Non-office	$14.4	$28.8	Avg	OJT
Waiter or Waitress	550	Non-office	$ 8.4	$14.4	Avg	OJT

GRAPHIC ARTS

JOB	NEEDED (000s)	LOCATION	ENTRY SALARY (000s)	MEDIAN INCOME (000s)	GROWTH RATE	TRAINING REQUIRED
CAG Layout Artst	40	Non-office	$12	$21.6	Fast	Jr Coll
CAG Terminal Input Artist	40	Non-office	$20.4	$21.6	Fast	Jr Coll
Computer Graphics Technician	150	Non-office	$24	$42	New	Jr Coll
Darkroom Laboratory Technician	—	Non-office	$ 8.4	$18	Slow	Voc

GRAPHIC ARTS

JOB	NEEDED (000s)	LOCATION	ENTRY SALARY (000s)	MEDIAN INCOME (000s)	GROWTH RATE	TRAINING REQUIRED
Engineering Draftsman	335	Non-office	$12	$26.4	Obs	Voc
Lithographer or Photoengraver	38	Non-office	$32.4	$45.6	Avg	Jr Coll
Painters, Sign	——	Non-office/ Mobile	$ 8.4	$18	Avg	Voc

INFORMATION AND MESSAGE DISTRIBUTION

JOB	NEEDED (000s)	LOCATION	ENTRY SALARY (000s)	MEDIAN INCOME (000s)	GROWTH RATE	TRAINING REQUIRED
Computer Terminal Distributive Information Processor	140	Office	$24	$42	——	Jr Coll
Computer Terminal Information Processor	270	Office	$24	$36	——	Jr Coll
Counter Clerk	89	Non-office	$ 9.6	$18	Slow	OJT
Electronic Mail Operations Specialist	300	Office	$22.8	$25.2	New	OJT
Mail Carrier	300	Mobile	$22.8	$25.2	Slow	OJT
Postal Clerk	281	Non-office	$21.6	$25.2	Slow	OJT
Receptionist	490	Office	$ 9.6	$14.4	Fast	OJT
Telephone Operator	192	Non-office	$ 9.6	$12	Slow	OJT

LAW AND JURISPRUDENCE

JOB	NEEDED (000s)	LOCATION	ENTRY SALARY (000s)	MEDIAN INCOME (000s)	GROWTH RATE	TRAINING REQUIRED
Attorney	372	Office/Home	$25.2	$72	Fast	Grad
Paralegal Assistant	——	Office	$10.8	$19.2	Avg	4yr Coll

LIFE SCIENCES

JOB	NEEDED (000s)	LOCATION	ENTRY SALARY (000s)	MEDIAN INCOME (000s)	GROWTH RATE	TRAINING REQUIRED
Animal Scientist	——	Farm/ Non-office	$16.8	$31.2	Avg	4yr Coll
Aquatic Biologist	——	Varied	$22.8	$33.6	Slow	4yr Coll
Biologist	66	Varied	$14.4	$42	Slow	4yr Coll
Botanist	——	Varied	$14.4	$36	Slow	4yr Coll
Microbiologist	——	Non-office	$14.4	$42	Slow	4yr Coll
Psychologist, Clinical	——	Non-office	$28.8	$48	Avg	Grad
Psychologist, Counseling	12	Non-office	$14.4	$26.4	Fast	Grad
Zoologist	——	Non-office	$14.4	$30	Slow	4yr Coll

MACHINE TRADES

JOB	NEEDED (000s)	LOCATION	ENTRY SALARY (000s)	MEDIAN INCOME (000s)	GROWTH RATE	TRAINING REQUIRED
CAD Product Design Technician	190	Non-office	$18	$33.6	Fast	Voc
CAM Machine & Manufacturing Materials Setup Mechanic	300	Non-office	$14.4	$24	Fast	Voc
CAM Production Scheduler & Progress Controller	90	Non-office	$14.4	$21.6	Fast	Voc
Patternmaker	4	Non-office	$21.6	$34.8	Slow	Apprent
Robot- Programmed Tool Handler	75	Non-office	$14.4	$21.6	New	OJT

MACHINING, METALWORKING, AND METAL FABRICATION

JOB	NEEDED (000s)	LOCATION	ENTRY SALARY (000s)	MEDIAN INCOME (000s)	GROWTH RATE	TRAINING REQUIRED
Assembler	1,014	Non-office	$ 9.6	$24	Slow	OJT
Auto Body Repairer	118	Non-office	$ 9.6	$18	Fast	Voc
Boilermaker	12	Non-office	$16.8	$26.4	Avg	Apprent

MACHINING, METALWORKING, AND METAL FABRICATION

JOB	NEEDED (000s)	LOCATION	ENTRY SALARY (000s)	MEDIAN INCOME (000s)	GROWTH RATE	TRAINING REQUIRED
Industrial Laser Process	600	Non-office	$36	$60	New	OJT
Jeweler	——	Non-office	$16.8	$24	Slow	Apprent
Locksmith	——	Non-office	$ 7.2	$21.6	Slow	Voc
Machine Operator	736	Non-office	$13.2	$39.6	Slow	OJT
Machinist or Job Setup Worker	658	Non-office	$24	$42	Slow	Voc
Millwright	92	Mobile	$12	$24	Slow	Apprent
Punch Press & Stamping Operator	183	Non-office	$24	$37.2	Slow	OJT
Sheet Metal Worker	112	Non-office	$21.6	$33.6	Slow	Apprent
Structural Metal Worker	58	Non-office/ Mobile	$18	$22.8	Slow	Apprent
Tool & Die Maker	138	Non-office	$25.2	$44.4	Slow	Apprent
Welder & Cutter	517	Non-office	$26.4	$33.6	Slow	Apprent

MANAGERS AND OFFICIALS

JOB	NEEDED (000s)	LOCATION	ENTRY SALARY (000s)	MEDIAN INCOME (000s)	GROWTH RATE	TRAINING REQUIRED
Apartment House Manager	——	Office	$ 7.2	$ 9.6	Avg	Voc
Automated Office Information Management Director	150	Office	$26.4	$60	New	Grad
Automated Office Records, Data, Information Security Manager	260	Office	$21.6	$30	New	4yr Coll
Automated Office Terminal/ Message Center Manager (Corporate Office)	500	Office	$21.6	$44.4	New	4yr Coll

JOB	NEEDED (000s)	LOCATION	ENTRY SALARY (000s)	MEDIAN INCOME (000s)	GROWTH RATE	TRAINING REQUIRED
Automated Office Terminal/ Message Center Manager (Single Office)	300	Office	$19.2	$25.2	New	4yr Coll
Bank Officer or Administrator	643	Office	$19.2	$34.8	Fast	4yr Coll
Blue Collar Worker Supervisor	1,300	Non-office	$19.2	$22.8	Fast	OJT
CAM Production Superintendent	90	Non-office	$18	$30	Fast	Voc
City Manager	4	Office	$39.6	$58.8	Fast	4yr Coll
Funeral Director	19	Office	$14.4	$33.6	Slow	Voc
Hotel Sales Manager	——	Office	$14.4	$24	Avg	4yr Coll
Office Manager	——	Office	$13.2	$19.2	Avg	4yr Coll
Restaurant Manager	——	Non-office	$16.8	$42	Avg	Voc

MEDICINE AND HEALTH

JOB	NEEDED (000s)	LOCATION	ENTRY SALARY (000s)	MEDIAN INCOME (000s)	GROWTH RATE	TRAINING REQUIRED
Audiologist	——	Non-office	$18	$32.4	Avg	4yr Coll
Cardiopulmonary Technologist	——	Non-office	$10.8	$30	Fast	4yr Coll
Computer Axial Tomography Technologist	25	Non-office	$14.4	$28.8	New	Jr Coll
Dental Assistant	96	Office	$ 9.6	$14.4	Fast	Voc
Dental Hygienist	26	Office	$13.2	$16.8	Fast	Voc
Dental Laboratory Technician	53	Non-office	$20.4	$36	Fast	Voc
Dentist	15	Office	$26.4	$66	Slow	Grad
Dietetic Technician	——	Non-office	$15.6	$28.8	Avg	4yr Coll
Dietitian	49	Non-office	$19.2	$31.2	Fast	4yr Coll
Electrocardiogram Technician	20	Non-office	$13.2	$21.6	Avg	Voc
Electroencephalographic Technician	5	Non-office	$14.4	$24	Avg	Voc

MEDICINE AND HEALTH

JOB	NEEDED (000s)	LOCATION	ENTRY SALARY (000s)	MEDIAN INCOME (000s)	GROWTH RATE	TRAINING REQUIRED
Emergency Medical Technician	120	Mobile	$12	$27.6	Fast	Voc
Geriatric Social Worker	450	Non-office/ Home	$18	$25.2	New	4yr Coll
Gerontological Science Aide	300	Non-office	$14.4	$21.6	New	Voc
Handicapped Compensating Technologies Diagnostician	80	Non-office	$15.6	$20.4	New	Jr Coll
Industrial Hygiene Technician	70	Non-office	$14.4	$19.2	——	4yr coll
Medical Laboratory Technician	205	Non-office	$14.4	$25.2	Fast	Jr Coll
Midwife	15	Home	$12	$24	Fast	Apprent
Nuclear Medical Technician	——	Non-office	$15.6	$21.6	Fast	Voc
Nurses Aide	928	Non-office	$ 7.2	$14.4	Avg	Voc
Occupational Therapist	24	Non-office	$18	$26.4	Avg	4yr Coll
Optometrist	8	Non-office	$24	$45.6	Avg	Grad
Orthodontist	——	Non-office	$14.4	$33.6	Avg	Voc
Pharmacist	104	Non-office	$25.2	$28.8	Avg	4yr Coll
Physical Therapist	57	Office	$20.4	$32.4	Avg	4yr Coll
Physical Therapy Assistant	——	Non-office	$ 9.6	$19.2	Avg	Jr Coll
Physician Assistant	51	Office	$21.6	$26.4	Fast	Jr Coll
Physician	239	Varied	$45.6	$88	Slow	Grad
Podiatrist	12	Office/Home	$26.4	$60	Avg	Grad
Positron Emission Technologist	25	Non-office	$14.4	$24	New	4yr Coll
Practical Nurse	550	Home	$10.8	$14.4	Avg	Jr Coll
Radiologic (X-Ray) Technologist	109	Non-office	$16.8	$22.8	Slow	Jr Coll
Registered Nurse	1,125	Varied	$16.8	$24	Avg	4yr Coll
Respiratory Therapist	50	Non-office	$16.8	$21.6	Avg	Jr Coll

JOB	NEEDED (000s)	LOCATION	ENTRY SALARY (000s)	MEDIAN INCOME (000s)	GROWTH RATE	TRAINING REQUIRED
Speech Pathologist	——	Non-office	$22.8	$30	Avg	4yr Coll
Surgical Technician	——	Non-office	$ 9.6	$19.2	Fast	Voc
Veterinarian	15	Non-office/ Home	$16.8	$68.4	Avg	Grad
Veterinary Assistant	——	Non-office/ Mobile	$ 7.2	$14.4	Avg	Jr Coll

MECHANICS AND MACHINERY REPAIRERS

JOB	NEEDED (000s)	LOCATION	ENTRY SALARY (000s)	MEDIAN INCOME (000s)	GROWTH RATE	TRAINING REQUIRED
Aircraft Mechanic	129	Non-office	$18	$28.8	Avg	Voc
Auto Mechanic	638	Non-office	$10.8	$16.8	Fast	Voc
Battery Technician, Fuel Cell	25	Non-office	$10.8	$16.8	New	OJT
Boatbuilder	——	Non-office	$12	$21.6	Slow	Apprent
Diesel Mechanic	——	Non-office	$12	$27.6	Fast	Voc
Heavy Equipment Mechanic	144	Non-office/ Mobile	$14.4	$20.4	Avg	Voc
Industrial Machine Repairer	523	Non-office	$19.2	$32.4	Avg	Apprent
Motorcycle Repairer	——	Non-office	$12	$19.2	Avg	Voc
Outboard Motor Mechanic	——	Non-office/ Mobile	$ 8.4	$19.2	Avg	Voc
Service Station Mechanic or Attendant	166	Non-office	$ 9.6	$14.4	Avg	PJT

MISCELLANEOUS TRADE AND NONPROFESSIONAL OCCUPATIONS

JOB	NEEDED (000s)	LOCATION	ENTRY SALARY (000s)	MEDIAN INCOME (000s)	GROWTH RATE	TRAINING REQUIRED
Child Care Worker (Household)	431	Non-office	$ 9.6	$12	Avg	OJT
Compositor/ Typesetter	54	Non-office	$21.6	$26.4	Obs	Apprent
Hairdresser or Cosmetologist	267	Non-office/ Home	$ 8.4	$16.8	Avg	Voc

MISCELLANEOUS TRADE AND NONPROFESSIONAL OCCUPATIONS

JOB	NEEDED (000s)	LOCATION	ENTRY SALARY (000s)	MEDIAN INCOME (000s)	GROWTH RATE	TRAINING REQUIRED
Housecleaner or Servant	491	Non-office	$ 8.4	$16.8	Avg	OJT
Janitor/Custodian	1,327	Non-office	$ 8.4	$15.6	Avg	OJT
Lithographic Press Operator	81	Non-office	$16.8	$20.4	Slow	Apprent
Masseur/ Masseuse	——	Non-office	$27.6	$32.4	Avg	Apprent
Packer or Wrapper (Not meat or produce)	600	Non-office	$10.8	$16.8	Slow	OJT
Pest Control Worker	40	Mobile	$ 8.4	$14.4	Fast	OJT
Printing Press Operator	178	Non-office	$20.4	$27.6	Slow	Apprent
Stock Handler	332	Non-office	$ 9.6	$14.4	Slow	OJT

MISCELLANEOUS PROFESSIONAL/TECHNICAL/MANAGERIAL OCCUPATIONS

JOB	NEEDED (000s)	LOCATION	ENTRY SALARY (000s)	MEDIAN INCOME (000s)	GROWTH RATE	TRAINING REQUIRED
Air Traffic Controller	29	Non-office	$18	$37.2	Slow	4yr Coll
Broadcast Technician	17	Non-office	$14.4	$16.8	Fast	Voc
Business Occupations Forecaster	75	Non-office	$20.4	$36	——	4yr Coll
CAD Engineering Software Specialist	360	Non-office	$22.8	$36	Fast	Jr Coll
CAD Product or Systems Inspector	280	Non-office	$14.4	$26.4	Fast	OJT

Occupation						
CAD Vocational Training & Educational Simulation Software Specialist	150	Non-office	$16.8	$22.8	Fast	Jr Coll
CAM Holographic Inspector	135	Non-office	$14.4	$25.2	Fast	OJT
CAM Manufacturing Material/ Finished Parts Traffic Controller	20	Non-office	$14.4	$16.8	Fast	Jr Coll
CAM-CAD Software Coordinator	80	Non-office	$20.4	$30	Fast	Jr Coll
Child Welfare Worker (Not household)	325	Non-office	$18	$25.2	Avg	OJT
Clergy Member	240	Non-office	$14.4	$30	Slow	Grad
Commerce Occupations Forecaster	60	Non-office	$19.2	$34.8	Avg	4yr Coll
Commercial Airline Pilot	82	Mobile	$37.2	$80.4	Avg	Voc
Computer Manufacturing Inspector	250	Non-office	$20.4	$38.4	Fast	Jr Coll
Computer Modeling & Simulation Technician	300	Non-office	$30	$48	New	Jr Coll
Computer Programmer	474	Non-office/ Home	$22.8	$32.4	Fast	Jr Coll
Computer Software Writer, General	1,830	Non-office/ Home	$24	$36	Fast	Jr Coll
Computer Systems Analyst	399	Office/Home	$24	$31.2	Fast	Jr Coll
Economic Occupations Forecaster	45	Non-office	$16.8	$22.8	Avg	4yr Coll
Economist	92	Office	$16.8	$30	Fast	4yr Coll

MISCELLANEOUS PROFESSIONAL/TECHNICAL/MANAGERIAL OCCUPATIONS

JOB	NEEDED (000s)	LOCATION	ENTRY SALARY (000s)	MEDIAN INCOME (000s)	GROWTH RATE	TRAINING REQUIRED
Educational Institutions Occupations Forecaster	20	Non-office	$14.4	$24	——	4yr Coll
Fishing Vessel Officer	5	Mobile	$14.4	$22.8	Avg	Jr Coll
Food Technologist	15	Non-office	$21.6	$36	Avg	4yr Coll
Industrial Occupations Forecaster	80	Non-office	$20.4	$30	Avg	4yr Coll
Industrial Relations Occupations Forecaster	50	Non-office	$16.8	$30	Avg	4yr Coll
Industrial Robot Production Technician	800	Non-office	$18	$28.8	New	Jr Coll
Key Punch Operator	200	Office	$18	$25.2	Slow	Voc
Librarian, Archivist, or Curator	165	Non-office	$16.8	$32.4	Avg	4yr Coll
Market Research Analyst	——	Office	$18	$33.6	Avg	4yr Coll
Military Occupations Forecaster	15	Non-office	$14.4	$24	——	4yr Coll
Parole Officer	——	Office	$10.8	$19.2	Slow	4yr Coll
Political Scientist	15	Office/Home	$18	$26.4	Slow	4yr Coll
Quality Control Inspector	——	Non-office	$ 8.4	$19.2	Avg	Jr Coll
Real Estate Appraiser	——	Non-office/ Mobile	$15.6	$21.6	Slow	OJT
Recording Engineer	——	Non-office	$ 8.4	$16.8	——	Voc
Robot Installation & Operations Technician	75	Non-office	$14.4	$26.4	New	Voc
Robot on-the-Job Programmer	125	Non-office	$14.4	$24	New	Jr Coll

JOB	NEEDED (000s)	LOCATION	ENTRY SALARY (000s)	MEDIAN INCOME (000s)	GROWTH RATE	TRAINING REQUIRED
Robot Repairman	100	Non-office	$16.8	$26.4	New	Voc
Sanitary Inspector	—	Non-office/ Mobile	$ 9.6	$19.2	Avg	4yr Coll
Social Worker	428	Non-office	$10.7	$32.2	Fast	4yr Coll
Telemarketing Computer Programmer	60	Office	$24	$42	New	Voc
Teletext Operations Supervisor	25	Office	$24	$40.8	New	Voc
Teletext Specialist —Software Programming	30	Home	$21.6	$36	New	Voc
Urban or Regional Planner	31	Office	$22.8	$42	Fast	4yr Coll
Urban Planner Occupations Forecaster	20	Non-office	$16.8	$25.2	—	4yr Coll
Vocational Counseling/ Training Occupations Forecaster	20	Non-office	$14.4	$24	—	4yr Coll

PHYSICAL SCIENCES AND MATHEMATICS

JOB	NEEDED (000s)	LOCATION	ENTRY SALARY (000s)	MEDIAN INCOME (000s)	GROWTH RATE	TRAINING REQUIRED
Actuary	11	Office	$15.6	$36	Slow	4yr Coll
Chemical Laboratory Technician	—	Non-office	$10.8	$20.4	Avg	Jr Coll
Chemist (except biochemists)	121	Non-office	$24	$42	Avg	4yr Coll
Geologist	36	Non-office	$24	$33.6	Avg	4yr Coll
Geophysicist	12	Non-office	$24	$33.6	Avg	4yr Coll
Meteorologist	—	Non-office	$19.2	$37.2	Fast	4yr Coll
Oceanographer	—	Non-office	$14.4	$20.4	Slow	4yr Coll
Physicist or Astronomer	35	Non-office	$18	$26.4	Fast	4yr Coll
Statistician	21	Non-office	$18	$34.8	Avg	4yr Coll

RECREATION AND ENTERTAINMENT

JOB	NEEDED (000s)	LOCATION	ENTRY SALARY (000s)	MEDIAN INCOME (000s)	GROWTH RATE	TRAINING REQUIRED
Actor or Actress	51	Non-office/ Mobile	$11.1	$22.3	——	4yr Coll
Announcer, Radio or TV	29	Non-office	$13.2	$42	Avg	Jr Coll
Athletic Coach	——	Non-office	$18	$30	Slow	4yr Coll
Disc Jockey	——	Non-office	$10.8	$33.6	Avg	Voc
Musician or Composer	45	Non-office	$16.8	$33.6	——	4yr Coll
Park Ranger	——	Non-office/ Mobile	13.2	$26.4	Slow	4yr Coll

SALES AND SERVICES

JOB	NEEDED (000s)	LOCATION	ENTRY SALARY (000s)	MEDIAN INCOME (000s)	GROWTH RATE	TRAINING REQUIRED
Advertising Worker	100	Office	$12	$48	Fast	4yr Coll
Auctioneer	1	Non-office	$ 7.2	$12	Slow	Voc
Auto Parts Salesperson	——	Non-office	$ 7.2	$12	Avg	Voc
CAD Training & Educational Materials Salesperson	95	Non-office	$14.4	$24	Fast	Jr Coll
CAG Sales Representative	30	Varied	$18	$36	Fast	Jr Coll
Collection Clerk	——	Office	$ 8.4	$15.6	Slow	Voc
Insurance Agent, Broker, or Underwriter	355	Office	$16.8	$48	Avg	4yr Coll
Model	——	Non-office	$14.4	$16.8	Avg	Voc
Real Estate Agent or Broker	356	Office	$15.6	$34.8	Fast	4yr Coll
Sales Agent, Stocks & Bonds	67	Office	$13.2	$60	Fast	4yr Coll
Salesclerk, Retail	2,345	Non-office	$ 7.2	$16.8	Slow	OJT
Sales Representative, Consumable Commodities, Wholesale	1,001	Office/ Non-office	$21.6	$39.6	Fast	Jr Coll

Sales Representative, Manufacturing	440	Varied	$19.2	$44.4	Fast	4yr Coll
Sales Worker, Consumable Commodities, Retail	3,300	Varied	$ 8.4	$16.8	Avg	OJT
Sales Workers, Services & Construction	222	Varied	$ 8.4	$20.4	Avg	OJT
Salesperson or Peddler	178	Varied	$ 9.6	$14.4	Avg	OJT
Telemarketing Advertising & Scenario Writer	110	Office	$21.6	$42	New	4yr Coll
Telemarketing Sales— Shipping, Billing Clerk, Supervisor	50	Office	$ 9.6	$21.6	New	OJT
Telemarketing Specialists, Recording/ Customer Order Takeoff	80	Office	$18	$36	New	OJT
Teletext Interactive Correspondent	30	Varied	$21.6	$30	New	4yr Coll
Teletext Specialist, CATV Liaison & Scheduling	30	Office	$20.4	$45.6	New	OJT
Teletext Specialist, Marketing	30	Home/Office	$21.6	$48	New	4yr Coll

SECURITY AND RELATED SERVICES

JOB	NEEDED (000s)	LOCATION	ENTRY SALARY (000s)	MEDIAN INCOME (000s)	GROWTH RATE	TRAINING REQUIRED
Correctional Institution Officer	169	Non-office	$14.4	$30	Fast	Jr Coll
Firefighter	197	Mobile	$16.8	$24	Fast	OJT
Policeman or Detective	707	Non-office	$18	$33.6	Avg	4yr Coll
Security Guard	548	Varied	$14.4	$21.6	Fast	OJT

STENOGRAPHY/TYPING/FILING

JOB	NEEDED (000s)	LOCATION	ENTRY SALARY (000s)	MEDIAN INCOME (000s)	GROWTH RATE	TRAINING REQUIRED
CAD Information Retrieval & Reproduction Clerk	300	Non-office	$12	$14.4	Fast	OJT
Court Reporter	——	Non-office	$14.4	$22.8	Avg	Jr Coll
File Clerk	191	Office	$ 9.6	$16.8	Obs	OJT
Legal Secretary	——	Office	$ 9.6	$21.6	Fast	Voc
Medical Secretary	——	Office	$ 8.4	$21.6	Avg	Voc
Other Information Center Terminal Operator	600	Office	$16.8	$27.6	New	Voc
Secretary or Stenographer	3,320	Home/Office	$10.8	$14.4	Fast	Voc
Transcribing Machine Operator	——	Office	$ 9.6	$14.4	Avg	Voc
Typist	630	Home/Office	$ 9.6	$14.4	Avg	Voc
Word Processing Operator	——	Office	$10.4	$15.6	Avg	Voc

TEXTILE/LEATHER MANUFACTURE AND REPAIR

JOB	NEEDED (000s)	LOCATION	ENTRY SALARY (000s)	MEDIAN INCOME (000s)	GROWTH RATE	TRAINING REQUIRED
Dressmaker & Seamstress (nonfactory)	49	Home	$12	$28.8	Slow	OJT
Sewer & Stitcher	788	Non-office	$10.8	$19.2	Slow	OJT
Tailor	48	Non-office	$ 7.2	$16.8	Slow	Voc
Textile Machine Operator	323	Non-office	$10.8	$20.4	Slow	OJT
Upholsterer	48	Non-office	$14.4	$20.4	Avg	Voc

TRANSPORTATION AND MATERIALS HANDLING

JOB	NEEDED (000s)	LOCATION	ENTRY SALARY (000s)	MEDIAN INCOME (000s)	GROWTH RATE	TRAINING REQUIRED
Bus Driver	193	Mobile	$12	$26.4	Avg	Voc
Crane, Derrick & Hoist Operator	148	Non-office	$14.4	$20.4	Avg	Voc
Fork Lift & Tow Motor Operator	366	Non-office	$ 9.6	$15.6	Avg	Voc
Freight, Stock, or Materials Handler	986	Non-office	$12	$28.8	Slow	Voc
Materials Utilization Technician	400	Non-office	$18	$28.8	New	Jr Coll
Sailor or Deckhand	17	Mobile	$18	$26.4	Slow	Voc
Travel Agent	52	Office	$12	$21.6	Fast	Jr Coll
Truck Driver	2,047	Mobile	$20.4	——	Avg	Voc

UTILITIES PRODUCTION AND DISTRIBUTION

JOB	NEEDED (000s)	LOCATION	ENTRY SALARY (000s)	MEDIAN INCOME (000s)	GROWTH RATE	TRAINING REQUIRED
Energy Auditor	150	Mobile	$14.4	$19.2	New	Voc
Energy Conservation Technician	1,500	Non-office	$15.6	$31.2	New	Voc
Hazardous Waste Disposal Technician	1,500	Non-office	$18	$33.6	New	Jr Coll
Waste & Water Treatment Plant Operator	41	Non-office	$14.4	$16.8	Avg	OJT

WRITING

JOB	NEEDED (000s)	LOCATION	ENTRY SALARY (000s)	MEDIAN INCOME (000s)	GROWTH RATE	TRAINING REQUIRED
Copywriter	——	Office	$ 9.6	$33.6	Slow	4yr Coll
Editor, Writer, or Reporter	220	Non-office/ Home	$14.4	$60	Fast	4yr Coll
Interpreter	——	Office	$10.8	$28.8	Avg	4yr Coll
Teletext Computer Specialist, Composition, Formatting & Editing	65	Office	$19.2	$48	New	4yr Coll

APPENDIX C:
THE JOBS OF THE FUTURE
CAREER GUIDANCE ASSAY

IF AFTER READING this book you are convinced that the time has come to find another career, there are four things you will have to do in order to make a successful transition:

First, look carefully at your own interests, abilities, values, and behavioral traits. In short, try to understand your own personality style. It doesn't matter how big a demand there is for accountants if you can't stand working with numbers. Conversely, for almost everyone, there is a well-paid, high-demand occupation that will make it a pleasure to go to work in the morning.

Second, take a look at the careers that might suit someone with your personality. Prepare a detailed profile of each job, paying special attention to the demands it will make on you and the training you will need to carry it out.

Third, compare what you have learned about yourself with each possible occupation. Then decide which job is best for you.

And finally, plan your route to your new career. Can you make the change with your current experience? Will you need professional training? If so, where can you find it? And can you learn on a part-time basis while earning a living?

This career-guidance inventory is designed to make this process faster, easier, more systematic, and more reliable. It was created by Dr. Cetron and college counselor James C. Gonyea as a supplement to Dr. Cetron's book *Jobs of the Future* (McGraw-Hill, 1984), a forecast of the 500 best employment opportunities of the 1990s. Part I contains a list of 264 job activities. Part II lists 11 work traits—characteristics that you may or may not want in your future occupation. In each section, you will be asked to decide how interesting or desirable you find the task or trait. By the time you are done, you should have a pretty good idea of where your preferences lie.

When you take the test, please remember that what counts is your level of interest in each activity or trait. It doesn't matter whether you have experience at investigating murders, whether you think you have any talent for acting, whether your friends would approve if you became a dishwasher in a restaurant, or even whether you could support your family while grooming dogs and cats. Would you find the activity endlessly fascinating or a colossal bore? That is all that should concern you at this stage.

Do not try to rush through the assay; snap decisions are seldom accurate when it comes to the delicate shadings of interest. Most people get better results if they break the test into two or three sessions.

Part I

Directions. Read each of the following activities, and among the following options, select the one that best describes your level of interest in the activity:
    4—Very Interesting
    3—Interesting
    2—Neutral
    1—Uninteresting
    0—Very Uninteresting.
Record your answer for each activity, and proceed to the next.

GROUP 1

3   1. Edit written materials for newspapers, magazines, or teletext transmission.
2   2. Teach art courses.
1   3. Teach or direct actors and actresses.
0   4. Design a new line of clothing for men or women.
3   5. Take photographs of people, places, or objects.
2   6. Use a computer to make signs, posters, or business letterheads and envelopes.
3   7. Write advertising slogans for sales commercials.
0   8. Model new clothes.
2   9. Write speeches for politicians or other people who speak in public.
2 10. Help design or edit computer graphic software programs.
1 11. Act in a play, movie, or television show.
1 12. Announce musical selections on a radio program.
2 13. Design interior living spaces such as living rooms and dining areas.
3 14. Make or repair jewelry.
2 15. Create attractive flower arrangements.
1 16. Design sets and props for theatrical stage productions.
3 17. Write books, newspaper columns, or articles for magazines.
2 18. Use computers to design and illustrate graphic art work or new products and materials.
2 19. Tell jokes or perform magic tricks for an audience.
0 20. Sing musical selections.
0 21. Perform modern dance routines.
2 22. Restore historic artifacts in a museum.
1 23. Supervise a computer-aided graphics department.
1 24. Illustrate greeting cards, calendars, or posters.
1 25. Write critical reviews of artworks.

2 26. Design and illustrate homes, clothes, furniture, office equipment, or other consumer products.

1 27. Announce the news, sports, weather, or musical selections, or introduce guests or contestants, on a radio or television program.

2 28. Play a musical instrument.

2 29. Prepare and stuff skins of birds and animals to make them look lifelike and natural.

3 30. Letter, paint, or decorate signs by hand.

2 31. Design packaging materials for manufactured goods.

1 32. Illustrate medical textbooks.

GROUP 2

1 33. Develop chemicals for new medicines.

1 34. Investigate new ways of breeding animals.

1 35. Diagnose and treat people who are sick or injured.

1 36. Perform chemical laboratory tests in a hospital.

2 37. Study the formation of mountains and rivers and the origin of minerals from the earth.

1 38. Repair and test biomedical equipment for use in a hospital operating room.

1 39. Treat people suffering from toothaches.

1 40. Test blood samples for signs of disease.

3 41. Develop ways for cleaning up the environment.

1 42. Compare the digestive systems of humans and animals.

1 43. Diagnose and treat animals that are sick or injured.

1 44. Investigate the atomic structure of various metals.

2 45. Study ocean plants and animals.

2 46. Develop new ways of preserving foods.

1 47. Develop programs to correct speech disorders.

1 48. Test human tissue samples in a medical laboratory.

GROUP 3

1 49. Grow farm crops and animals.

1 50. Supervise a dairy farm.

1 51. Exercise horses before a race.

1 52. Pick farm crops.

2 53. Manage a landscaping company.

1 54. Investigate ways of growing larger vegetable plants.

1 55. Care for animals in a kennel.

1 56. Cut trees in a forest.

3 57. Raise trees and shrubs for landscaping purposes.

1 58. Care for animals in an animal farm or park.

1 59. Groom dogs and cats.

2 60. Remove diseased limbs from a tree to save its life.

1 61. Manage and care for trees in a forest.

1 62. Raise chickens for commercial sale.

4 very interesting
3 Interesting
2 neutral
1 Uninteresting
0 Very uninteresting

63. Help an animal doctor care for sick or injured animals.
64. Care for lawns, shrubs, and flowers.

GROUP 4

65. Maintain law and order and protect the rights and property of people.
66. Guard prison inmates.
67. Investigate a murder or robbery case.
68. Guard passengers and property on a commercial airline.
69. Protect forest lands, fish, and wild animals from illegal poachers.
70. Guard swimmers in a public pool.
71. Investigate a narcotics case to find drug pushers.
72. Fight fires in homes and other buildings.

GROUP 5

73. Design new electrical or electronic machines and equipment.
74. Create computer-assisted-design software programs.
75. Survey a section of land and mark it off for construction.
76. Fly a commercial airplane.
77. Help construct a building by laying bricks.
78. Inspect manufactured goods produced by a computer.
79. Examine a building for sources of wasted energy.
80. Drive a tractor-trailer truck.
81. Use a computer to keep track of inventory parts in a large warehouse.
82. Repair electrical or electronic household appliances.
83. Operate road-paving equipment.
84. Clean homes or office buildings.
85. Use computers to design new machines, tools, and equipment.
86. Repair and service computers.
87. Use a computer to prepare architectural or mechanical blueprints.
88. Make dental plates and false teeth.
89. Repair a damaged automobile body.
90. Operate a boiler to produce heat and hot water.
91. Install computer and word-processing equipment in offices.
92. Survey the ocean floor for construction purposes.
93. Supervise the shipping and receiving of materials in and out of a business.
94. Operate equipment to develop film, broadcast radio or television programs, or transmit electronic mail.
95. Design new automobile engines.
96. Operate a dishwashing machine.
97. Create new ways of designing buildings, bridges, or landscape formations.
98. Install or repair laser-optics equipment and machinery.
99. Control airplanes arriving at and departing from an airport.
100. Pilot a ferryboat.

3 101. Repair heating and cooling equipment, automobile and motorcycle engines, or industrial and office machines.

| 102. Investigate new uses for nuclear energy.

(103. Inspect telephone lines for damage.

(104. Record musicians or singers in a recording studio.

\ 105. Install robotic equipment and machines.

2 106. Prepare food and bakery goods.

| 107. Install and repair telephone equipment.

| 108. Repair and service television broadcasting equipment.

| 109. Design machines that can "think" like human beings.

| 110. Make maps of earth and ocean features and terrain.

/ 111. Install mechanical devices to save energy in homes.

/ 112. Pilot a fishing vessel or pleasure craft.

/ 113. Operate a printing or sewing machine.

/ 114. Operate machinery to treat water in a purification plant.

/ 115. Prepare meals for people on special diets.

(116. Help design braces and artificial limbs for people with physical disabilities.

(117. Install television cables.

| 118. Use chemicals to control insects and other small pests.

| 119. Operate a crane to lift construction materials to the top of a building.

/ 120. Lubricate machinery and equipment in a factory.

GROUP 6

\ 121. Supervise workers assembling computers.

(122. Operate a drill press to bore holes in plastic or metal.

\ 123. Inspect new cars on an assembly line.

| 124. Trim books in a bookbinding factory.

(125. Operate machinery to make metal parts.

\ 126. Operate machinery to make synthetic cloth and textiles.

| 127. Install and service computerized machines that make manufactured goods.

| 128. Spray-paint appliance parts in a factory.

(129. Assemble atomic nuclear fuel cells.

2 130. Develop and process photographs in a darkroom.

(131. Test electronic parts before assembly.

| 132. Operate laundry and dry-cleaning equipment.

2 133. Test diesel engines after assembly.

/ 134. Supervise chemical-processing workers.

(135. Operate a machine to bend metal.

(136. Wrap manufactured goods for shipment.

GROUP 7

| 137. Interview college students about financial aid.

3 138. Keep records of all purchases and sales for a business.

| 139. Operate a cash register in a restaurant.

140. Help travelers register for a hotel room.
141. Take notes during a court trial.
142. Type letters, forms, lists, and other material on a typewriter or word processor.
143. File forms and letters in an insurance office.
144. Supervise workers who are using computers to do word processing.
145. Keep payroll-account records up-to-date and process payroll checks.
146. Help bank customers deposit or withdraw money.
147. Help callers place long-distance phone calls.
148. Take notes in shorthand and type a copy for mailing.
149. Operate a computer to obtain previously stored information.
150. Deliver messages from one office to another.
151. Type letters, file reports, and schedule appointments in a business, medical, or legal office.
152. Maintain records of hospital patients.
153. Deliver mail on foot or by automobile.
154. Greet people entering a place of business and direct them to the person they came to visit.
155. Sort mail in a post office.
156. Take people on a guided tour of a famous city.
157. Conduct simple medical exams, such as taking blood pressures and temperatures, in a doctor's office.
158. Investigate the credit history of a person attempting to finance a car.
159. Maintain a file on people who have not paid their city water bills.
160. Keep score at a professional basketball game.
161. Interview people for a political survey.
162. Supervise workers engaged in preparing videotext information for a cable television company.
163. Operate a computer to read and validate checks in a bank.
164. Purchase retail merchandise for a department store.

GROUP 8
165. Sell computer-aided graphic and design software programs to industrial engineers.
166. Sell time on a cable television station to local merchants.
167. Sell merchandise at a public auction.
168. Advise people about the kind of life insurance they should buy.
169. Buy wholesale goods and materials and resell them to retail stores.
170. Help individuals lease a car.
171. Buy clothing for a major department store.
172. Help travelers plan their vacations.
173. Sell computer-assisted-design software programs to engineering firms.
174. Sell advertising space in a national magazine.
175. Help couples who are soon to be married purchase wedding services and arrangements.
176. Sell computers to business and industrial clients.

GROUP 9

177. Design a recreational program for children.
178. Give haircuts.
179. Drive a school or public bus.
180. Make drinks for customers in a bar or restaurant.
181. Massage a person's body to relieve tension and fatigue.
182. Guide visitors on a tour through a factory.
183. Design new hairstyles.
184. Provide funeral services to the public.
185. Take food orders and bring prepared meals to customers in a restaurant.
186. Carry suitcases for hotel guests.
187. Teach children various recreational games and crafts.
188. Serve food to customers in a cafeteria.
189. Sell gas and oil to people operating motorboats.
190. Record and process purchase orders received over the telephone.
191. Carry golf clubs for a golfer.
192. Serve meals to airline passengers.
193. Give scalp and facial treatments in a beauty shop.
194. Escort patrons to their seats at a ballet.
195. Collect cash and make change for customers buying goods in a department store.
196. Entice visitors to participate in games at an amusement park.

GROUP 10

197. Provide religious guidance and counseling services.
198. Provide bedside care to hospital patients.
199. Use special equipment to test the health of a person's heart.
200. Counsel people about their career direction.
201. Help someone overcome a physical disability.
202. Assist a surgeon in an operation.
203. Help individuals overcome emotional or social problems.
204. Use X-ray or other machines to analyze the internal workings of the human body.
205. Test a person's hearing.
206. Help families solve personal problems.
207. Teach handicapped children.
208. Care for the elderly in a nursing home.

GROUP 11

209. Write instructions to control the operation of a computer.
210. Teach physical education to high school or college students.
211. Manage a residential apartment house or condominium.
212. Design a security system for protecting classified business information stored in a computer.

213. Manage a bank.
214. Prepare financial records for a business.
215. Direct a social-service or welfare agency.
216. Teach people how to use computer-assisted-design software programs.
217. Design an advertising campaign for a new product.
218. Plan and manage business or political conventions.
219. Manage a hotel or motel.
220. Write an insurance plan to protect the health of workers in a factory.
221. Design a manual or computer system for collecting data and information.
222. Teach high school students.
223. Study the history of people or governments.
224. Defend a person in court.
225. Investigate the reasons people buy various consumer products.
226. Manage the personnel hiring, firing, and labor relations of a company.
227. Direct a community health-protection agency.
228. Write feature articles for a television news program.
229. Raise money for a charitable organization.
230. Examine a company's waste-disposal system to determine if it complies with the law.
231. Manage a restaurant.
232. Study the political behavior of individuals and groups.
233. Design a computer program to teach people how to use a computer.
234. Classify and catalog books in a library.
235. Determine which occupations will be needed in the future.
236. Gather information about a crime for use in a court of law.
237. Manage the student records and registration department of a college.
238. Determine the value of a building or residential home.
239. Inspect the sanitary conditions of restaurants.
240. Develop statistical life-expectancy theories and models for insurance companies.
241. Promote a local company by speaking at various public functions.
242. Help control the flow of illegal immigrants into the country.
243. Represent the legal rights of a company involved in a tax audit.
244. Supervise a crew of telephone salespeople.
245. Plan the orderly growth and development of a city.
246. Teach vocational subjects, such as carpentry, auto-body repair, practical nursing, or cooking.
247. Study the causes of good and bad economic conditions.
248. Identify business-related occupations of the future.
249. Direct the activities of a funeral home.
250. Buy and sell stocks and bonds.
251. Direct the activities of a museum.
252. Translate a foreign language into English.
253. Determine the best media source for an advertising campaign.
254. Investigate employee-safety standards in a factory.

255. Design informational teletext programs (video newspapers, catalogs, and magazines) for cable television viewers.
256. Examine the investment records of a bank.

GROUP 12
257. Coach a school, college, or professional athletic team.
258. Perform stunts in a movie.
259. Umpire a baseball, basketball, or other professional game.
260. Play professional golf.
261. Become a professional athlete.
262. Ride racehorses.
263. Play professional tennis.
264. Scout college and semipro athletic teams for potential professional athletes.

Part II

Directions. Listed below are eleven features of particular jobs which people seeking a new career often consider important. Selecting those work traits which you prefer will make it easier to zero in on occupations that match your interests, needs, and preferences.

1. *Reasoning Ability:* Reasoning can be defined as the ability to understand concepts, principles, logic, data, information, and/or scientific knowledge. Some occupations will require you to deal with very abstract and difficult-to-understand concepts, while others involve only simple, easy-to-understand, commonsense principles. Listed below are three levels of reasoning ability that might be required in your new occupation. Please select the one you would prefer in a job.

High Reasoning Ability: the kind of reasoning required of such workers as physicians, engineers, psychiatrists, airline pilots, mathematicians, and college professors.

Moderate High to Average Reasoning Ability: the kind of reasoning ability required of such workers as teachers, managers, secretaries, bookkeepers, audiovisual-equipment technicians, electricians, and automobile mechanics.

Low Average to Low Reasoning Ability: the kind of reasoning ability required of such workers as farm workers, assembly-line workers, parking-lot attendants, dishwashers, sales-counter clerks, and inventory stock clerks.

2. *Mathematical Ability:* Many occupations require at least some ability to solve problems using numbers and numerical concepts as clues and tools. Mathematical ability can range from easy-to-understand arithmetic to such

abstract and difficult-to-understand concepts as calculus and statistics. From the list below, please select the level of mathematical ability which you would prefer your new job to require in order to handle the work successfully.

High Mathematical Ability: the kind of math ability required of such workers as mathematicians, physicists, architects, statisticians, scientists, psychologists, and engineers.

Moderate High to Average Mathematical Ability: the kind of math ability required of such workers as nurses, medical-laboratory technicians, financial-aid counselors, high school teachers, librarians, motel managers, and sales representatives.

Low Average to Low Mathematical Ability: the kind of math ability required of such workers as timekeepers, office-machine operators, automotive-parts clerks, kitchen helpers, bellmen, and dry-cleaning-machine operators.

3. *Language Ability:* Language ability can be defined as the capacity to use accepted and correct sentence structure, punctuation, and spelling as well as to have a well-developed vocabulary and appreciation of literature. From the list below, select the level of language ability you would prefer your job to require of you.

High Language Ability: the kind of language ability required of such workers as authors, magazine editors, professional writers, college professors, and professional speech writers.

Moderate High to Average Language Ability: the kind of language ability required of such workers as surveyors, commercial drafters, computer programmers, scientific or medical laboratory technicians, police officers, kindergarten teachers, and ship pilots.

Low Average to Low Language Ability: the language ability required of such workers as acrobats, dancers, water-meter readers, bank tellers, mail carriers, and groundskeepers.

4. *Aptitudes.* Using one of the five rating levels below, rate your skill level in each of the 11 aptitudes listed below.
Skill Rating Scale:
1—High Level
2—Above Average Level
3—Average Level
4—Below Average Level
5—Low Level

Intelligence: general learning ability. The ability to "catch on" or understand instructions and underlying principles; the ability to reason and make judgments.

Verbal: the ability to understand the meaning of words and to use them effectively. The ability to comprehend language; to understand relationships between words and to understand the meaning of whole sentences and paragraphs.

Numerical: the ability to perform mathematical operations quickly and accurately.

Spatial Perception: the ability to think visually ("see" pictures in your mind) of geometric objects and forms. The ability to "see" the inside and outside of objects in your mind; to be able conceptually to turn them around; and to understand the way objects fit together without actually seeing the objects.

Form Perception: the ability to perceive pertinent detail in objects, pictures, or graphic materials. The ability to make visual comparisons and discriminations and see slight differences in shapes, shadings of figures, and widths and lengths of lines.

Clerical Perceptions: the ability to perceive pertinent detail in verbal, tabular, or written materials. The ability to observe differences in written copy, to proofread words and numbers accurately, and to find errors in arithmetic computation.

Motor Coordination: the ability to coordinate your eyes and hands (or fingers) rapidly and accurately in making precise movements with speed.

Finger Dexterity: the ability to move your fingers to manipulate small objects rapidly and accurately.

Manual Dexterity: the ability to move your hands easily and skillfully, to work with your hands in precise and accurate movements.

Eye/Hand/Foot Coordination: the ability to move your hands and feet together in accordance with visual prompting or stimulation in accurate, precise movements.

Color Discrimination: the ability to perceive or recognize similarities or differences in colors, or in shades or other values of the same color; to identify a particular color, or to recognize harmonious or contrasting color combinations, or to match colors accurately.

5. *Values:* Listed below are twenty-four possible job characteristics often found to be important when people select a career direction. Review the list, and select up to five which are important to you and which you would like your ultimate job to satisfy.

1) Adventure and excitement.
2) Change and variety.
3) Competition with other workers.
4) Opportunity for creativity and self-expression.

5) Decision-making power and authority.
6) Flexible work schedule.
7) Opportunity to help others and society.
8) Personal freedom and independence.
9) High intellectual stimulation and development.
10) Luxurious work surroundings.
11) High salary.
12) Opportunity to persuade and influence the opinion of others.
13) Physically strenuous work.
14) Precision (detailed) work.
15) Contact and involvement with the public.
16) Public recognition, esteem, and prestige.
17) Routine (repetitive) work.
18) Seasonal work.
19) Solitary work (little contact with other employees and/or the public).
20) Travel.
21) Working under pressure, stress, or in emergencies.
22) Working mainly with your hands (equipment, tools, and machinery).
23) Working mainly with data, information, and/or numbers.
24) Working mainly with people (helping them solve problems and/or satisfy their needs).

6. *Physical Demands:* Listed below are six forms of physical demand which may be important to you and your future job. Read each section, and select those which are important to you.

1) *Strength:* While all jobs require workers to lift, carry, push, and/or pull objects to some degree, it is a long way from lifting pencils and opening file drawers to loading a delivery truck with bags of cement. Select the strength level below which you would prefer.

Sedentary: very light lifting or carrying (usually under 10 pounds) and light pushing or pulling.

Light: frequent lifting or carrying of objects (usually under 20 pounds), a significant amount of walking and standing and/or sitting with a degree of pushing or pulling with the arms or legs.

Medium: lifting or carrying of objects that usually weigh 25 to 50 pounds.

Heavy: lifting or carrying of objects that usually weigh 50 to 100 pounds.

Very heavy: lifting or carrying of objects that usually weigh over 100 pounds.

2) *Climbing and Balancing:* Check Climbing and Balancing if you *do not want* an occupation that requires a good deal of climbing and/or balancing in order to complete the work successfully.

3) *Stooping, Kneeling, Crouching, and/or Crawling:* Check this answer if you *do not want* an occupation that requires a good deal of stooping, kneeling, crouching, and/or crawling in order to complete the work successfully.

4) *Reaching, Handling, Fingering, and/or Feeling:* Check this answer if you *do not want* an occupation that requires a good deal of reaching, handling, fingering, and/or feeling in order to complete the work successfully.

5) *Talking and/or Hearing:* Check this answer if you *do not want* a job that requires a good deal of talking and/or hearing in order to complete the work successfully.

6) *Seeing:* Check this answer if you *do not want* a job that requires special seeing skills (beyond normal seeing ability), such as clear vision (near or far), depth perception, wide field of vision, and/or color vision to complete the work successfully.

7. *Environmental Concerns:* This section deals with the nature or condition of the surroundings in which you would work. Listed below are nine environmental situations which may be important to you and your ultimate job. Review the list, and select those items which you *do not want* in your ultimate occupation.

1) Work that is primarily indoors.
2) Work that is primarily out-of-doors.
3) Work that is evenly split between indoors and out-of-doors.
4) Work in extreme cold temperatures.
5) Work in extreme hot temperatures.
6) Work in wet and humid conditions.
7) Work with a lot of noise and vibration.
8) Work that may be physically hazardous to your health.
9) Work where fumes, odors, toxic conditions, dust, and poor ventilation are present.

8. *Vocational Preparation Level:* All occupations require some time learning and preparing yourself to handle the work. Some occupations require very little preparation time (a few hours to a few days), while others may require up to ten years or more of preparation time. Review the four training periods below, and select the one you prefer.

Very Short: training that may last a few minutes, a few hours, or anywhere up to thirty days.

Short: training that may last anywhere from one month to one year.

Medium: training that may last from one to four years.

Long: training that may last from four years to over ten years.

9. *Data, People, and Things:* All occupations can be defined in terms of how much involvement or interaction a worker has with data (knowledge and numbers), people, and things (physical objects, tools, and machinery). In any occupation, a worker could be required to deal with a high, moderate, or low level of data, people, and/or things.

1) *Data:* Select the level below which best describes how much involvement you would like with knowledge and numbers.

High Level: This level would require you to gather a great deal of information about your work, to understand this information, and to make judgments based on what you have learned. This level requires a high level of reading comprehension, reasoning ability, and logical thinking skills.

Moderate Level: This level would require you to gather an average or moderate amount of information about your work, and to make basic judgments from what you have learned. This level requires an average amount of reading comprehension, reasoning ability, and logical thinking skills.

Low Level: This level would require you to gather only a small amount of information about your work and to make simple judgments from what you have learned. This level requires a below-average amount of reading comprehension, reasoning ability, and logical thinking skills.

2) *People:* Select the level below which best describes how intimately or deeply involved you would like to be with people.

High Level: This level would require that you engage in personal and intimate subjects with the people you work with. For example, you might be required to help people improve their personality or behavior or work out serious marital, emotional, or sexual problems. Or you could be required to help people develop a strong religious faith and relationship with God. Sometimes the subjects you discuss with your clients may be emotionally uncomfortable for them, as well as for you, such as in the case of dealing with child-abuse victims or criminals.

Moderate Level: This level would require that you engage in some personal and intimate subjects with the people you work with, but not to the extent described above. For example, you might be required to help people improve their educational development, social-relationship skills, or personal appearance. Also, you might be engaged in interviewing people regarding employment, a bank loan, or their need for social services.

Low Level: This level would require little more than meeting and greeting people. In this level, you would have very little contact with people, and what contact you might have would be very brief and consist of little more than casual conversation.

3) *Things:* Select the level below which best describes how much involvement you would prefer with objects, tools, machinery, and the like.

High Level: This level would require that you work closely and intimately with machines, tools, equipment, and other tangible objects. The main focus or purpose of your job would be to set up, adjust, control, and/or operate various machines, tools, equipment, and so on. These "things" are usually very complex, requiring precise operation standards, and require special skills and training.

Moderate Level: This level would also require you to work with machines, tools, equipment, or other tangible objects, but not to the extent described above. While these "things" would help you accomplish your work, they would not be the main focus or purpose of your job. These "things" are moderately complex, requiring some operating standards, and may require some special skills and training.

Low Level: This level would not require you to deal with any special machines, tools, or equipment other than the common items most people use in the course of their work, such as calculators, telephones, or an automobile. The main focus or purpose of the job would be dealing with data and/or people, not with "things."

10. *Temperaments:* Succeeding at many occupations requires workers to possess certain personality traits. Listed below are ten common personality traits found to be important in many occupations. Review each trait below, and select those which you believe you characteristically display in your work behavior.

1) The ability to accept responsibility for the direction, control, or planning of an activity.

2) The ability to interpret feelings, ideas, or facts in terms of personal viewpoints.

3) The ability to influence the opinions, attitudes, or judgments of other people.

4) The ability to make generalizations, evaluations, or decisions based on sensory (feelings) and judgmental (not actual proved facts) criteria.

5) The ability to make generalizations, evaluations, or decisions based on measurable or verifiable criteria.

6) The ability to deal with people beyond simply giving and/or receiving instructions and information.

7) The ability to perform repetitive work, or to perform continuously the same work, according to set procedures, sequence, or pace.

8) The ability to perform under stress when confronted with emergency,

critical, unusual, or dangerous situations, or situations in which working speed and sustained attention are "make or break" aspects of the job.

9) The ability to handle situations which require precise attainment of set limits, tolerances, or standards.

10) The ability to perform a variety of duties, often changing from one task to another of a different nature without loss of efficiency or composure.

11. *Work Site Location:* Listed below are five options concerning the physical location or place of your work. Select one option which best represents where you would like your work to be located. Choose only one option.

Office (located within your employer's office area).

Off Site (Your work area would not be located within your employer's office area, but would be located elsewhere on the employer's property).

Home (located within your personal home).

Farm.

Mobile (You would have no fixed office or work-area location).

You can use this assay on your own as a starting point for self-analysis, but it was really designed to be evaluated by professionals. If you would like help from qualified career counselors, write down your answers to the questions above and send the results to Jobs of the Future, Inc., 101 North Highland Street, Arlington, VA 22210. They will develop a profile of your personality style and mail you a report on the occupations which they believe you should consider as career goals. (Please include a self-addressed, stamped, business-size envelope and a check or money order for a $21 service fee; allow four to six weeks for processing.) You may be surprised and pleased by what you learn.

INDEX